Body Voice Imagination

David Zinder's *Body Voice Imagination* is written by one of the master teachers of the Michael Chekhov technique of acting training. It is a comprehensive course of exercises devoted to the development of actors' expressive creative expressivity, comprising both *ImageWork Training* and the seminal exercises of the Chekhov Technique. These techniques can be applied to performance through a discovery of the profound connections between the actor's body, imagination, and voice.

This new edition has been fully updated, with revisions and new material:

- updated exercises, reflecting developments in David Zinder's own *ImageWork Training*;
- a detailed description, with exercises, of *ImageWork*'s connection with the Chekhov Technique;
- a new chapter, bridging the gap between training and performance.

Body Voice Imagination develops both a comprehensive physical training system and an emphasis on practical character work. This authoritative program of "pre-Chekhov" training is furnished with essential notes and advice from the author's vast store of experience.

David Zinder, Professor Emeritus of the Tel Aviv University Department of Theatre Arts, was a founding member of the Michael Chekhov Association, and has over three decades of experience in actor training and directing. Today he is a freelance international director.

Body Voice Imagination

SECOND EDITION

ImageWork Training and the Chekhov Technique

David Zinder

 Routledge
Taylor & Francis Group

LONDON AND NEW YORK

First published 2009
by Routledge
2 Park Square, Milton Park, Abingdon, Oxon OX14 4RN

Simultaneously published in the USA and Canada
by Routledge
270 Madison Ave, New York, NY 10016

Routledge is an imprint of the Taylor & Francis Group, an informa business

© 2009 David Zinder

Typeset in Univers and Avant Garde by
Book Now Ltd, London
Printed and bound in Great Britain by
TJ International, Padstow, Cornwall

British Library Cataloguing in Publication Data
A catalogue record for this book is available from the British Library

Library of Congress Cataloging in Publication Data
Zinder, David G., 1942–
Body voice imagination / David Zinder.
—2nd ed.
        p. cm.
Includes bibliographical references and index. 1. Acting. I. Title.
PN2061.Z54 2009
792.0'28—dc22
2008047319

ISBN10: 0–415–46197–9 (hbk)
ISBN10: 0–415–46198–7 (pbk)
ISBN10: 0–203–87819–1 (ebk)

ISBN13: 978–0–415–46197–9 (hbk)
ISBN13: 978–0–415–46198–6 (pbk)
ISBN13: 978–0–203–87819–4 (ebk)

For Leah
. . . let me count the ways
Impossible!
There are too many to count—a life's worth . . .
and it's here—on every page.

Contents

Preface to the Second Edition

The first edition of this book comprised a highly detailed cycle of "instrument training"—*ImageWork*—which took teachers, actors and directors up to, but not into, work on character, text, or the practical application of this training in rehearsal or performance. Having been re-introduced to the Chekhov Technique thiry years after I first heard of Michael Chekhov, and subsequently learning the details of the Technique from the master teachers, the late Mala Powers, Joanna Merlin, Ted Pugh, Fern Sloane, Lenard Petit, and the late Jack Colvin, among others, I discovered that this form of training, which I had developed more or less on my own from many different sources, was intimately related to the inspired precepts of the Chekhov Technique.

Now, after years of teaching *ImageWork* in tandem with the Chekhov Technique, and learning year by year just how strong the bond was between my work and that of the Master, it was clear to me that beyond the training I must also elaborate on the deep connections between the two forms of training: how *ImageWork* is a comprehensive preparation for the Chekhov Technique, and how the major elements of the Chekhov Technique follow naturally out of *ImageWork Training*. This is what I have attempted to do in this revised edition.

Re-reading a text that was written nine years previously to prepare it for a new edition is an exciting challenge. Having been invited by Routledge to prepare this new, expanded edition, I took the opportunity to revise the original, cutting exercises which, in the organic nature of theatre training, I found that I no longer use, combining others which, in the first flush of writing, I separated artificially, and expanding on those which have developed over the years in directions different to those foreseen when I originally wrote them down. The result, I hope, is a leaner, clearer version of the original with the essential addition of the connection to the Chekhov Technique.

Amusez-vous bien!

Tel Aviv, September 2008

Pre-text

Consider this image:

> The eye of the artist concentrates on his pencil, the pencil moves—and the line dreams.

This is the way the painter Paul Klee described what happens at the very instant of artistic creation: how it is prepared for and made welcome; how it is recognized when it appears and given space to occur; and how it is managed in time until the creative impulse is exhausted. This seemingly simple act of drawing a line— picking up the pencil, holding it over the blank page, concentrating on the point, and allowing the line to "dream" itself into a work of art—requires an infinitely delicate balance between technique and inspiration, control and release, containment and freedom, consciousness and unconsciousness. It's as easy and as difficult as pushing a soap bubble: push it too hard and it will burst; push it too gently and it won't move at all. Avoiding both, yet applying sufficient pressure and energy so that it moves in the chosen direction requires delicacy, determination, strength, and concentration.

Yet look carefully at this chronology of artistic creativity: after concentrating on the point, and letting the tip move, there is a breathtaking leap of faith: allowing the line "to dream." That interstice, that infinitesimal space between technique and inspiration, between waking and dreaming as it occurs in the body, voice, and imagination of the actor, is the subject matter of this book.

Consider another image:

> An actor standing absolutely still in front of an audience, not moving a muscle, rendering an expression, nor uttering a sound, yet affecting the spectators to tears or laughter.

On the face of it this seems impossible, more a contradiction of theater than an affirmation. And yet, this "silent" moment is in many ways a very pure, very condensed form of the art. It is, in the language of theater technique, a profound moment of psychophysical "connectedness," when self and other almost become one, coruscating in our perception like an optical illusion—occupying the same time and space, but foregrounding now one, now the other, imperceptibly. If we ignore for a moment voice or language, which in any case are not absolute requirements for a moment of theater to take place, everything that makes up an act of theater is there: *presence*, *form*, *resistance*, *enigma*, and *contact*. This concept of "the unmoving actor moving an audience"—sheer performative *presence*—suggests a paradigm of acting that is the other touchstone of this book.

What follows here, then, is an attempt to deconstruct the process of creativity and the phenomenon of presence in actor training, to reveal what can be revealed about the way they work, and then to suggest ways of learning their components through a detailed training procedure. Having found through my own experience what I believe to be a coherent through-line of training for actors, my hope is that this book will be able to provide actors, directors, and teachers with new insights into the mysteries of the actor's creative instrument, and to suggest new ways of shaping them into an enduring technique. By making the elements of the actor's creativity visible and trainable, the ultimate aim of this book is to help actors develop their creative individualities step-by-step to the point where technique is forgotten and becomes one with the talent it supports; to the point where they can stand confidently on that threshold of artistic endeavor so evocatively described by Herbert Blau: "on the edge of a breath, looking."

Introduction

Fundamentally, this is a book about Training: the development—or *formation*, in the more evocative French term—and fine-tuning of the actor's instrument and basic creative tools through the systematic acquisition and maintenance of techniques. Through this concept, the book centers on the three things that have been—and still are—the abiding passions of my professional life: the endless fascination of the creative moment as it unfolds in the time/space of performance; the never-ending mystery of presence radiating from an actor profoundly connected in body, voice, and imagination; and the inspiration and guidance that is to be found in the work of Michael Chekhov.

When all is said and done, this book is also an offer, a suggestion, a highlighted guide along the path that I have taken and have found so enriching; one that still fills me with wonder and excitement forty years down the road from the time I began my professional involvement in theater. It is also a book about all the many wonderful artists, teachers, mentors, colleagues, and students who have taught me so much, and in so doing helped shape my vision of theater training.

Since the book outlines a trajectory of learning in a controlled environment—a theater school, a professional workshop process, or the training of a theater group—it is angled primarily—but certainly not exclusively—toward the teacher or the director. Throughout its different sections I have attempted to weave together theory and practice, influences and discoveries, methodology and exploration in order to give directors, teachers, and actors the fundamentals of the exercises at hand, as well as the logic behind them, the mechanisms that make them work, and the pitfalls that tend to beset them. The idea behind these elaborations is not to set out any finite forms for these exercises, but, on the contrary, to give teachers, directors, and actors the benefit of everything I have learned about them through many years of trial and error, so they can concentrate on the core benefits of each exercise. Implicit in all this is the heartfelt urging to anyone who uses this material to expand and develop these exercises and to use them as a guide for a flight into new, uncharted areas.

While *the creative moment* and *presence* are well-known terms in the field of Training, the name Michael Chekhov is less so, and too often still elicits a routine response, "You mean Anton, don't you?" So a word or two about this unusual man is in order.

Michael Chekhov came into my life in two stages that were separated by nearly thirty years of acting, directing, and teaching. I first heard of him at the fledgling Department of Theater Arts at Tel Aviv University in 1963, from the founder of the department and my first teacher, Peter Frye, who had studied with Chekhov briefly in New York in 1941.[1] Thirty years later, at the 1993 conference of the Association for Theater in Higher Education, in Philadelphia, I began to understand a connection to his technique that had apparently always been there. After a work-shop I gave in my *ImageWork Training*, I was told by Mala Powers (the executrix of Chekhov's intellectual estate and the moving force behind the publication of the Chekhov "bible" *On the Technique of Acting*) and her student and Chekhov practi-tioner Lisa Dalton, that everything I demonstrated in the workshop was identical to central elements in the Chekhov Technique. This revelation was followed by a period of questioning and learning, during which, with the help of many of my present colleagues in the Chekhov work, I rediscovered and re-embraced the work of this extraordinary man and understood for the first time just how closely related my work was to his. In an unusual process of synchronicity, my development in the theater ran parallel to Chekhov's work—ever since that memorable evening when Peter Frye sowed the seed by asking me to do a Psychological Gesture for *Richard III* in the dilapidated prefab hut in Jaffa where I took my first steps into acting.

Unfortunately, Michael Chekhov's fascinating biography is beyond the scope of this book. Suffice it to say that he was Anton Chekhov's nephew, a brilliant actor whom Konstantin Stanislavsky called his "most gifted pupil," and an extraordinary teacher who, over a period of forty-five years (he died in Hollywood in 1955 at the age of sixty-four), developed a unique and comprehensive technique for the devel-opment of the creative actor. If I were asked to sum up all of Chekhov's teachings in a nut-shell I would take two quotes from his own writings. The first is, "A gesture is a psychology," and the second, "The actor imagines with his body." Psychology in the theater, according to Chekhov, is not a question of intellectual analysis but of movement and gesture. Whatever you want to know about the character you are playing you will be able to find easily—not through extensive intellectual analysis ("table work"), but through a series of physical techniques.

And the reason for that, Chekhov suggests, is the profound connections that exist between the moving body of the actor and her imagination. Note the following from *On the Technique of Acting*:

> The inner life of the images, and not the tiny experiential resources of the actor should be elaborated on stage and shown to the audience. . . .
>
> The acceptance of this independent world of imagination, the ability to penetrate through the outer appearances of the vision to its inner, fiery life, the habit of waiting actively until the image is right, brings the artist to the verge of discovering new and hitherto hidden things.
>
> (5)

This brings us to the full quote referred to only briefly above, which is,

> The actor imagines with his body. He cannot avoid gesturing or moving without responding to his own internal images. The more developed and stronger the image, the more it stimulates the actor to physically incorporate it with his body and voice.
>
> (95)

These two keys, the physical and the imaginative, that Chekhov discovered in his own brilliant creations at the Moscow Art Theater and later as a director and a teacher, he eventually elaborated into a complete Training in *To the Actor* in 1953, which was revised after his death and published in 1991 as *On the Technique of Acting*, which was re-issued in an expanded version in 2002. This is a training that combines detailed physical awareness with many techniques for using the active imagination of the moving body as a primary creative tool. And it is along these lines that my concept of theater training developed over the years, informing my work and this book—a training that places enormous emphasis on the development of a finely tuned and highly expressive body that combines with a profoundly resonant, actively communicative imagination in order to tap the springs of creativity and make them powerfully present in the performance space.

My retroactive acquaintance with the Chekhov Technique has given my work amplitude and context, and many of this brilliant actor/director/teacher's extraordinary insights on the actor's creativity are to be found—directly or indirectly—in almost all of the exercises outlined here. Yet, as I hope you will see, I believe I have extended this form of training into many different areas of the actor's creative work through a structured acquisition of techniques for expanding the actor's understanding of his creative/expressive mechanisms.[2] If anything, this book is a tribute to Chekhov through what I believe is an expansion of his ideas into new areas of training. I can only hope that this work will underscore and illuminate

Chekhov's unique contribution to the understanding of the creative processes of the actor, and open up the possibilities of following his lead into what he called the "Theater of the Future."

Notes

1   He is the only student mentioned by name in *Lessons for the Profesional Actor* by Deirdre Hurst du Prey (New York: PAJ, 1985), the chronicle of Chekhov's November 1941 workshop in New York.
2   For the sake of convenience in the avoidance of gendered—and hence sexist—terminology, throughout this book the term *actor* will refer to both men and women. For most pronouns in the book, a random choice of gender has been made.

PART 1

Logic

CHAPTER 1

The Logic
of Training

An untrained body is like an untuned musical instrument—its sounding box is filled with a confusing and ugly jangle of useless noise that prevents the true melody from being heard.

—Peter Brook

Training does not guarantee artistic results. Rather, it is a way of making one's intentions coherent.

—Eugenio Barba

Training, in any form it may take, is based on the understanding that the basic elements of the actor's creative individuality can be trained in preparation for the actor's work on all the other elements of theater such as character, scene, and text. This involves a training of the most fundamental elements of the creative instrument—the actor's three basic expressive tools, the *body*, the *voice*, and the *imagination*—and two basic skills: *radiation* (Chekhov's term for the actor's ability to project performative expression over a distance), and *creative cooperation* (the ability to create together with others: the director, fellow actors, and, most importantly, the spectators).

These strategies are the subject matter of the systematic training structure, which I refer to here as the "Logic of Training." These are procedures that are aimed at developing in the actor an awareness of the *separate* performative expressivity of the body, the voice, and the imagination, then providing performers with an understanding of the mechanisms involved in connecting them into a complex but coherent whole that generates a performative presence. These procedures also address themselves to a training of the skills required for the actor to be open and available to work creatively with all the other people involved in the theatrical event in order to allow the communion of theater to occur.

Trajectories

What we are talking about in fact is a kind of tightly knit, progressively stepped training structure, with some fairly profound aims—no less than "developing creativity." So the obvious question—and the most difficult one—is, Where do we start? If we consider training as a series of structures, each one addressing a different aspect of the actor's creative instrument, we can, I believe, discern a number of parallel "trajectories" that provide the beginning of an answer to that question and a framework for the process:

- from body to voice to imagination;
- from physical to physical/vocal to physical/vocal/verbal;
- from the abstract to the concrete.

These trajectories are, in fact, different cross-sections of the same thing: the body of the training. They coexist and complement each other extensively throughout the process, and are extremely helpful in determining the sequence of the training, the order of the exercises in a given session, and the inner structure of the exercises themselves. In other words, embracing these trajectories can give a period of actor training a built-in "logic" that is very helpful in determining the structure of a training program.

From body to voice to imagination

This trajectory traces the sources of actor training back to the purely physical, with work on voice and the imagination coming in only later in the process. There are a number of reasons for this, and here they are, in reverse order—proceeding from the last of these elements to the first.

Of all the actor's tools, the imagination is the most powerful and complex, but at the same time it is the most difficult to tap into or hold onto. This in itself is reason enough, I believe, to leave work on the imagination to an advanced stage of training. But there is also this very simple fact: the actor's imagination can only be perceived in performance when it is made present by the actor's body in space. How to *em-body* this wonderful tool; how to carry it into the audience's perception and maintain its presence there in a powerfully effective way over a given period of time—seems to me to be the foundation that must be laid before any attempt is made to train the actor's imagination for creative work.

Voice, as we shall see later, is the *product* of the moving body, and therefore it, too, requires a trained body before it can be worked on as a separate technique. And in *The Open Door*, quoted above, Peter Brook tells us that "since what frightens people most of all today is speaking, one must begin neither with words, nor ideas, but with the body. A free body is where it all lives or dies."[1]

All of which brings us to the outline of one of the training trajectories that informs this book: starting from the body, moving into voice work on a solid basis of the well-trained body, and only then moving into the fascinating, elusive, complex, and profound terrain of imagination.

From physical to physical/vocal to physical/vocal/verbal

These trajectories overlap in many significant ways, and in fact coexist as distinct procedures in the training. The distinctions that I have drawn among them offer, I hope, a more comprehensive, multilevel overview of the training offered here. This trajectory looks at the same parameters set out above in the first one, but charts the progression of the training from a slightly different angle—that of the relationships among body, voice, and language. The basic premise here is that actor training needs to steer clear of voice, words, or text for as long as possible, and to develop the training in that order: from the purely physical to the discovery of the sound produced by the moving body, and only then using the well-trained, deeply *connected* body and voice to support the actor's work with words, language, and text.

In the filmed version of Nikos Kazantzakis's *Zorba the Greek* there is a moment when Zorba, unable to contain his excitement about the plans for the lumber cableway, rushes out into the night and dances wildly on the beach. Collapsing finally in exhaustion, sweat pouring down his face and a beatific/apologetic smile on his face, he explains his ecstasy to his buttoned-up English friend: "When a man is full, what can he do? He dances!" When words fail, the only resort is to choose a "denser" form of expression that will say it *all*: dance—or, closer to our purpose, nonvocal movement and gesture. Translating that into training strategies means that the physical/nonverbal mode is where it all begins. Having the confidence of a well-trained, highly expressive body allows the actor to bring in voice—not for its verbal content, but for its deep connections to the actor's rhythm, pace, and breathing, and, at the end of the process to apply the knowledge she has gained to words and text. This, then, is the outline of the second training trajectory, one that moves from training the body to training the connections between body and voice, and, only at the end of the process, to connecting it all to words and language.

But this trajectory also brings into focus the curious paradox between the "density" of performative expression, as in Zorba's dancing and its "revelation factor." Basically, it goes like this: the denser the mode of expression, the more it both reveals and hides the inner life of the actor. How does this work? Up on her feet and expressing herself only through movement, gesture, and facial expression, in other words working almost directly from the subconscious to the physical without the mediation offered by voice, or, particularly, by language, the actor has absolutely no place to hide. "Revelation," under these circumstances, is almost infinite. And yet the opposite is no less true—since purely physical expression is far less precise than language or voice, it is susceptible to multiple interpretations, so that under the same circumstances of physical expression, the actor is actually *protected* from any kind of uncomfortable personal exposure. This "multiple inter-pretability" offers the performer many more shelters from unwanted revelation and exposure than vocal or verbal expression, and ensures his or her relative "safety."

An example from my own days as a theater student at Manchester University in the 1960s is a good case in point. In those early days of the Drama Department, there was a regular Wednesday evening event we called The Studio Group—an open framework for our own creative initiatives. Not long after we launched this fixture, I created and performed a one-man movement piece that I titled *One Act of Self*. It was a fairly desperate piece about the loneliness of a young man in an alien environment, far from his home, family, and friends. After the performance, one of my friends—the only person I was truly close to at the time—told me she had been shocked by the glaring transparency of the piece, and wondered how I dared bare my soul so completely in front of so many strangers. I was totally amazed because until she mentioned it I had not thought of the piece as being so powerfully revealing. However, listening to her I realized—after the fact—that she was absolutely right, and I began discreetly canvassing some of my other class-mates to hear their impressions of what they had seen. I was in for yet another surprise: all of them offered many very different interpretations of my perform-ance, but none of them said anything that even remotely resembled the acute discomfort Carry felt as she watched me supposedly "baring" myself so devastat-ingly before them. Now, forty years later, I know what happened: the high "revela-tion" value of the dense, nonverbal movement piece indeed "bared my soul" to someone with privileged information about my emotional state of being and a similar psychological makeup. Yet this same density also sheltered me completely from any gossipy interpretation by people less close to me. Somehow, as I was preparing the piece, I must have understood that I was, in my own modest way, emulating Antonin Artaud's paradigm of acting and "signaling through the flames," yet, at the same time, remaining almost totally protected from the fire.

This paradox of density and revelation led me to an inescapable conclusion: if the physical/nonvocal mode is the densest, the least controlled, the most highly revealing, and yet at the same time the "safest" or least threatening, then it seems like a very good place to start a program of training. Since the densest form of performative expression—the physical/nonvocal—releases the greatest degree of inner life, revealing and sheltering at the same time, it also helps develop in actors a facility for expressing their emotions, sensations, images, memories, and fantasies through physical action and gesture, and sharing them fairly securely with their observers. At the same time, it provides them with an understanding of the kind of confident vulnerability that they need in order to become sensitive and communicative artists. Once a basic level of proficiency has been achieved in this technique, actors can then move in stages to the other two modes, the physical/vocal mode and the physical/verbal—or textually-connected—mode, both of which require increasing levels of skill and a constantly growing willingness to touch upon, and express, highly personal imagery.

Finally, following this trajectory in a training group is also particularly conducive to the creation of an ensemble relationship. Acquiring the ability to reveal aspects of one's inner life with a fair degree of security is of vital importance, both to the development of each individual actor and to the development of trust and freedom within an ensemble (and an acting class, for all intents and purposes, is an ensemble). This trajectory of physical/nonvocal to physical/vocal to physical/verbal, allows the actors to develop the confidence of revelation gradually, in a training environment that is as supportive as it is demanding, and in so doing, to open themselves up freely and creatively to their partners and colleagues.

From the abstract to the concrete

This third trajectory, which informs the training concurrently with the two previous ones, is slightly different, and, rather than addressing the physical aspects of the work, suggests, in effect, a strategy for the development of the "habit of creativity" at every point along the other two trajectories. Since the actor's creativity is the central issue of this training, the application of this trajectory to the Logic of Training is as rigorous as possible.

Pablo Picasso once remarked how much he envied the creative freedom of his two young children, Claude and Paloma, as they scribbled away with childish abandon in his studio. "I have spent a lifetime trying to learn how to paint like they do," he said. What Picasso envied in his children was their ability to maintain a direct line of communication from a totally unfettered imagination to graphic expression, blissfully ignorant of "rules" and unencumbered by inhibitions or emotional stumbling blocks—in short, their absolutely natural hold on a precious commodity: creative freedom.

There is a logic at work here that I have found very useful in training actors. In order to help actors achieve a deep understanding of their creative individualities, and in order to provide them with techniques that will lead them to the highest level of their art, the training process that they undergo must first of all help them explore different strategies for understanding what creative freedom is all about. Before they learn about limitations, they must experience the sheer joy of creative/improvisational freedom, in all its variations. Only after they have developed the *habit* of that kind of freedom can they go on to one of the most important lessons of all: how to retain that same creative joy and freedom even within the tightest structure (of text, costume, mise-en-scène, lighting, music cues, etc.), or the most limited forms of expression.

The conclusion, once again, seems inescapable: every segment, indeed every exercise, in the Logic of Training should remain free-form for as long as possible, devoid of anything "concrete" such as words or props, or the kind of structured movement found in mime or "imaginary object" exercises. Miming the opening of a box of matches (for some reason the all-time favorite "imaginary object"!) is an exercise in prestructured memory, in which the entire development of the move-ment sequence is known in advance, allowing no room for improvisation or inven-tion. Beginning a movement/phrase from a physical impulse and giving it leave to *find its own form* in total improvisational freedom until it is over is an abstract exer-cise in creative freedom, one that provides the actor with a limitless variety of choices as the movement/phrase unfolds from one second to the next. The same principle underlies almost every sequence of exercises in the book, and is a crucially important element in the Logic of Training.

These three trajectories of the training intertwine and coexist naturally in the training offered here. The first two suggest different "takes" on the progression of the physical work into work on the imagination and the relation of all these to voice and language, while the third, "From the abstract to the concrete," informs them all equally, as an overall strategy of training for the development of creative freedom.

Improvisation technique

These trajectories of training are colored throughout by three "primary colors" of the actor's craft that run through them all, and will be referred to frequently in the exercise section in the Part 2 of this book, "Praxis." These three "colors" are (1) *connectedness*—the powerfully radiating "oneness" of body, voice, and imagina-tion in the performed moment, and the hoped-for end result of this entire process of training; (2) *repetition*—the one thing an actor does more than anything else throughout his professional life; and (3) *improvisation/creativity*—the inseparable, virtually indistinguishable "tandem." As we shall see, the first two—*connected-ness* and *repetition*—appear as distinct elements in the training, and are taught through specific exercises. The *improvisation/creativity* tandem, however, is much more difficult to pin down because it in fact informs everything in the training. Indeed, since this training hardly deals with language, and certainly does not go as far as dramatic text, and since the root subject of the training is the actor's crea-tivity, the principal technique employed throughout the entire spectrum of the exercises is improvisation. How this works requires a brief explanation.

Looking into moments of improvisation, I was uncovering patterns related to every kind of creativity. . . . I came to see improvisation as a master key to creativity. In this sense, all art is improvisation.

—Stephen Nachmanovitch

Improvisation is . . . immediate and organic articulation; not just a response, but a paradigm for the way humans reflect (or create) what happens . . . In that sense, improvisation may come close to pure "creativity."

—Anthony Frost and Ralph Yarrow

Stephen Nachmanovitch's arresting suggestion that improvisation is the "master key to creativity" does indeed place this element of performance in a very different perspective, as does Anthony Frost and Ralph Yarrow's claim that improvisation is close to "pure 'creativity.'" *Improvisation*, as I understand it and use it in training, is the visible aspect of creativity—a "technique"—and it is both a framework and a deeply embedded infrastructure for virtually every element in this training. It is only through improvisation/creativity technique that the creative moment can be seen as it unfolds again and again in workshop, rehearsal, or performance. It is only through solid grounding in the improvisation/creativity tandem that the workings of that all-important ingredient of creativity—the imagination—can be revealed and turned into an "on-tap" technique.

While Nachmanovitch provides an inspiring description of the component elements of the creative moment ("Mind at Play," "Disappearing," "The Power of Limits," "The Power of Mistakes," "Form Unfolding"—to mention just a few of his chapter headings), he does not directly address a central issue: can the components of improvisation as he identifies them be trained as individual techniques in their own right? This process whereby the unformed suddenly becomes form—where free-floating, unconnected elements in our psyche leap synaptic gaps in our brain to become entirely new and unplanned entities in the performance space—can this be taught and turned into a practical, permanently available, technique?

Well, thirty years or so of dealing with the formation of actors, and investigating the question of creativity through teaching and directing, have taught me two closely related things: (1) that the process of creativity is so fundamental to the life of an artist that no self-respecting training program can afford *not* to teach it, and (2) that talent, or innate creativity, cannot be taken for granted as a preexisting condition, an untouchable gift from the gods, and therefore it must be trained—formed—until it becomes a *habit*. How to do this is the tricky part. Practically speaking, just like Konstantin Stanislavsky's suggestion that the best way of comprehending a "beat" in a play is to give it a name, so too the mechanisms of improvisation/creativity technique can be trained if they can be named. The moment you are able to abstract a "technical" aspect of creativity from the whole and give it a name, you can almost always find activities (= exercises) that will model that same technical element in a different context, and lead you to an understanding of the way it actually works in practice. From there it's only a small step to the creation of training procedures that will help impart this understanding to others and teach them how to acquire these component elements of creativity.

An example from a well-known film—a celluloid moment deconstructed into segments—can perhaps give us some idea about this process of "naming" leading to the development of training procedures.

Most action films are instantly forgettable, and, in most cases, by the time the credits come on, we are hard-pressed to remember anything at all of all the mayhem we have just witnessed. And yet, scanning my memory for a compact example of the elements of improvisation/creativity technique, a scene from an *Indiana Jones* film kept coming to my mind. In what is most probably a highly selective recreation of this scene, I recall that at some point in his adventures, the fabled "archaeologist" Indiana Jones finds himself on a long rope bridge spanning a deep chasm and a crocodile-infested river, blocked by two sets of "bad guys" advancing on him from either side. As I remember it, there is a moment when despite—or perhaps because of—the seeming impossibility of his predicament, a tiny smile flashes onto actor Harrison Ford's mouth, as he actually *relaxes* for a fleeting second and says, "Oh shit!" But there is a devilish gleam in his eye. A great improviser, the wheels have begun turning rapidly in his head as he thinks positively, seeking a creative way out of this apparently no-win situation. I have a clear sense that his mind is racing, but that it all begins in that moment of relaxation—a kind of Zen-oriented Soft Focus—when he frees up his gray matter in order to allow it to concentrate on *nothing*, and by so doing opens up the possibility of concentrating on *everything*. In my fanciful recreation of the scene, neurons begin firing, multiple lines of information leap over myriad synapses at the speed of thought, as "Indy" ranges creatively over every possibility, even the most outlandish, and the little smile seems to indicate that the incorrigible optimist is allowing himself the luxury of believing that—even in those dire circumstances!—the right combination will drop into place as long as he keeps all lines open and remains *disponible* (that multilayered French word implying openness, availability, readiness, and willingness, all in one). In other words, as the music crests, and the saber-wielding nameless ones close in from both sides along the precarious rope bridge, the ever-resourceful archaeologist remains *open*—willing to consider absolutely any option until the very last instant, when he must select one of the many he has scanned in the blink of an eye.

Strangely, whenever I recall this moment, all I can bring to mind is the moment *before* the decision. I can't for the life of me remember what the intrepid archaeologist actually does to extricate himself from his rope-bridge predicament. Thinking about it for a minute, I realize that it is not at all surprising that what I retained in my memory was the *search* and not the decision. It's that moment *before*, that potential-packed second when all the options are open and a choice is about to be made—*that's* what fascinates me. Why? Because that is the Zero Point, the heart of any investigation into the creative moment; the moment of the purest, greatest creativity; the stillness that belies movement, the highly-charged median point between one action and another when fateful decisions are being weighed in the imagination. It is a moment of elation, of clarity, of incisive excitement when the creative organism is totally focused, poised to make a decision (Herbert Blau's "on the edge of a breath, looking") and absolutely confident in its ability to follow through on whatever impulse may appear.

Deconstructing this admittedly selective recollection of that moment on the bridge yields, then, an initial crop of "names": *Soft Focus*, *Openness/Availability* (Disponibilité), *Zero Point*, *Action in Stillness*, *The Moment Before*, and *Creative Flow*. But there is more to be gleaned, for our purposes, from the "Indiana Jones-on-the-bridge" syndrome.

In another memorable celluloid moment relevant to this investigation, Frank Finlay as Iago in Laurence Olivier's *Othello*, has a moment when, considering all the balls he has up in the air as part of his growing plot, he taps his temple and says " 'Tis here, but yet confused." Our hero on the bridge, Indiana Jones, also does not have a complete plan of action. He can project the outcome of his choices only as far as that first gesture—cutting the rope or burning it away—but no further. Having committed himself to action, and absolutely confident that his creativity will supply him with the complete solution at the last instant, he has to be prepared himself to step beyond the point of no return. And this is where he engages my interest again, because he now has to actually shift into action—he has to lift a foot in the air and move himself into a state of imbalance (what Eugenio Barba calls "precarious balance"), which, as we shall see, is virtually the precondition for any creative choices to be made. Once all of these are in place, there is only one more thing to do—to step into the unknown.

Here, then, through this recollection of moments on film, is the *creative moment*, deconstructed into a sequence of strategies, which, I believe, can be translated into exercises and trained separately in a very pure form: *Readiness*, *Foot-in-the-Air*, *Creative Imbalance*, and *Stepping into the Unknown*, which can all take their place now in the growing nomenclature of the creative moment.

But theater, as we all know, is an instantly perishable art, so beyond making the creative moment appear, we also have to learn how to seize it before it vanishes (remember that great idea that flashed into your mind, and, before you could write it down, disappeared—*forever*?), and learn how to manage the riches we have mined in order to give form to the products of our creative imagination—as they are happening. And, voilà—three more names appear, giving us a complete cycle of creativity: *Recognizing*, *Seizing*, and *Managing* the creative moment.

It is possible to learn through repetition to recognize the onset of a creative moment. It is characterized mainly by a sense of potency, of infallibility, of great clarity and supreme ease. Once the moment is recognized, seizing it generally requires no more than surrendering to it, allowing it to be, or as Jerzy Grotowski has taught us through his concept of the actor's "*via negativa*", not preventing it from being there. However, it is the idea of "managing" the creative moment that gives us pause. Can we really say "managing" and a "creative moment" in the same breath? Aren't they mutually exclusive? For the answer to that one, let's go back to the soap-bubble image again (from p. x in the Pre-text) and ask the obvious question: Given that a soap bubble (= the moment of improvisation/creativity) is infinitely fragile and likely to vanish at the slightest provocation, can it in fact be pushed? Can it be made to move without bursting it into oblivion? The answer is yes, but—as in the reply to the famous question about how porcupines make love—very carefully! Pushing it too hard will burst it; pushing it too gently will not give it enough energy to move. Pushing the soap bubble—or generating the creative moment—with a delicate touch and a careful combination of push and release, *just so*, imparting a constant momentum without bursting the loveliness—that is the form of "management" I am talking about when I speak of "managing the creative moment."

And there is more. For all its sublime pleasures, no matter how beautiful or powerful a creative moment is, it is, at the same time, an organic process that emerges, rises, peaks, and must eventually fall. And yet, because of its beauty and profundity, we feel bound to try and keep it vibrantly alive as long as possible. This provides us with two more names: Exhausting or Squeezing the moment—making it last as long as possible—and only then initiating the next creative cycle, so that the state of improvisation/creativity we are in can go on without missing a beat. And here we have it—the complete cycle of creativity: Disponibilité, *Zero Point*, *Creative Imbalance*, *Recognizing and Seizing the Creative Moment*, *Stepping into the Unknown*, then *Managing the Creative Moment*, *Exhausting the Moment*, and finally *Initiating the Next Creative Cycle*.

And just before we leave this naming process, there is one more aspect of improvisation technique that must be considered. Managing the creative moment in time is never a one-sided event. Much of what happens between our conscious selves and our subterranean creative forces depends for its success on an ongoing "dialogue" between the intrepid soap-bubble pusher and the intrepid soap bubble itself. From this we derive one more name to add to the list: the well-known element of *Give and Take*, or as I will be calling it, *Initiating/Yielding* about which much will be said later on.

Improvisation/creativity informs every area of the training trajectories. It is the basic technique that is used to perform all of the exercises. This being the case, Improvisation Technique—as such—is not taught as a distinct element in the training—it *is* the training. And the above deconstruction was carried out not in order to reveal what cannot be revealed—namely, the mystery of the creative process, but to identify its component elements, which will appear, in one way or another, in virtually all the exercises that make up the Logic of Training.

This process of naming is an attempt to distinguish between many mutually embedded concepts, and this makes any attempt to arrange them in order of priority extremely difficult. Here then is a brief recap of the elements of improvisation/creativity technique, arranged in the order in which they appeared above:

The first principles of improvisation technique

Soft focus

Openness/Availability (Disponibilité)

Zero Point/The Moment Before

Readiness/Action in Stillness

Creative Imbalance

Stepping Into the Unknown

Creative Flow: Recognizing, Seizing, Managing the Creative Moment

Initiating/Yielding (Give and Take)

Exhausting (Squeezing) the Moment

Initiating the Next Creative Cycle

This is not an exhaustive list, but on the face of it, there seems to be a glaring omission: spontaneity. Since this is supposedly the very matter and substance of improvisation, its absence here requires a brief explanation. Basically, I don't think spontaneity can be taught. Telling someone to "be spontaneous" is like ordering someone to relax—in both cases other techniques must be brought into play in order to facilitate either spontaneity or relaxation. Consequently, spontaneity itself is not a technique; rather it is the result of the successful application of many of the techniques mentioned above. Learning how to become "available," how to generate a moment of "creative imbalance," how to "step into the unknown," how to work whatever is happening from one split second to the next—all these add up to learning how to "be spontaneous" for theatrical purposes. When we work on a text and search for our character's superobjective, we are constantly reminded to use a verb implying an action—"to rule," "to protect"—rather than a verb relating to a state of being—"to be a king," or "to be loved." This same logic applies to any attempt at identifying the "action" of an improvisation: it is not "to be spontaneous," which cannot be taught, but "to step into the unknown," which can.

This is the basic theory and structure underlying the Logic of Training that I am proposing here. And yet, however inspiring the theory may be, translating these organic, creative precepts into the essential linearity of a book form is always a major challenge that requires some attention. That is where I would briefly like to take you now, in the hope that these clarifications will help turn the exercise section of the book into a useful tool.

Note

1   Peter Brook, *The Open Door: Thoughts on Acting and Theatre* (London: Methuen, 1995), 77.

CHAPTER 2

Training into Writing

One of the most treacherous pitfalls, which, unsought for, lie in wait in descriptions of exercises and advice for performers, derives from the fact that it is a book, things must be placed one after another. They cannot be interwoven.

—Eugenio Barba

Training from a book

As Eugenio Barba notes above, training sessions are notoriously hard to write down. In *The Presence of the Actor* Joe Chaikin goes even further, claiming that workshop exercises are untranslatable "internal territory" and simply cannot be written down in any practical form. Unlike a book, where there is no choice but to list exercises one after the other in some kind of linear order, a workshop is an organic, multileveled process that often deals simultaneously with many different strands of the same weave. What is more, new exercises, or variations on existing ones, are forever being developed in the real time of the workshop session as part of a natural process of growth, so trying to write all of this down at the same time that it is growing is like Alice's predicament toward the end of her fantastical sojourn beyond the looking glass: the faster I run the more I stay in one place. There is also a Pirandellian Catch-22 at work here: trying to "immortalize" in writing what is essentially a labor of creative art means dooming it to a life outside of time—to a kind of death.

So what are we to do? In order to offset the unavoidable linearity of a book, I have chosen to provide detailed accounts of the way in which each of these exercises works in practice, together with suggestions for modifying them in response to changing circumstances or major brainstorms. Ideally, the Logic of Training outlined here should be used as a framework and an incentive for further development, and all its parts should be interwoven individually by the teacher/ director to suit the particular temperament of the group in training. This should be done wisely, with what might be called *professional prudence*—after all, as you will see, the sequential structure of the training I am suggesting is a very important aspect of the work—but it should be done nonetheless. This is the only way to ensure a creative flexibility in the work, as opposed to the uncreative, deadly strictures of adherence to chapter and verse.

The basics

Seminality

In their excellent study *Meyerhold: Eisenstein and Biomechanics*, Mel Gordon and Alma Law bring the following quote from the writings of Vseyolod Meyerhold:

> In my Biomechanics, I was able to define in all twelve or thirteen notes for the training of an actor. But in polishing it up I'll leave perhaps no more than eight.

And in their unique *Dictionary of Theatre Anthropology*, Eugenio Barba and Nicola Savarese have this to say about training:

> It is possible to make a long training with even a very small number of exercises . . . It is like the meaning of a sentence which, in spoken language, is not only the result of syntax but also of the stress and tone which underline certain words. So it is in training, where the same chain of exercises takes on various logics, depending on the accents used.

The concept of training in this book—the Logic of Training—is very much the result of a process of reduction similar to those referred to by Vsevolod Meyerhold and Eugenio Barba. As my own interests as a director and a teacher increasingly spiraled in on the actor's presence and the workings of the creative moment in theater, I found that more and more of the exercises I had been using in various stages of the training actually applied, on a deep level, to those two all-important aspects of the actor's art—*presence* and the *creative moment*. At about the same time, I also began to notice that the exercises I had dropped from my training all had something in common: they either lacked a truly profound connection to these two seminal concerns, confused the issue through a lack of clarity or a duplication of other exercises (in most cases it was the duplication that *caused* the lack of clarity), or else addressed themselves to some form of self-indulgent "experience" rather than to technique-oriented training. The result was a growing understanding that I could in fact use fewer and fewer exercises and still help my actors achieve the same, if not better, results—with considerably less confusion. All that was needed, I soon discovered, was a throughline—a logic—that would enable me to extract different training procedures from slightly varied applications of the same exercises. Removing all the excess, I found myself using a select number of exercises, which I began referring to as "seminal" because each one can be used for many different aspects of the training, depending on the "accents" used in presenting and sidecoaching them.

This, then, is the format offered here in the training section: exercises that contain multiple *Emphases* relating to many different aims of the training—presence, connectedness, improvisation/creativity technique, radiation, and so on—all of which can be used repeatedly, throughout the training period, to train now one, now another of these elements separately. In the training section, all of these potentials are listed and described in some detail under the heading "Emphases" at the end of each exercise.

Structure

> Structure ignites spontaneity. . . . Limits yield intensity . . . containment of strength amplifies strength. Commitment to a set of rules . . . frees your play to attain a profundity and vigor otherwise impossible. . . . Form used well can become the very vehicle of freedom.
>
> —Stephen Nachmanovitch

> Training is improvisation which is structured by the application of principles.
>
> —Roberta Carrieri (The Odin Theatre)

Creativity in theater, or in any art form, for that matter, is so wondrously mysterious, imprecise, and indefinable, that the last thing we need to do is make it even more mysterious through vague terminology or a lack of clarity and structure in the training. As Stephen Nachmanovitch suggests in the quote above, it is only through adherence to form or a set of rules that we can create the special "space" our creative potential needs in order to touch the depths. By the same token, a lack of structure, or the lack of clearly defined parameters either for single exercises or for a full sequence, leads only to a kind of amorphousness, or, as Grotowski used to call it, "plasma." Unstructured training can yield deeply moving moments in the workshop, but care should be taken: sheer creativity is very seductive! Without the scaffolding of structure and clarity, training can provide actors with any number of one-shot "beautiful experiences" that may have their own merits but that, I believe, fall short of providing the kind of discipline that is truly conducive to a career of creativity in the performing arts. If the practical applications of theater training are not made absolutely clear by the structure of the teaching, the distinctions between training for a professional career in the performing arts and the related but different fields of psychodrama or group dynamics break down.

All of these considerations have prompted me to include in this book many suggestions relating to the structural aspects of the training, the clarity of the presentation, recommendations about the progression from one exercise to the next, how exercises can overlap and interweave in different stages of the process, and suggestions about how each area of training and its specific exercises can be introduced, sidecoached, and evaluated.

There is one more consideration of prime importance to be taken into account in this context of structure. Training involves an accumulation of experiential knowledge over time. Each step in the trajectories set out in Chapter 1, then, needs to be "layered" into the performer's organism to serve as a basis for the next step in the training. The fundamentally experiential nature of this knowledge means that it is not physically recorded in any way, leaving it vulnerable to the vagaries of memory. A clearly delineated structure—a logic—that moves in "memorable" steps from one level to the next is, I believe, invaluable for actors in training. More than anything else it clarifies the process and provides the actors with readily available points of reference back and forth along an easily traceable line of development. As Eugenio Barba notes in *The Paper Canoe* apropos the work of the actor, "The performer's action is *real* if it is disciplined by a score" (122). Later Barba adds, "The performer's soul, intelligence, sincerity and warmth do not exist without the precision forged by the score" (*The Paper Canoe* 122, 128).

And yet, when all is said and done, structure should never turn into an end in itself, nor should teaching become pedantic as a result of blind adherence to structure. In the incorrigibly improvisational mode of the Israeli lifestyle there is a saying: "Every plan is the basis for a change of plans." The same should apply here: for all the emphasis on structure and applicability, every workshop plan should be no more than that—an outline that is clear enough to define the goals but also flexible enough to accommodate the particular development of any single actor or group of actors in a given class.

Synchronicity and symbiosis

In 1990 I took part in a conference called "Beyond Stanislavsky", which was organized by the Liège-based Centre des Récherches Théâtrales. The conference was devoted to modes of acting training that were different from the prevailing adherence to the Stanislavsky System or its Method variation. Among the teachers was one of Russia's greatest movement experts, Andrei Drazhnin. To my utter amazement, during the course of the workshop, he put us through the paces of an exercise that was identical—not similar, *identical*—in almost every single one of its details to an exercise that I *know* I invented one night in the privacy of my home.

This was a humbling and at the same time enlightening experience, because it brought home to me two very important observations: (1) unintentional synchronicity in training procedures is as natural as it is unavoidable; (2) teachers working in the same field, out of the same basic concepts, will almost invariably come up with similar or even identical solutions for training problems. This, in turn, produces an almost natural flow and exchange of information between teachers of similar performance inclinations, an exchange that can occur through personal contact—as was the case with my meeting with Drazhnin—or over great distances through a commonality of interests, that is, a synchronicity. All of this is by way of saying that the exercises in this book belong to a certain form of training that is certainly not mine alone (and my "retroactive" Michael Chekhov connection is proof enough of that), and that many of the procedures and exercises outlined here owe a great deal to other teachers and artists whom I either worked with, or who influenced me through their writings or training. What makes this book unique, I hope, is the way I have melded all of these influences with my own accumulated experience to create this Logic of Training.

Now that the stepping-stones are in place, let's begin moving across the water, first of all setting out some of the basic requirements for a successful training.

CHAPTER 3

Technicalities

What follows here is an attempt to guide the reader into the exercise section of the Logic of Training with the help of a frame of reference that lays out the way the book should be used, and describes an optimal *Setup* for teaching these training concepts.

Fundamentals

The concept: The systematic, step-by-step design of this book and the highly detailed elaboration of my own personal experience with these exercises is my way of attempting to make a book feel like a live workshop. Hopefully, this will give the reader an indication of the way this training develops in the real space of a workshop.

Read the whole thing: The multiple applicability, or multilayered "seminality," of these exercises necessitates a detailed description of the activities, procedures, variations, and points of emphasis, as well the relevance of these exercises to different aspects of performance. Have patience! Read the whole description of an exercise before trying it out.

Resonance: Some of these exercises may work differently for you from the way I describe them here. There is only one absolute guideline to follow: *resonance*. If a particular training procedure resonates in your system, ties in easily with your teaching, your directing concerns, or your feel for acting processes, try it, see how it works, and shape it to serve *your* purposes. Then apply the golden rule of acting: if it works, use it; if it doesn't, throw it out!

The learning trajectory 1:   The cumulative nature of the training creates a unique dynamic: sometimes, in a three-hour session, only the last few minutes may yield an illumination or a useful experience; in a six-month training session, only the last day may be truly enlightening. Bearing this in mind helps develop professional patience and the diligence needed to seize seconds or minutes of valuable insight when they happen.

The learning trajectory 2:   The order in which the exercises of the training appear in the book is, more or less, the order in which I introduce them in the training process. In practice, of course, workshop sessions are based on a complex structure composed of ongoing and new exercises in a fairly precise overlapping structure. Therefore, the succession of exercises is punctuated by a number of proposals for integrating various training procedures at critical junctions in the process.

The learning trajectory 3—platform and variations: There are many exercises in the book that serve as "platforms" for any number of variations. This is not only a mechanism of this training, but a recommendation for further developments and explorations of the potentials of specific exercises.

Exercises as models of behavior: This is a useful way of describing the concept of training through exercises. The parameters of each exercise create a learning structure, or "model of behavior," that the actors *have to use* in order to learn something about their creative selves.

The Actor's Catechism: Because these models of behavior are essentially experiential—like everything else in theater—and have no existence beyond their duration in time, actors have to develop a mechanism for turning the "behavior" into a learning experience. One of the ways of doing that is by developing the habit of questioning themselves about processes *as they are experiencing them*, with questions like, "What am I *doing* when I do this?" "What have I done to make this happen?" "What do I have to add to make this happen?" This is the habit of ongoing "personal research" that I call *The Actor's Catechism*.

Nota Bene (henceforth *NB*)
Often there are no answers to the questions asked during an exercise, or else actors may intuit an answer or feel it as a resonance without being able to articulate it in words. Just asking the question is the important thing, so that the process of seeking an answer will be engaged. The query itself is often enough to focus our attention on the training benefit of the process we are undergoing.

Continuity and sequence: Since the accumulation of experience is the fundamental dynamic of this process, continuity and sequence are of the utmost importance, both on the part of the teacher and on the part of the participants. This is one of the reasons why this kind of training should, ideally, take place consecutively and intensively, in a workshop format of frequent and extended work sessions.

Critiques: Exercises have no value unless they are discussed for their intrinsic level of achievement and put into a context of the training and their practical application to the actor's craft and artwork. Therefore, group critique sessions after every exercise and after every sequence of exercises, plus extended critique sessions at the end of cycles of work, are absolutely indispensable as a way of incorporating the work and bringing each section or each exercise to an effective closure.

Evaluation: There is a very simple, commonsense rule of thumb that I try to teach actors: the spectators—in the theater, the workshop group, or in the class— are *always 100 percent right*! There is absolutely no way to counter anyone's subjective evaluation of an exercise, nor does it serve any conceivable purpose to try to rebut a critique, save perhaps to assuage a bruised ego. All one can do is listen to the evaluations and treat them all with equal respect. "Comments," Yoshi Oida says, "might not be 'true' but they are useful."[1] He adds, "Even a distorted mirror is better than no mirror at all." As experience grows, so too does the self-critical faculty of the actor and, with it, the ability to learn from everything—everything!—an actor hears from colleagues and teachers. In my own work, most of the evaluation is generated through group critiques. In this way, after performing a piece of work, actors receive a broad spectrum of evaluations from the group that usually covers most aspects of the performed event. It is up to the actor then to weigh the relative merits of all the comments, and extract what are, for him or her, the most constructive elements. Clearly, this requires a great deal of maturity and honesty, and as a result, it is a very important part of the performer's development process. Finally, as the training proceeds and certain fairly clear performance parameters, such as *Connectedness*, *Seduction* (the level of attention created by the work), *Variety*, and *Centers* become practical measures used regularly by the group for evaluating the effectiveness of any given exercise, the margin of subjectivity is narrowed.

Diaries: Since the accumulation of experience is so important, human memory so fallible, and personal interpretation of creative events so crucial, I always recommend to my actors that they keep a diary of one kind or another to note their experiences throughout the training. I generally ask my actors to put their diaries somewhere handy so that they can get to them quickly and easily if they need to record something. As I see it, this notation is so important that I encourage my actors to do it at any time, and not to regard these "diary moments" as a break in the flow of the work. Once the actors learn to use this option wisely, it becomes a highly effective aid in their training.

The work space

The emphasis on physical expression that runs right through the training places a premium on having a space that is suited for movement. This means a large studio with a sprung wooden dance floor. Concrete or tiled floors—even those covered with linoleum—can cause damage to knees and ankles over an extended period of time, and they certainly limit physical expression. The studio should be big enough (e.g. ten meters by eight) to accommodate the entire group on the floor at once in group exercises and to allow for the distance work required in some of the exercises.

It is best if the work space has a high ceiling and, if possible, no unprotected windows, light fixtures, mirrors, or anything else equally breakable. At least one of the more important recurring exercises in the training—Throwing Sticks—has occasionally resulted in some unfortunate personal experiences with broken light bulbs, and therefore provides a strong incentive to bear this warning in mind. Most importantly, there should be *no mirrors*! Or, if there are any in the space, they should be equipped with curtains to cover them so that the actors cannot spend any time observing themselves as they move. Mirrors distort, hypnotize, and otherwise distract actors in their work on the studio floor. What is more, actors are their own worst spectators *and* critics!

Rules of conduct

There are a number of simple rules that should be followed in order to make the training effective.

NB

Each of the following suggestions is the result of many years of experience working in this area of actor training, and trying to find the best ways to make the creative moment welcome in the work space. After all, we are dealing with a very rare, easily frightened "soap bubble," and any distraction to its delicate flight may cause it to burst and disappear forever. Therefore, it is very important to make every effort we can—before entering a creative situation—to prepare for that moment.

Physical preparedness and stamina: Actors should always be in top form for a workshop session so that they will be able to reap the greatest benefit from the training. This means, among other things, not eating heavily before the class and having plenty of water available in the studio. Occasionally, the continuity required to make a particular training procedure fruitful will require up to three hours of consecutive work with no break, and this should be borne in mind as an option. Breaks are no less a part of the structure of a workshop than the exercises. Actors who step out of the work space—for whatever reason—before a scheduled break will often require up to ten or fifteen minutes to reorient themselves in the working atmosphere.

Transformation: Not too long ago I observed an acting class where one of the participants entered the work space, took off his sunglasses, and walked right onto the floor in his street clothes, a bulging wallet in one pocket, jangling keys in another, and a cell phone dangling from his belt. This is perhaps a fairly extreme exception, and perhaps more of a reflection on the teacher than on the student! Nevertheless, it is a telling case in point. Going into a training session requires the actor to undergo a transformation, to "cross the threshold," as Michael Chekhov used to call it, or, in Eugenio Barba's terminology, to shed the diluted, unfocused "daily" self that the actor comes in with from outside, and take on an "extradaily" self that is prepared to engage in creative work. These are all highly evocative concepts that help define the initial transformation that an actor has to undergo in order to embark on the pursuit of his craft. After all, transformation is what an actor does, and there is absolutely no reason for so important a part of the actor's craft to be regarded as something that occurs only during a performance in front of an audience. It is, rather, a *habit* that should be acquired, a way of thinking about and treating the art form—and it begins in the studio space. Therefore, every time actors prepare to go into the work space they should make a habit of undertaking a minimal transformation, at the very least by changing one item of apparel.

Working clothes: Since this training work is very physical, heavy and/or constricting material (e.g. denims or corduroy) should be avoided. By the same token, apparel that requires frequent adjusting or is likely to come undone in one way or another during strenuous physical activity should be also avoided. Tights or light cloth pants should be worn with a T-shirt or a loose—light—sweatshirt (the heavy, baggy ones hinder movements and blur the actor's form in space, thus reducing overall expressivity). I generally do not recommend working in shorts.

Bare feet: Yes and no. Yes, because the contact of the entire foot on the working space should be unmediated and an integral part of the body's physical expressiveness. No, because a light dance shoe offers almost the same sense of the floor and the same degree of expressiveness, and at the same time, offers some protection from occasional accidents. Whatever you choose, sneakers with thick inflexible soles should be avoided at all costs.

Accoutrements: Rings, watches, bangles, earrings, and so on should all be shed before actors enter the work space. The various talismans people wear in their daily life—around their wrists or necks; on their ears, fingers, or anywhere else— form a protective barrier that shelters them by constantly reaffirming the self they like to present to the world at large. If actors are going to reap any benefits from a training process, they must be prepared to present themselves to the work free of masks, unprotected and vulnerable. Rather than emphasizing the self they have fashioned and with which they confront the world more or less successfully they must deliberately make themselves vulnerable—so that they can be available for whatever surprises come their way in the course of the training. And it should go without saying that large dangling earrings, floppy necklaces, massive pointed rings, SCUBA-diving watches, or multiple nose-piercings are downright dangerous to work with in strenuous movement exercises!

Kneepads: *A must* in the advanced movement exercises. They provide a good measure of protection and greatly increase actors' willingness to take physical risks. The kneepads should be the soft ones like those used in volleyball, not the hard plastic ones used for roller-skating.

Masters, teachers, mentors, and guides

My early versions of *ImageWork*, my "retroactive" Chekhov connection, and finally, the present form of *ImageWork Training* based on this Logic of Training, are all the result of the way many different influences coalesced within me over a lengthy period of time. Consequently, large parts of this book owe their existence to teachers, mentors, colleagues, "accidental guides," and generations of student actors. So before I go into the praxis that they, to a large extent, gave me, a heart-felt word of thanks is due.

Among the most notable of these teachers were Peter Frye, my first mentor in the theater and a lifelong friend until his death a few years ago; the brilliant and eccentric Stephen Joseph, who, in Manchester in the 1960s, provided me with striking examples of the extraordinary power of images; my dear friend Jacki Kronberg, who, so many years ago in Jerusalem, gave me the precious gift of improvisation technique and my first systematic training in theater; Joe Chaikin and Bruce Meyers who, in an exhilarating workshop in the Jerusalem Khan Theater in 1979, pointed me in the direction of body–voice–imagination connections in acting training; Eugenio Barba and the actors of the Odin Theater—Iben, Torgeir, Roberta,

Julia, and all the others—who in the thirty-odd years of our acquaintance, have proven to be an inexhaustible source of practical guidance and inspiration; and Tony Cots, one of the "accidental guides," a former Odin actor who, not long after he left the Odin, reinforced in me a fundamental understanding of Training as a concept in the life of the actor.

Then there is what Eugenio Barba fondly calls "The Chekhov cabal"—the teachers of the Chekhov Technique around the world from whom I have learned so much: Joanna Merlin, Jack Colvin, Mala Powers (all three of whom studied with Chekhov in Hollywood in the 1950s; sadly, both Jack and Mala passed away since the first writing of this book), Lenard Petit, Ted Pugh, Fern Sloane, and Andrei Malaev-Babel, all from the United States; Jorg Andrees and Jobst Langhans from Berlin; Sarah Kane and Graham Dixon, from the United Kingdom and Australia; Slava Kokorin and the late Nelly Dugar-Jabon from Siberia; Andrei Kirilov from Russia; and Per Brahe from Denmark. Finally, there is Avinoam, a former student of mine, who years ago resisted my directorial probing of his work on the character of John Proctor in *The Crucible*, with the admonition "Leave me my secrets!" and in so doing taught me an important lesson in the nature of the relationship between actor and teacher/director, and also a very profound lesson in the fundamental dynamics of creativity in the theater. He belongs to the scores of students I have worked with over so many years at the Department of Theater Arts at Tel Aviv University, and many other places all over the world, all of whom have proven to me, in the clearest possible way, the aptness of the Talmudic saying, "I have learned from all those who have taught me, and from my students most of all."

All of these teachers appear here in these pages—some by name, most of them anonymously—and to all of them I owe a great debt of gratitude, the profundity of which is difficult to express in words.

Finally, a special note of thanks to Miri Regendorfer, Dalit Gurfinkel, Limor Ben-Shushan, Tamar Samuel, Guy Weiner, and Mischa Ruzetsky, all of whom appear in the photographs in these pages.

Note

1   Oida, Yoshi, and Lorna Marshall, *The Invisible Actor* (London: Methuen, 1997), 53.

PART 2

Praxis

PART 2

Praxis

CHAPTER 4

The Exercises

CROSSING THE THRESHOLD

Here we go, taking a first step from the periphery of the theory into the praxis that is the heart of this book. Taking a deep breath, I cross the threshold, stepping out into a *terrain inconnu*: the translation of a lifetime of live work with moving, sounding, speaking actors in the real space and time of the rehearsal room/studio space, into the linear, two-dimensional finality of a book. *Bon voyage*!

1. CROSSING THE THRESHOLD

This is a vitally important way to start *any* training session or class work. It is the essential transformation actors should undergo before entering into their creative work. Once introduced, this should be the standard opening for every workshop session.

> ### Activity
>
> The actors are asked to line up around the perimeter of the work space. Then they are urged to take a moment for themselves, and whenever each feels ready to step into the space, remain there in silence until the entire group has joined them in the space. The workshop session begins when everyone has crossed into the work space.

Hugh O'Gorman from Cal State Long Beach, includes this important addition to his explanation of the exercise: suggest to your actors that as they are standing with their backs to the wall, they are facing an invisible membrane, so that stepping into the space also involves moving through that membrane into a very different kind of space.

Finally, habit is a great deadener, so as you work through your training sessions, suggest to the actors that they choose a different place to enter from each time.

BREAKING THE ICE

The first meeting of an acting class or a working group of actors has only one main function: to get to the second session! That is why before we set out along the trajectories of training, some ice must be broken.

Some of these icebreakers are used only once, at the very first workshop session. This does not mean that they cannot or must not be used ever again. If there is good enough reason to repeat them at any point in the training, go ahead and do so!

Names and variations

What follows are a variety of exercises based on the use of the actors' names, with the following applications:

- A quick way to get everyone to learn the names of all the members of the group.
- An introduction to some first principles: openness, vulnerability, body language, self-confidence, and Give-and-Take, or, as I shall be referring to it: initiating-and-yielding.

2. CIRCLE OF NAMES

Setup

The entire group stands in a loose circle, facing inward.

Activity

An actor moves into the center, and, moving to his left does the following: he stops in front of each one of the other actors in order, faces him or her, creates and holds eye contact, offers a hand for the other actor to shake, and says his first name only. The actors approached by him on the periphery maintain eye contact, hold the offered hand, and then give the actor *his own name* back ("David"—"*David*"). There is often some initial confusion as to what name should be given in response. Make sure it is clear to the actors standing around the circle that they do not offer their own names, but instead are repeating the name offered to them by the actor in the center of the circle.

Only when this exchange of handshake, eye contact, and name has been completed—and not before—can the actor in the center break the contact, and move to the next person. When the first actor completes the circle of participants and returns to his place in the circle, the actor on his right gets into the circle to begin her circuit.

Notes

1. Only one actor enters the circle at a time, and total silence—apart from the exchange of names—should be maintained throughout the entire exercise.
2. Full-frontal body language is maintained at all times, so that the actors will have to deal with direct confrontation and commitment. This temporary bond between the two partners should remain complete—eye contact, hand-shake, full-frontal body language—until the actor in the center gets his name back.
3. No time limit should be set for when a name is given or returned. This will ensure that the encounters, however they proceed, will be a true expression of the moment.
4. I would suggest that (a) the teacher/director should stay out of the circle, unless he or she feels compelled to take part in the round of introductions (being watched by the teacher/director from outside the circle gives the entire process a very important edge that disappears if the teacher/director participates in the circle itself); and (b) there should be no sidecoaching during the activity—just let it follow its own course.

Emphases

This is only an "icebreaker" and therefore there is no "right" way of doing it, nor is there any need for it to be talked about afterward. The following elements, however, should be pointed out:

1. *Basic Give-and-Take.* In a very primitive form, this is an exercise that underlines one of the fundamentals of the training: Give-and-Take, or, as I will be referring to it from here on: *initiating and yielding.*
2. *Creative imbalance.* Creativity occurs at moments of imbalance. Symmetry and balance are usually deadening in this respect. In this exercise the imbalance is more of an "inquietude" brought about by being alone in the center of a circle surrounded by strangers. You have no way of knowing how your name will be received, nor—more disturbingly—how it will be given back to you. All this generates an anxious imbalance that is a prerequisite for creative work.

3. CRAZY NAMES AND VARIATIONS

This is a follow-on exercise with variations, all of which use the same basic concept—eye contact, handshake, and the exchange of names—but with a twist.

Setup

The actors are now free to move through the entire space with no limitations.

Activity

This is the same activity as before—eye, hand, and name contact—but with a few changes:

- The exchange now is like a proper introduction: one actor gives her *full* name—first and last names—and the other actor replies with *his own full name.*
- The event takes place on the run, with everyone moving rapidly, even "hysterically," through the space.
- The two actors going through their introduction must complete it—exchanging with each other both first and last names—before breaking contact and running off to find someone else.
- The participants repeat the entire introduction procedure at each encounter, no matter how many times they meet each other—even if they find they are introducing themselves to the same person three times in a row.
- Emphasis should be placed on the "hysterical" element of the exercise, with everyone desperately seeking someone to introduce themselves to and with absolutely no time to think about it!

A "Freeze!" command should be given every few minutes. Upon hearing it the actors must do just that—freeze completely, with no sound or movement—and remain frozen until the "Continue!" signal is given. When they continue, the actors must pick up from exactly where they left off, both physically and verbally. This is the quirk in the game that gives it an edge of uncertainty—and an added challenge.

Example

I have just grabbed a partner's hand, made eye contact, and begun saying my name when the "Freeze!" command is given. I stop immediately, midshake, midname; instead of completing "David Zinder" I stop at "Dav—". When the "Continue!" signal is given, I complete the handshake, and pick up the introduction from exactly the same point where I "froze" it—the last syllable of my first name: "—id Zinder." The freeze, then, is like a bubble, a moment out of time, a gathering-in of energies. After running furiously around the space, frantically grabbing hands and making endless introductions—expending energy—I now have to stop everything, regain control, and hold it all in, savoring the expectancy, the tense wait for the explosive release that will follow the "Continue!" signal.

Notes

1. The exercise is aimed at freeing up a new group and is therefore blatantly hysterical. Speed is essential as a device for encouraging openness. The actors should be exhorted to run as quickly as they can all the time—without compromising the *complete* exchange of eye contact and names.
2. At the breakneck speed of this exercise, the full-frontal body language of the previous exercise is simply not possible, so forget it. However, all the other elements of the Give-and-Take must be there in full: eye and hand contact must be held until the last syllable of the returned name is uttered.
3. Tell the actors that you want to be part of every introduction, so they should shout their names out loudly so that you can hear them. The noise generated by the group adds excitement, energy, and an element of distraction that enhances the need for concentration.
4. Sidecoaching during the running of the exercise is virtually impossible, so coaching remarks should be given before the exercise or during the

freezes. Regarding the freezes, tell the actors that it requires them to reverse the flow of energy, from outward into the run and the vigorous vocal encounters, to an inward holding-in of energies. Point out to the actors that they should freeze without letting arms or hands dangle after they stop, and without looking at the teacher/director. Tell them that if the "Freeze!" command catches them with a foot in the air, they should first put it down and then freeze.

Emphases

1. *Play.* This is very much a game that involves a certain challenge, high-energy physical exertion and just plain *fun!* The importance of play as an element in creativity training simply cannot be emphasized enough, and it therefore serves as a good opening—an intimation of things to come.
2. *Speed as opposed to thinking.* As in many other improvisation exercises, speed is introduced here in order to help the actors bypass the actors' analytical/protective thinking mechanisms.
3. *Control.* The actors are required—despite the frenetic pace of the exercise—to execute a complete exchange of eye contact, handshake, and name exchange before breaking away. What is more, through this exercise, they take a first step toward physical awareness and control, since they are required to move very swiftly from heightened physical activity to a total freeze.
4. *Repetition.* This is the first example of the element of *repetition* in the training. The actors are repeating an event over and over again—introducing themselves—and they should be urged to approach it each time as if it were "the first time," even if they meet the same person four or five times during the course of the exercise.

NB

In the entire trajectory of this training, knowledge and understanding are cumulative and are acquired through the "layering" of training experiences, one on top of the other. Therefore, when elements like *repetition* appear in any exercise—even one that does not directly address the experience of repetition—they should be pointed out so to further the accumulation of "layers" of knowledge. This is like clicking "Save" in a computer program: the idea goes into a file in the actor's mind, and is always there as a point of reference that will be engaged automatically, even when the teacher/director does not specifically point it out.

Variation 1—Alice in Wonderland

1. The same as above, "hysterical" running, eye and hand contact, and a complete introduction—first and family names—but with this difference: at each encounter, the partners must now invent *totally new names* for themselves. Actors are allowed only one name per encounter, and—to keep them inventive—they are absolutely *forbidden* to repeat a name they have already used, or even names they have heard others use in passing. Like Alice in *Through the Looking Glass* walking with the fawn through the enchanted wood, this exercise offers the actors the exhilarating possibility of being vulnerable by virtue of being nameless. Here it comes with a twist: in this enchanted wood, the actors are *repeatedly* nameless except for the tiny moments when they meet other nameless ones and briefly—very briefly—acquire an identity. The actors should be sidecoached to pay attention to this feeling of vulnerability in the nameless limbo.

Notes

1. Any name at all can be used—male or female names, off-the-wall gibberish inventions, friends' names, movie stars', politicians'—anything.
2. Remind the actors to wait until the moment of contact or the moment they hear their partner's new name before deciding on a name to give back. They should try to experience the exhilaration of being "empty" by virtue of being "nameless," and avoid protecting themselves by preselecting a stock of names and pulling them out one after the other.

Emphases

This early exercise already has a seminal quality, and can be used to stress a number of fundamental elements of improvisation technique.

1. *Second to second (a.k.a. "moment to moment")*. In improvisation technique, choices are made from split second to split second, and not like the well-known "moment to moment" of scene work. Having no control over the space, over whom they will meet, or who the others will be when they meet them, the actors have no option but to remain "open" and make split-second decisions on the fly.
2. *Creativity*. Here we go! In one of the very first exercises in this long process of training, the actors are instantly involved in *creativity training*—inventing new names for each encounter on the run. It is, of

course, too early to talk about this in any way as creativity training, but it, too, can be a point of reference for future exercises.

3. *Vulnerability/Stepping into the Unknown.* The *Through the Looking Glass* syndrome mentioned above.

Variation 2—Class reunion

Here there is a shift of focus that changes the flow patterns in the space. The actors are now told that all the encounters take place at a class reunion, twenty-five years after graduation. The dynamics of this are very familiar to anyone who has ever attended one but should be explained to young actors who have never done so: someone from your distant past suddenly recognizes you underneath the graying hair, the paunch, and the bifocals, and makes a bee-line for you from across the room, crying out ecstatically, "David *ZINDER*!!" and shakes your hand out of its socket. As he is flying toward you, arms outstretched for the inevitable embrace, you cudgel your brains trying frantically to remember this person's name, and then, at the last second, just before embarrassment sets in, it hits you, and you shout, "Aaron *KATZ*!!"

This dynamic of the reunion causes an extraordinary shift of energies in the space: Alice's "enchanted wood" turns totally crazy, as actors now run around the space frantically, with absolutely *no* identity, waiting for someone to tell them who they are. What is more, when an actor "recognizes" a long-lost pal and runs over to greet her, glee-fully calling out a name, the runner, having delivered the name, now has to wait, holding his partner's hand until she "recognizes" the runner and gives him a name.

Note

Be careful! This variation tends to get out of hand easily, as the actors get hooked on the reunion thing, start slapping each other on the back, hugging each other, and regaling each other with "stories of long ago"! This should be avoided since it dissipates the "identity-seeking" energies and turns the exercise into a simple improvisational moment of no partic-ular merit. Emphasis should still be placed on the openness and vulner-ability occasioned by the lack of identity, until each actor is met and "named."

Summary

Once these four name games have been played, the actors, flushed and excited with the strenuous physical activity and the craziness of the many surprising names they have concocted, should be totally relaxed. If this is a new group, they have not only learned each other's names, but have also seen something of each other's personalities as they responded to the different forms of the exercises. And here we are—through these playful introductions—a group of strangers set out on the way to becoming an ensemble.

The NameBalls exercises

While the preceding names exercises are usually a one-time event, used only at the first session of a workshop sequence, the next family of exercises, the NameBalls exercises, is an ongoing series that eventually becomes an integral part of what is known as the *WarmUp Sequences* throughout the training. Michael Chekhov made extensive use of balls exercises in his warm-up sessions with actors, and the following exercises are some of the variations that I use and recommend. At the beginning of every session, I generally put a pile of balls in the center of the space as a kind of focal point of concentration for the actors as they take their "moment" before crossing the threshold. Used at the opening of every session like this, the NameBalls exercises become a kind of daily reacquaintance for the actors with themselves and their colleagues just before they embark on their creative work together.

4. NAMEBALLS

Setup

The entire group stands in a loose circle in the work space. The balls should preferably be juggling balls—cloth bound and with a bean filling—but any small balls will do.

Activity

The exercise begins with one ball, thrown from one person to another across the circle. An actor throwing the ball says her first name, so that the ball "carries" the name, so to speak, to the catcher.

Gradually, more balls are introduced until there is roughly one-third as many balls as participants (e.g. eighteen participants, and six or seven balls).

Notes

1. The name is "attached" to the ball and its resonance in the air should "last" until it is caught on the other side of the circle.
2. The balls should be thrown easily, with a full commitment of the body, so that they arrive gently, *with no forward impetus*, at their target. This makes them easy to catch. It helps to tell the actors to throw the balls *upward* instead of *across*, so that they free-fall into the catching hand.
3. The catch is the beginning of the next throw, so it should be done with the entire body, not just with the hand. As the ball is caught, the actor catching it should continue the momentum of the caught ball into a backswing while scanning the circle for a pair of eyes to "lock onto" for the next throw (see Figures 1 and 2).
4. The name that is "thrown" with the ball should be called only as the ball is on its way, not as a wake-up call for a potential catcher.

NB

One of the easiest ways to introduce this concept of "the catch is the beginning of the throw" is by telling the actors to make the catch *soundless*. Instead of stopping the ball loudly with the palm of their hand, and then beginning the backswing, the actors should concentrate on taking the ball from the air right into the backswing of the next throw. The sidecoaching, then, is, "Catch the ball silently, with your whole body—not just with your hand."

Emphases

In this early, icebreaking phase of the work, there are only two *emphases*: fully giving and receiving the names of the members of the group, and the physical precision that is required to throw the ball with just enough impetus so that it arrives at its target with zero momentum—to facilitate the "catch as the beginning of the next throw." This element should be mentioned here, but don't spend too much time on it. In any case you will be throwing balls at every session.

Figure 1 Nameballs I.
The catch . . .

Figure 2 Nameballs I.
. . . into the throw.

Variations

The variations, of course, are endless—beginning, perhaps first of all, with using the name of the *catcher* rather than that of the thrower—once again not in order to attract attention but just to make the connections. Other possibilities include saying "good morning" in fifteen different languages, to having a word-by-word conversation among the group, and so on. The thing to remember when inventing these variations is that they, too, are a part of the larger Logic of Training, and therefore must feed *organically* into the rest of the work planned for that day.

Summary

Most of the icebreakers and name-learning exercises are used in the first few sessions in order to make acquaintances, free up the atmosphere, and get people to begin to learn something about each other. But these exercises are also the first thread in the weave, and should be used to introduce the tone, terminology, *emphases*, and fundamental nature of the work that has begun.

And the first step beyond making preliminary introductions is a detailed sequence of exercises, that is called the WarmUp Sequence, but that is, in fact, the substance of the first and highly important phase of the Logic of Training.

THE WARMUP SEQUENCES

When actors are instructed to take free time for personal warm-ups before a class or a rehearsal, it usually results in a series of vague, formless stretching by actors trying to look as if they know what they are doing and secretly praying for someone to actually tell them what to do. They wander aimlessly around the room, moving their arms importantly above their heads, shifting their necks from side to side, cracking their knuckles, looking for spots on their faces in the first available mirror, or just lying down on the floor in some form of meditation—in short, doing little to prepare themselves for the work of creating art.

In an effort to provide actors with a useful structure for warm-ups, I began to develop a structured warm-up sequence that in time became the actual substance of initial training procedures. This sequence has, therefore, a double function: it serves as a "platform" for introducing virtually every important aspect of the Logic of Training, and it provides the actors with a structure for warm-ups.

These exercises, which are taught in a structured sequence, are designed to be *repeated at every session* throughout the training. Among other things, this brings home the concept of *repetition training* at a very early stage, and in a very simple and straightforward way: if the actors aren't able to imbue daily repetitions of fairly basic exercises with a sense of first-time freshness and enthusiasm, they'll find the rest of the work very hard going indeed. To avoid too rigid a repetition, as the workshop process progresses, I occasionally introduce new elements into the sequence, or mix-and-match the existing ones. As we shall see, this warm-up sequence eventually returns to its source, turning into a fifteen-minute "free time" warm-up, but based on a clear structure for preparing the psychophysical organism of the actor for creative work.

The WarmUp Sequence has two sections: the Physical WarmUp and the Creative WarmUp. The first addresses the foundation of the actor's work—pure physicality—while the second is aimed at awakening the actor's creative organism through physical awareness and an integration of the body/imagination tandem. When run in this order—from Physical WarmUp to Creative WarmUp—the warmup sequences take the actor in stages from the "daily" self into the "extradaily" self, and from "extradaily" self into the "creative" self, preparing the actor's entire creative organism for the pursuit of art.

Despite the heavy reliance of these sequences on physical expression, this approach to actor training is not designed solely for the purpose of what is known as "physical theater." It is, rather, a training of the actor's creative instrument, designed to inculcate in the actor the "habit" of creative freedom through an understanding of the creative process while at the same time equipping him with a large measure of precise control—through awareness—over creative expressivity. All of this works to fine-tune an actor's technique to serve *any* form of theatrical expression.

The Physical WarmUp/DangerWorks

There is a basic semiological premise that underlies this first segment of the training and it goes like this: The moment an actor becomes visible to the spectators in the performance space, *everything* she does is meaningful because it is instantly and continuously interpreted by spectators intent on deciphering the signs emanating from the stage. Therefore, if actors want to have some measure of control over the effects/signs they produce at any given moment of their performance, they must develop a very high level of physical awareness.

The first section of the WarmUp Sequence is the beginning of the physical/nonvocal trajectory of the training, and is aimed at helping actors acquire the technique and habit of total physical awareness. The emphasis here is solely on the actor's body, generating a growing awareness of the form of the body in space, and leading eventually to a high degree of control over performative expression.

Many of the exercises in this section come under the heading of "DangerWorks Exercises," and this requires a brief explanation. The term *DangerWorks* is both metaphoric and real—up to a point. For actors to be prepared to use themselves as the material of their art, to develop the kind of openness needed for spontaneity and creativity, and to experience the heightened sensitivities that are required for seizing the creative moment, they must be prepared to render themselves vulnerable, to take risks—in other words, to place themselves in some form of danger. In the same way that regularly changing clothes before entering the work space cumulatively enhances the actor's understanding of transformation, the risk-taking involved in the following exercises cumulatively enhances the actor's grasp of creative daring, of "Stepping into the Unknown"—developing a fearless desire to reach, again and again, a state of creative vulnerability. All this begins very simply—with a clap and a sound.

5. THE ENERGY CIRCLE

This exercise is a very useful way of introducing the basic concept of DangerWorks, and getting the group's energy level up and going for the rest of the session. After an initial learning period, I generally move this exercise to the end of the workshop session, where it functions as a ringing—literally!—closure for the workshop session (see Figure 3).

Setup

The actors start in a loose circle—"loose" being the operative word, because they will need space between each other.

Activity

A handclap and a loud, energetic vocalization—"Ha!"—are passed among the participants in a number of variations.

The basic form of this exercise is as follows: one actor begins by giving the handclap and the sound simultaneously—*as a single gesture*—to the actor on his right in the circle. The receiving actor responds by turning fully to his right and sending the handclap and "Ha!"—the sound/gesture—on to the person on his right, who sends it on to the person on his right, and so on around the circle in one direction, as fast as possible without either anticipation or delay.

Figure 3 Energy Circle. The catch . . .

Notes

1. The idea is to get a rapid, rhythmical flow of handclaps and sounds going around the circle without a break. Only when this has been achieved can the variations noted below be introduced.
2. The handclap and sound should be a single, sweeping movement, not divided into a "receiving" from the person on the left and "sending" to the person on the right.
3. The "Ha!" sound should remain the same loud neutral sound throughout, without any personal modifications.
4. The sound/gesture should be vigorous, powerful, loud, and compact—involving a total commitment of body and voice. Watch out for actors who just turn their heads rather than their whole body, or those who "toss" the handclap to their right without committing their body to the action.
5. Sidecoaching here should be used to keep the tempo up, and to ensure the effortless flow of sound and movement around the circle.

Emphases

1. *DangerWork.* The giddy feeling of anticipation, trying not to drop the beat and to keep the sound/gesture moving rapidly—all these feed into a heightened sense of risk.

2. *Energy*. This is, literally, the name of the game, the high-energy flow providing the basic structure of the exercise. That is why the sound/gesture must be full and strong as it moves around the circle.
3. *Readiness*. The First Rule of Improvisation. This is a good place to introduce this seminal concept, as it relates to the waiting, in a state of *Readiness*, for the exact second when the sound/gesture is given, neither anticipating that split second nor delaying the continuation of the sound/gesture around the circle.

On the above "platform" we can load the following variations.

6. ENERGY CIRCLE—REVERSE FLOW

This can be introduced only after the Energy Circle platform has been practiced for a while, and the group has managed to generate a rapid rhythm and high-energy flow. It is important to check the quality of readiness (refraining from anticipation) and the quality of flow (refraining from allowing a thinking process to delay the physical reaction) before going on to the next form of this work.

Setup

The actors are in a circle, as above.

Activity

The same compact sound—"Ha!"—and clap, moving from one performer to another, but with one difference: instead of going around the circle in a repetitive and easily anticipated pattern, the participants can now choose either to send the sound/gesture on around the circle or to give it back to the person who gave it to them.

Notes

1. The change of direction is introduced only after the group has set up a rhythmic, energetic tempo in one direction around the circle.
2. To avoid a "ping-pong" effect, which leaves the rest of the group idle, the sound/gesture may be handed back and forth between any two actors only twice.
3. My suggestion: the teacher/director should take part in the game as one of the participants in the circle, to initiate the changes of direction "from the inside" when the time is ripe.

Emphases

1. *Readiness*. Readiness takes a quantum leap in this version, as the actors no longer have the luxury of waiting for the sound/gesture as it makes its way around the circle to them, but must constantly remain alert and ready. This a good place to introduce the *Actors' Catechism*, and urge the actors to examine the sensation of readiness by asking themselves: "What am I doing in order to be 'ready'?"

2. *Concentration*. The rapid pace of the exercise and the potential for surprise embodied in the option of returning the sound/gesture occasionally cause actors to "lose it," and either to send the clap in one direction and the "Ha!" in another, or to "Ha!" and clap twice—for instance, to the person who gave it to them and to the person on the right. This is a heads-up exercise that requires keeping your wits about you; the faster the sound/gesture goes around the greater the readiness/concentration challenge.

3. *Feeling of Ease*. This is a seminal Michael Chekhov concept, which will be mentioned frequently throughout the training, and it should therefore be introduced as early as possible. Everything an actor does in workshop, in rehearsal, or in performance—even the most demanding action—should have a quality of lightness and ease about it. Concentration supported by a Feeling of Ease will ensure an easy flow of high-level energy—and fewer mistakes.

7. ENERGY CIRCLE—ALL DIRECTIONS

The most complex variation on the theme, which moves all the *Emphases* mentioned above into a new dimension.

Setup

The actors are in a circle, as above.

Activity

As above, first get the rhythm going in one direction, then add the possibility of returning the gesture, then add one more option— sending the sound/gesture *across* the circle, to someone far away.

Notes

1. A funny thing happens in this variation: actors seem to think that it takes time for the sound/gesture to cross the circle. The result is that whenever the gesture is sent across the circle, the pace automatically slows down as everyone "watches" the gesture float, like an imaginary ball, from one side of the circle to the other. This, of course, defeats the whole purpose of the exercise. Remind your actors of the physical speed of sound and light, and tell them that the gesture moves just as quickly *across* the circle as it does *around* it, then stress again the need to maintain the original single-direction pace of the claps.
2. In this variation, emphasis must be placed on eye contact and a strong desire to get your gesture to your target. This concept of precision is an important one and will be dealt with extensively throughout the book.

NB

In all these variations, if one of the actors loses concentration, either everything comes to a confused stop or a number of gestures start going around the circle in different directions in a frenzy. This is where another basic principle of improvisation technique should be noted: *ensemble responsibility*. The object of the exercise is to keep the sound/gesture going around or across the circle at a high level of energy without missing a beat. If someone mixes things up, *someone else should pick it up immediately*, so that the group rhythm doesn't falter. The whole group does not have to wait until the person who lost the beat regains her composure and starts again; anyone with presence of mind can send out a gesture in some direction to get the energy flow back on track.

---

8. STACCATO/LEGATO

This is an exercise created by Michael Chekhov, and used in many variations from the early days of the Chekhov Studio at Dartington Hall in England (1936–39) to Blair Cutting's Chekhov Studio in New York in the 1980s. I learned it from my colleague in the Chekhov work, Lenard Petit. Staccato and Legato are also recurrent definitions of movement qualities in the Chekhov Technique, and will be appearing frequently in connection with any number of exercises in the training.

The beauty of this exercise is the energy flow that it develops in each of the actors individually, and the sense of ensemble that it helps develop in the entire group as they do the work in unison. Its tight, totally fixed structure fits in perfectly with what I have said about repetition training, and the challenge it poses to discover new reasons and a freshly recurring drive for doing the same thing over and over again—not only from one day to the next but also within the same exercise done on any given day.

This exercise can be, and sometimes is, explained in spiritual terms. For me, working so close to the sources of artistic creation is mystery enough, so I assiduously avoid additional mystification in the instructions I give to my actors for *any* of the exercises in the book. Suffice it to say that the six-direction movement sequence does involve a strong affirmation of the actor in space—right, left, up toward the sky, down toward the earth, backward, forward—and it is based on two contrary and complementary tempi: *staccato* and *legato*.

Setup

The group is spread out more or less evenly in the work space, all facing the same direction, with plenty of individual space around each member of the group. If necessary two or three lines may be formed (see Figure 4).

Figure 4 Staccato/Legato.

Figure 8 Staccato/Legato: Down.

Figure 9 Staccato/Legato: Forward.

Figure 10 Staccato/Legato: Backward.

Notes

1. It is helpful if the teacher/director leads this exercise at first, either facing the group, or facing forward in the same direction as the group. After a few weeks of work I generally ask a different actor to lead the exercise each day.
2. The movements in this sequence should be sharp, clear, and full, with a sense of energy gathering, flowing, and being sent out from the feet through to the fingers and beyond.
3. Between moves in any direction there is a still point that is neither a remnant of the previous movement nor a preview of things to come, but a moment on its own, a gathering of energies—a "Zero Point."
4. The actors should be sidecoached to hold the peak stretch of each position very briefly and send out a concentration of energy as far as the wall of the studio or even beyond it.
5. When using directional words ("right!," "left!," and so on), there should be no drop of vocal energy in the legato part. If this happens—as a result of the slower pace of the movements—point it out and urge the actors to keep the vocal energy at the same level throughout.

Emphases

1. *Sustaining and Radiating.* This exercise is a good vehicle for introducing these two fundamental concepts of the Chekhov Technique that relate to rhythm and to the extension of the actors' presence into space. Since these refer to what I have called "seminal" concepts that will appear in many different contexts repeatedly throughout the training, it is important to make them a part of the actors' vocabulary early on. Here they refer to the holding of each stretch at its peak and on sending out a flow of energy in the direction of the movement.
2. *Chekhov's "Four Brothers."* This is the title given by Chekhov Technique teachers to Michael Chekhov's four touchstones of creative work: *The Feeling of Beauty*, *The Feeling of Ease*, *The Feeling of Form*, and *The Feeling of the Whole*. We have already mentioned *The Feeling of Ease*, and this is a good opportunity to mention the other three "brothers," since they will soon become a central part of the WarmUp Sequences. The idea is derived from Chekhov's contention that, as artists, everything we do—*everything!*—is "a little work of art" and therefore should be imbued with these four fundamental aspects of art: beauty, ease, form, and wholeness (or entirety).
3. *The Zero Point.* This is the still, potential-packed moment between each stretch, and another fundamental concept in the training. This is an important element of the creative moment, and will be dealt with extensively later.

StickWork and Soft Focus

Before continuing with the exercises, a word about these two important concepts.

StickWork

In the field of Training, there are endless variations in the use of sticks. I initially learned the ones appearing here from Tony Cots, formerly of Eugenio Barba's Odin Theatre, at a conference on acting held in Saintes, France, in 1990. Over the years it has become one of the most important elements of the DangerWorks section in the training.

When I demonstrated various versions of this exercise at the 1993 conference of the Association for Theatre Higher Education in Philadelphia, an audible gasp arose from the audience, followed by sotto voce comments about the kind of insurance we must carry in Israel for our students. So—a word of explanation is in order.

This is indeed an exercise with a seemingly obvious potential for physical injury. However, in the many years that I have been using it in the training, with literally hundreds of acting students and actors of all ages and levels of experience in Israel, Europe, the Far East and the United States, there has never been a single injury. The worst thing that has ever happened was an occasional mild knock on the head, and the occasional broken light fixture or mirror (that being a danger of a different order, depending on how superstitious you are!). On the other hand, the benefits of this exercise—in terms of concentration, coordination, readiness, group trust, and ensemble training—are enormous and far outweigh its possible hazards.

This disclaimer notwithstanding, it is most definitely a risky exercise, and the basic technique should be strictly enforced. What is more, each of its stages should be introduced gradually and with care, only after the training group has achieved a high degree of proficiency in the preceding stage. Actors with problems of depth perception (as a result of any difficulty with proper bifocal vision) or poor hand–eye coordination should be excused, unless they have developed a proven ability to locate the relative position of objects in space, or shown ability to learn how to catch the sticks effectively.

Finally, once again we are in a seminal exercise, which I use regularly as part of the daily warm-up throughout the time I am working with a group. The "platform" and its variations branch out to numerous aspects of the training depending on how it is sidecoached. Where it should appear in the WarmUp Sequence and how it should be used will be detailed below.

Soft Focus

The requirements of the StickWork exercises place us smack in the middle of the dilemma of the multiplex nature of training versus the linear structure of a book on training. Soft Focus is a fundamentally important, and highly useful, technique that is used practically and metaphorically throughout the entire Logic of Training—and is absolutely necessary for the StickWork exercises. I usually introduce the concept of Soft Focus in the walking exercises, which come later in this book, but which, in a workshop situation, run concurrently with StickWork. So, here, before its *organic* place in the training, is the explanation of this seminal technique.

Basically, Soft Focus is a technique for "relaxing" the actors' vision, making their peripheral vision as effective as frontal vision. In other words, by focusing on nothing in particular they are able to focus on everything. This makes it possible for a great deal of spatial and kinetic information to be received and processed simultaneously—and effortlessly.

In our daily lives, we use only about a 70–80-degree field of vision, and normally, our peripheral vision is not actively engaged. Once we learn how to use our periph-eral vision actively, we expand our field of vision to at least 180 to 200 degrees. This is easily demonstrated: place two actors about three meters apart; stand directly between them so that the three of you are on a straight line; then look straight ahead and try to "relax" your sight to take them in on the periphery of your field of vision. Then, maintaining this "relaxed" but enlarged peripheral vision, try to see how far forward you can move before the two figures on either side of you totally disappear from sight. The results are often surprising!

Since the StickWork takes place mostly in a circle, but also in a random flow of actors in space, Soft Focus provides us with absolutely necessary nonstop flow of information from a very large field of vision, and all this without turning our heads or locking our sight in any one direction. In this way we are able to take in, process, and react to an enormous amount of information on the go, swiftly and effort-lessly. This is the reason why this technique is so important for almost every aspect of the Logic of Training, and why it must be introduced before embarking on the StickWork exercises.

To introduce Soft Focus, give the actors the following instructions:

- Bring your hand up in front of your nose, about 15 centimeters away, and concentrate on the lines of your palm.
- Drop your hand and stay focused on that spot in front of you where your palm was a moment ago. Bring your palm up again to check the focus, then drop your hand.

- Note that while the head is kept erect, the gaze in Soft Focus is angled slightly below the horizontal.
- Walk through the space trying to maintain that focal point and experience the Soft Focus, the simultaneous processing of frontal and peripheral information.

Technicalities

1. The sticks used in these exercises should be made of smooth, splinterless wood about 2 centimeters in diameter, with rounded ends, and should not exceed 120 centimeters in length—about the size and shape of a broomstick. They should be as light as possible, but, in order of priority, resistance to breakage is much more important than weight. Pinewood, for example, breaks easily and should not be used.
2. Since all the variations of the StickWork involve throwing these sticks from one actor to another, all breakable items in the work space—mirrors, lighting fixtures, sound systems, and so on—that are within reach of a badly thrown stick or a missed catch should either be removed or protected.

NB

DON'T FORGET: Acting studios are not immune to Murphy's Law! If a stick *can* break a mirror, a light fixture, or a CD player—*it will*. So cover them or get rid of them before you begin.

StickWork grows in stages, and involves a number of variations on one basic action: throwing these fairly long, hard, and somewhat unwieldy sticks from one actor to another. The number of variations on this basic idea is almost limitless, and the validity, or usefulness, of any given variation as a training should depend on: (a) whether it is basically safe, and (b) how it fits in with the overall training rationale. The variations should be introduced in the right place, as part of a logic of training, and not just for the fun of throwing sticks around.

Emphases

Since the points of emphasis here apply equally to almost all the variations of this exercise, I will note them here, before we begin, and add more as they present themselves.

One very important aspect of this exercise relates back to one of the trajectories of training we discussed in Chapter 1: from the abstract to the concrete. Apart from all the practical *Emphases* listed below, this exercise is purely physical, and as such, purely abstract since it neither engages the imagination nor excites any deep emotional content.

The *Emphases* are as follows:

1. *DangerWork.* Goes without saying.
2. *Concentration.* Goes without saying.
3. *Readiness/alertness.* Goes without saying.
4. *Physical coordination and control.* If actors are to be aware of their performative expression at all times, they must learn—through training and repetition—what it is that they do when total physical control and awareness are required of them. In this exercise, coordination is at a premium, and getting the stick across the circle in a very precise manner, to an exact point near one's targeted partner, requires—and trains—physical control.
5. *Soft Focus.* Remind the actors of its main benefit: by concentrating on nothing in particular one concentrates on everything equally. As the number of sticks flying through the air at any given moment increases, the actors must be totally aware of *all* of them simultaneously, while at the same time maintaining precise eye contact with their targeted partners. Normal vision simply won't do here, and Soft Focus is the answer.
6. *Trust.* The risky nature of the exercise makes trust a prime ingredient from the outset. As you will see, in the advanced versions, the sheer complexity of the exercise demands total trust between all the members of the group.

NB

This is a good opportunity to begin making early connections between training and performance. Throwing sticks seems about as far removed as possible from the actual work an actor does on stage, but acting is not only learning the lines or "getting into the part." It is also coming in on cue, following the agreed upon mise-en-scène, hitting the upbeat of the music, and staying in the narrow beam of light coming in from the wings—all at the same time. This kind of precision and total concentration on many disparate activities requires an ease, a technique for multiple and simultaneous focus, and a sense for precision that is provided as a "model of behavior" by many different elements of StickWork.

---

9. THROWING STICKS—BASIC TRAINING

This is the basic platform of the StickWork family, upon which everything else will be built.

Notes

In order for the actors to exercise maximum control over the trajectory of the stick the following instructions should be noted:

1. The stick should be grasped down low—about a palm's width (10–15 centimeters) from one end (see Figure 11). Throwing the stick while holding it any higher will cause it to revolve around its midpoint in the air. This makes it hard to catch and downright dangerous.
2. The stick should be thrown gently *upward* at about a 45-degree angle, with a sweeping motion of the arm, followed through by the body—like a pitch in softball, horseshoe pitching, or bowling (see Figures 12–14). Ideally the thrown stick should reach the peak of its trajectory about three-quarters of the way across the circle, and revolve slightly so that the base of the stick—the same end that the thrower held—lands gently in the receiving actor's hand like this:

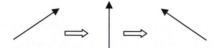

   This way the receiver can catch the stick easily, and, in one flowing movement, use the momentum of the catch to begin a new throw.
3. *No javelin throwing or shotputting!* Those forms of throwing are *dangerous* because they give the stick too much momentum and are basically uncontrollable.
4. Speed is not an issue in this exercise—but safety is. So, if a stick is badly thrown, the receiver should catch it any way she can and adjust her hold on the stick *before* returning it.
5. If the space is large enough, the group can split off into pairs and practice throwing the sticks from one to the other. At this stage it should be emphasized that eye contact must be "locked in" before any stick is thrown, and both actors should concentrate on making the throws as precise as possible and on making the catch a part of the throw. As in the NameBalls exercises mentioned earlier, the action should be a flow of movement back and forth, with the stick constantly in motion (unless the hold on the stick needs to be adjusted—which takes priority over *everything*).

Figure 11 Throwing Sticks: Holding the stick low down.

Figure 12 Throwing Sticks: Backswing.

Figure 13 Throwing Sticks: The throw, angled up.

Figure 14 Throwing Sticks: Following through.

10. STICKS IN A CIRCLE

Beyond the "basic training," we now move into the exercises.

Setup

The group should stand in a loose, spacious circle.

Activity

One stick is introduced, and thrown across the circle from one actor to another. In this first version the thrower has many "targets" to choose from, and the concept of "giving eye contact" should be introduced: once the exercise has begun, everyone should concentrate on the thrower and actively offer eye contact, so that he does not have to search for a receiver.

Gradually, over a number of sessions, more sticks are introduced and thrown *simultaneously* across the circle of actors, until the group works its way up to the point where the number of sticks in use is half the number of the actors in the group (e.g. six sticks for a group of twelve). As each additional stick is introduced, time should be taken to get used to the added complexity.

As soon as one more stick is introduced—not to mention two or three—many training elements kick in, and the exercise begins its life in the workshop as a multiplex model of behavior. Soft Focus, concentration, timing, precision of physical energy, control, coordination, rhythm, and eye contact are all heightened as the space is gradually filled with flying sticks.

NB

If the space is large enough and the circle doesn't begin to flatten out into an oval, this exercise can be worked comfortably with groups of up to fourteen. Whatever the number of actors in the circle, watch out for reduced sight lines, which can make a risky exercise downright dangerous.

Notes

1. *Remember*—when the group gets good at it, they should not get carried away by their supposed virtuosity. This is not a juggling class; virtuosity is not the issue, and *safety is an absolute prerequisite*. The exercise is practiced only so that the actors can learn something about their art, not in order to prepare them for a life in the circus.
2. Additional sticks are added *gradually*, only as the group's proficiency and confidence grow.
3. As more and more sticks are introduced, timing of the throws becomes a paramount issue, and this should be sidecoached with: "Choose your moment."
4. *Total silence* should be maintained. (Talking or joking around while sticks are flying through the air is not very healthy!) This also applies to vocal reactions of any kind ("oops!," "sorry!," or the like) to missed catches or flubbed throws. This exercise does have elements of a game, but it is not done for fun. Keep the atmosphere cool and professional, and keep vocal responses out of it.

NB

As a general rule, I try to teach my actors to overcome their natural habit of apologizing for bad throws or catches. Saying "I'm sorry" is a very natural human response, but when it happens in the work space, the "extradaily" training persona instantly disappears, and the daily, protective, inhibited, head-centered self appears. At that very same instant one stops learning. I am not suggesting that actors should forget all their manners and treat each other impolitely, but in the work space, actors should relate to each other *professionally*, not *personally*. So, if someone throws a stick badly, he shouldn't apologize, but just try to do it more precisely the next time. Once actors get into this habit, it does wonders for the atmosphere of professional concentration and dedication in the work space.

5. This is the time to introduce the idea of making eye contact. Since the idea is to generate a flow of sticks back and forth across the circle, no one holding a stick and ready to throw it should have to wait even a second for a potential receiver's eyes to lock on to. This can only be achieved if the actors actively give eye contact as soon as they themselves are empty-handed. (The sidecoaching I usually use here is "Give your eyes.") An actor not actively involved in throwing or receiving a stick should be actively involved in trying to make eye contact with someone with a stick. This way—even with a large number of sticks in play—no one will have to wave, whistle, shout, or otherwise draw attention to herself—and distract everyone else in the process. As each actor goes into a backswing for the throw (Figure 12), she must, at the same time, seek out a pair of eyes to lock on to, so that there will be no break in the flow.

6. When all the sticks are in play and the problem of finding someone to throw to becomes acute, actors can exchange sticks with each other, but *this should be done only when the group has reached a good level of basic skill without such exchanges.*

7. As the actors' confidence and ability grows they can be challenged to cut their margins of safety and raise the "danger quotient" of the exercise. This should, of course, be done *very carefully*, but sticks can be thrown with minimal intervals, or on near-miss trajectories with other sticks. At this stage, the importance of such elements such as concentration, timing, rhythm, precision, trust, Feeling of Ease, and Soft Focus grows by leaps and bounds. The more sticks there are in the space, and the more proficient and daring the group becomes, the more important the group's sense of rhythm becomes. Eventually, in a well-trained group, the entire circle—sticks and actors—breathe together in a common rhythm, and watched from afar, the entire exercise turns into a beautiful dance!

Emphases

Apart from the points of emphasis noted at the beginning of the StickWork section, this exercise emphasizes rhythm, timing, and a Soft-Focus incorporation of the entire circle of actors and sticks. All these become major players, and should be pointed out as highly important elements in the behavior being modeled here.

11. STICKS AND BONES

This slightly facetious title describes the most complicated, dangerous, and beautiful version of StickWork. It should be introduced only after the group has reached a high level of proficiency and confidence in the most advanced version of Sticks in a Circle, and the actors are capable of using the maximum number of sticks with ease, timing, and a good sense of group rhythm.

When introducing this version of the exercise, we begin again with one stick. Only after a number of "basic training" sessions can more sticks be introduced, adding them one at a time over a number of sessions each time, up to half the number of the participants.

Setup

As before, the group should stand in a loose, spacious circle.

Activity

The actors in the circle now throw the sticks as before, but once the thrower is sure his stick is on target—and *while it is still in the air*—he runs across the circle after the stick to a new place next to the person he threw the stick to. As more and more sticks are added, the space inside the circle becomes filled with flying sticks and running bodies, becoming extremely complex, changeable, and unpredictable.

Notes

1. However hazardous this exercise might seem, it is in fact quite easy. With a physically well-coordinated group of twelve or fourteen actors, and a gradual increase in the number of sticks, you should be able to work this exercise with up to six or seven sticks.
2. *Never throw on the run*! This is dangerous because doing so increases the momentum of the stick. So—the actor should first throw, then take a beat (no more) to check that the stick is on target, and *then* run.
3. The golden rules for crossing the space after a stick are:
   - After throwing the stick, cross the circle on the run, calmly and without panic, with total application of Soft Focus. In order to cross the space safely you have to be able to process simultaneously a great deal of real-time information—from all sides of the circle. This is precisely what the Soft Focus technique is for.

- *Don't hesitate*! Other actors are counting on your rhythm, and will expect you to move across the circle *in one go* right after throwing your stick. That will be part of their calculations for the timing of their own throw and run.
- Don't try to protect yourself as you cross the circle. If you throw your arms around your head or duck under your arm as you're running *you won't be able to see anything*! This will either get you nowhere or get you hurt. Keep your head up and take in all the information.
- *Expect the unexpected*! "Readiness," said Hamlet, "is all." Use Soft Focus on the entire space, and process everything as coherent, integrated, multiplex information.

4. Once again there should be complete silence! The level of concentration required for this exercise is very high. Timing your throw with other sticks either already in the air or about to fly as well as with earthbound bodies running around the circle is extremely demanding. Distractions are dangerous! There is also no need for reactions of any kind (laughter, giggling, joking, cursing, apologizing, etc.) when a stick flies out of the circle to the wall, hits the ceiling, or barely misses someone; just keep at it—quietly, professionally, seriously.

5. The space is in fact only seemingly chaotic: after all, there is method in the madness—everyone is adhering to the same set of rules for throwing, running, and receiving.

NB

One of the most difficult things to teach actors in relation to this exercise is not to gasp in shock when a stick is badly thrown. An audible gasp during the exercise is like having a backseat driver shout "Watch out!" as you're driving. Not knowing *what* to watch for, you may cause an accident by turning your head to ask what the problem is, or turning the wheel sharply in one direction when the problem is in *another* direction. If, on the other hand, your driving companion says urgently but quietly, "There's an old lady on your right!" or simply points in the direction of the hazard and says, "Look out over *there*!" you will be able to deal with the emergency much more calmly and efficiently. The same applies to this stick exercise. In cases of dire emergencies, the silence can be broken and actors warned about an incoming stick. But even then, always prefer a calm response over a generalized gasp of horror.

---

6. When the number of sticks in play nears or reaches the maximum, there will be a problem finding someone to throw to. Everyone will be in the

process of throwing, receiving, or running. The need to give eye contact will become so much more important, and thus needs to be stressed.
7. At this stage the circle also begins to lose its shape, so keep reminding the actors to adjust back into a complete circle.

12. STICKS IN SPACE

This is a much less structured version of StickWork, and generally should only be used with a group that is well trained in all the other versions. The relative ease of this version turns it into just plain fun—which is why I usually use it to end this part of the WarmUp Sequence.

Setup

The actors move freely, on the run, through the work space.

Activity

The sticks are now thrown from one actor to another on the run (NB: see note 3 below!). Starting with two sticks, more and more are gradually introduced. In this version, many more sticks can be used; in a group of twelve you can use up to seven or eight—or even ten.

Notes

1. Emphasize running at random—changing directions all the time—over herd-like running in a circle.
2. The actors' concentration, coordination, and physical precision can be challenged here by encouraging "immediate throws": sticks should be thrown the instant they are caught. (Sidecoaching: "Don't hold on to a stick for more than a second!")
3. Since the sticks are now being thrown on the run, the way to reduce their forward momentum is by not really throwing them, but "leaving them in the air" in the general direction of the targeted actor. This means throwing the sticks *straight up*, perpendicularly, and letting the inertia from the forward body movement take them to the target.

Emphases

1. *Timing.* Since the sticks are thrown on the run, timing and eye contact are critical. Randomly shifting distances, speed, and the visual "noise" of all the movement in the space train a different, high-speed sense of timing.

2. *Spatial awareness*. Running at random in the space while looking for and catching sticks, and at the same time not bumping into anyone, requires a higher degree of ease and a heightened sense of spatial awareness through a sophisticated combination of Soft Focus and true focus.

3. *Readiness/alertness*. Moving from the Sticks in a Circle exercise into this barely controlled chaos is like moving from Tic-Tac-Toe to Rubik's Cube. All-around alertness, at a much higher level than before, is the name of the game. Multiplex information-processing on the run is what's happening. For sheer exhilaration there is hardly anything that compares to a group of actors "in the zone" of this exercise, controlling space, time, movement, and the seeming chaos of multiple sticks flying in the air—and all with consummate ease!

Summary

Once the group overcomes any initial apprehension about working with the sticks, and the hesitation that attends each new and more difficult version, this exercise is an invaluable tool for creating an atmosphere of clear and cool concentration, devoid of any psychological or imaginative overlays. This is the beauty of the exercise—its total physicality. There is only one thing to concentrate on: getting the stick to your partner precisely and gently, with clear eye contact and—as far as possible—no mistakes. Done well, it is an exhilarating opening for the creative work at hand, generating a crystalline concentration and a razor-sharp readiness. What more can one ask of a warm-up exercise?

The walking exercises

Like Marcel Duchamp's *Fountain*, the "ready-made" urinal that became a major work of contemporary art merely by having been chosen by the artist and displayed in a gallery, so too the simple ready-made act of walking can be elevated to the degree of a seminal training exercise by being brought into the studio space and given the quality and structure of extradaily activity. The "studio version" of simple everyday walking that follows, and its variations, are among those multifaceted, seminal exercises that feed into many basic training concepts—depending on how they are sidecoached.

The initial training benefit that can be derived from the walking exercises is the focus they give to the actors' energies. Even the simple, basic form of the exercise helps the actors spiral in on their performative selves; tones up their concentration and awareness of space, self, and others; and gives the actors a "kick" of DangerWork that is a wonderful preparation for the work ahead.

NB

The profound relation of these exercises to so many of the most fundamental aspects of the Logic of Training requires extensive explanation. Please read the *entire* section on walking exercises before setting out on your walk.

---

13. MINI-MAXI PACING

Setup

The actors spread out in the entire work space. (If this exercise is done—as I generally do it—after the Staccato/Legato exercise, they are already spread out in the room.) If the group is small (up to eight people), or if the work space is larger than 8 by 10 meters, the exercise space should be limited to a square of roughly 6 by 6 meters in the center of the room. If the actors have too much space to move around in, much of the "danger" inherent in this exercise disappears.

Activity

Standing in their own space around the room, and knowing that they are about to walk, the actors should be sidecoached to pay attention to the desire to walk as it wells up inside them before taking their first step: They are then told, "When you can no longer hold back the desire, move smoothly into a very slow walk."

The initial slow walk should be maintained as a definite pace for as long as possible. When the actors find their concentration on the chosen pace wandering, they should "step it up," accelerate into a slightly more rapid walk that is also controlled as a definite pace, and maintain that for as long as possible. This process continues until the actors, each in his or her own time, reach the fastest possible walk— but *without breaking into a run.* Running is a total release of energy that denies the structuring element of pace that is so important here.

Once they have reached this very fast walk and sustained it for as long as it interests them, the actors now initiate a reverse process, "stepping down" the pace gradually until they reach the same motionless point where there is a desire to walk—when the energy of the walk is still resonating in the body, but there is no forward movement. (This is usually apparent when the actors stop but are still leaning forward slightly.) When this resonance, too, drains away and the desire to move fades, they should sit down wherever they are in the space.

NB

As the training progresses, this exercise can be given a framework through the introduction of Chekhov's "Four Qualities of Movement," *molding, flowing, flying, radiating*, as a way guiding the actors through the transitions from one pace to another. These qualities are described by Chekhov in *On the Technique of Acting, in* pages 45–48, and they relate to levels of resistance, *molding* being the mode of the greatest resistance, and *radiating* being the mode of no resistance at all. Shifting from one quality to the next should be guided initially by the teacher/director, and the actors should be asked to pay special attention to the different sensations aroused by the change of pace brought about by the change of quality. As their proficiency grows, the teacher/director should sidecoach the actors to examine the diapason of each quality: how many variations does *molding* have before it turns into a *flowing*? How finely can *flowing* be sliced before it becomes *flying*? And so on.

Notes

1. Before beginning the exercise, the actors should check their Soft Focus using the method indicated earlier. If at any time an actor feels he has lost the focal point in front of his nose that enables his Soft Focus, he can lift his palm up in front of his face to realign the focal point.
2. Remember: the line of the Soft Focus gaze is just below the horizontal, i.e. head up and gaze directed slightly downward. This is a general aid to the Soft Focus, but it also prevents any kind of eye contact, which is important here.
3. The transition from the desire to walk to the walk itself should not be a jerk into motion, but rather an easy transition. Once the actors generate a desire to walk they are already walking, and they must them simply move into it smoothly.

4. The first pace of the walk should be a very slow, fully articulated walk, i.e. not a *slow-motion* walk which involves exaggerated movement and a great deal of physical tension.

5. The second cycle of the walk—stepping the pace down from the fastest walk to zero—is not a relaxation; on the contrary, it is a *concentration* (see the Hunt and Pounce exercise below).

6. The actors should be directed to pay particular attention to the moments of transition built into the exercise: the nonmoving "desire to walk" at the beginning, the shifts in pace (*molding, flowing, flying radiating*), the high-revving "engine in neutral" at the end of the walking, and the moment at the end when the forward momentum drains away altogether. These too are preliminary instances of the Zero Point.

8. Throughout this exercise, in all of its stages, the actors should be instructed as follows:

   - Keep your Soft Focus at all times; take in the whole space and all the moving bodies without looking at them.
   - Make each pace as interesting as possible for as long as possible. Once the teacher/director introduces the Four Qualities of Movement the challenge is built-in: how long can we make any given pace—molding, flowing, flying, or radiating—last?
   - Don't touch anyone, and try not to get involved in evasive steps that will affect your pace. If you are on a collision course with someone, instead of shuffling your feet, or making tiny steps to one side to avoid the collision, change direction and pass smoothly by, or turn on the spot as many times as necessary to avoid the collision.

Emphases

1. *Readiness*. The First Rule of Improvisation and the principal training objective of the exercise. Since the actors have no control over their space, the only way for them to work the space successfully is by honing their sense of readiness to a very fine point and being ready for any eventuality. In a world that is *all* surprises, there can be *no surprises*.

2. *Feeling of Ease*. The way to prepare for every eventuality is by developing a Feeling of Ease. This and the previous emphasis on readiness are the most important aspects of this exercise: experiencing a model of behavior that approximates the second-to-second decision making that is at the heart of the creative process. Doing this over and over again generates an instinctive understanding of the concept, and raises actors' willingness to place themselves in creative "danger," "vulnerability," or "imbalance."

3. *Pure physicality*. The effectiveness of this exercise derives from this

attribute. There is nothing to it but a walk with certain rules, and this generates a heightened awareness of body, movement, and space.

4. *Spatial awareness/Soft Focus.* Soft Focus enhances the actors' grasp of movement patterns in space, and raises the level of their attention to their surroundings. When it becomes a habit, it helps maintain an easy, full awareness of minute changes in physical, aural, or material patterns on stage.

5. *Stepping into the Unknown.* The Second Rule of Improvisation, and in many ways, the most basic improvisational strategy, is: First make a move, then find out where your body is going, and then take responsibility for it by shaping the outcome of your choice as you are moving.

6. *The Four Qualities of Movement.* As noted above.

14. WALKING VARIATIONS—DIRECTION CHANGES

This is a follow-on exercise from the basic Mini–Maxi Pacing, which upgrades the DangerWorks factor, leading to an even more heightened awareness of space, instantaneous decision making, and, most of all, readiness.

Setup

As in the previous exercise, the actors are spread out in the work space.

Activity

Once the basic concept of the Mini–Maxi Pacing with Soft Focus is understood, the risk factor of the exercise is notched up: now the actors are asked to repeat the entire process—from the desire to walk, through the paces to the fastest walk, and back to zero—but to add sudden, random shifts of direction throughout the entire process.

Over a period of time, as the actors repeat this exercise again and again, they should be encouraged to take greater and greater risks and cut their margins of safety. They can, for example, play "chicken" with each other—set a collision course with another actor and delay the turn away from the collision to the very last possible split second. They should make a habit of heading directly into a knot of actors, keeping all options open, and trusting on finding a way smoothly and effortlessly through the traffic jam of bodies without dropping a step or making emergency adjustments of any kind.

NB

Other ways of raising the DangerWorks stakes in this exercise is by sending an actor through the rapidly walking group with his eyes closed (an exhilarating experience for the actor crossing the circle blindly, too!) or allowing individual actors in the group intermittently to close their eyes—only one actor at a time, of course!

Notes

1. The actors should get into the habit of making these sudden shifts of direction at all times, from the very slow walk to the very fastest walk, and challenging their readiness by moving back and forth through the center of the group and not remaining safely on the periphery.

2. Remind the actors repeatedly throughout the exercise that there is always a solution to any traffic problem. Walking backward, stopping, or making little shuffling steps to avoid a collision are not options. They can turn or veer right or left, or turn around on the spot—any of these as long as they maintain their pace.

NB

The surest sign of actors' being surprised—not "ready"—is when you hear the soles of their feet slapping on the floor as a sudden adjustment is made to avoid a collision. Watch out for that. Actors should also be reminded not to make small steps out of pace or stop even briefly to let someone pass just to avoid a collision. *There is no room in this exercise for courtesy or good manners*; it's not about that. It's about constantly moving forward toward some passionately sought goal without involving anyone else on the way, and maintaining a determination of purpose throughout, regardless of any obstacles that may be encountered. Finally, in all of this—don't forget the Soft Focus! This kind of total concentration is not head centered; what it requires is for the actors to use their entire organism to take in everything with a great sense of ease so that the space may be traversed as efficiently as possible.

---

3. The actors should be urged to walk quietly by dividing their body weight evenly over the entire sole of the foot, from heel to toe. This ensures that even the heaviest person in the group will move through the group with a light, easy walk that in itself is a form of readiness. The idea is a flow of

energy *upward* toward the head and beyond as they are walking, not downward toward the floor.

4. Watch out for signs of tension in the body language: clenched fists, heads down on the chest, necks tight, hunched-up shoulders. These reduce the actor's overall readiness and should be pointed out so that the actor can relax them and maintain his Feeling of Ease at all times.

5. Make sure that the actors do not break into a run at the fastest pace.

Emphases

1. *Stepping into the Unknown.* With the walking space now completely chaotic, and every change of direction a "step into the unknown," this element is "modeled" throughout the exercise.

2. *Improvisation/DangerWork and repetition technique.* The concept of keeping all options open until a choice is unavoidable is an important model of improvisation technique. It is also a DangerWorks technique that gives actors the skill to treat every moment on stage—even one they have been through hundreds of times before—as totally new and unpredictable.

3. *Feeling of Ease.* The object of the exercise is to engage both Soft Focus and The Feeling of Ease so that body and eyes become a totally integrated information-gathering organism. Scouting ahead with the eyes at a different rhythm from the body, or tensing the body in any way, is counterproductive.

15. THE HUNT AND THE POUNCE

This is another way of using this same exercise for slightly different—and very specific—training purposes. This variation emerged out of occasional remarks by actors, who often found that, when they reached the end of the Mini–Maxi Walk, instead of being at the height of readiness and concentration, they felt loose, relaxed, and unfocused instead.

NB

The following version of the Mini–Maxi Pacing involves a direct appeal to the imagination, but the imaginative part of the exercise should be downplayed as much as possible. Any attempt to "play out" a mimed or imagined "hunt" should be avoided at all costs. It is only a mindset, a frame of reference, for the walk.

Setup

The actors spread out in the space, ready to begin the walk.

Activity

This is a two-part exercise. Read the whole description first.

Part 1—The Hunt: For this version, the entire Mini–Maxi Pacing exercise is now described as a hunt, the only problem being that the hunters do not know what it is they are looking for or where this thing—whatever it is—is located. (NB: in order to give the actors as much imaginative freedom as possible, don't describe this "thing." Refer to it only as a "thing"—not a "monster" or a "creature.") Their task then, in the first part of the exercise, is to locate the prey, approach it, and be ready to confront it, following this step-by-step progression that must be closely sidecoached, as follows:

Step 1: Before moving out, prepare yourself by centering and readying yourself for the task at hand.

Step 2: Now start moving very slowly, because the first thing you have to do is get a "fix" on your unknown prey. Since you have no idea what you are looking for, or where to look for it, use your *entire body* as a sensor, and keep changing directions at random, "sending out" your senses in an effort to pick up the slightest indication of a presence.

Step 3: You get a vague sense that the "thing" is close by, but you still don't know where it is. Increase your pace gradually, to close the distance to the prey, changing directions all the time to try and locate the direction of the strongest "signal." Walk as lightly as possible to avoid creating vibrations that might alert the prey to your presence.

Step 4: The sense of the prey's presence is now very strong. Still shifting direction to get the strongest signal, you move into the fastest possible walk in order to bring yourself within striking distance.

Step 5: You're now *very* close, and you begin to slow down in order to reduce your "signature" in space and at the same time remain within striking distance. *Remember*: you have absolutely no idea what it is you are looking for or where it is at any moment, so all you can do to protect yourself is be ready. (NB: at this point, remind the actors to use the Actor's Catechism—"What am I doing to make myself ready?".)

Step 6: You're *very* close now so slow down to near-zero. When your sense of the prey is at its strongest, stop; reduce your spatial signature to zero. This way you can keep the element of surprise on your side. Now, get ready for the main event—the *pounce*. This "thing," whatever it is, is very near. You have to be totally ready for it, totally attuned to your body/sensor, and ready to jump in any direction at any second—either for protection or for the kill.

This is where Part 1—The Hunt, ends: the actors are standing in the space, totally alert, their bodies focused outward in the space.

Emphasis

Readiness. Stalking this "prey" through the space, with a single-minded sense of purpose—that is, not getting involved with all the other bodies moving through this space—and a constant radiation of the senses out into the space leads the actors through the imaginative structure to a very pure, total state of readiness. Using the active questioning technique of the Actors' Catechism to try and understand what they are experiencing *as they are experiencing it* is the only way they will be able to benefit from the exercise.

Part 2—The Pounce: Having brought the actors to this point, you now take them one step further into this exploration of pure readiness.

Activity

At the end of the hunt the actors are spread out in the space, vibrating with readiness, waiting for the slightest trigger to make them pounce. At the sound of a hand-clap they are to jump as far, as fast, and as hard as they can—either for the "kill," or to protect themselves from a surprise first strike by the unseen prey.

Clap; let the actors complete their reaction—jump to "kill" or jump to save oneself from being "killed"—then sidecoach with, "You missed. Don't move! You have to 'reacquire' your prey, get a 'fix' on it, and at the same time protect yourselves by being totally ready, just like before—even in that uncomfortable position."

Clap again; let the actors pounce, then repeat the sidecoaching. Do this two or three times. The last time, give the following side-coaching:

- You missed, and you are getting the sense that "it" isn't there anymore—but you may be mistaken. Bring yourselves *slowly* back into an optimal standing position, but make the shift to standing *without losing the edge of readiness*. It's "kill or be killed," and you still have to be prepared for anything at any second.
- Ask yourselves now, "How do I remain *totally ready* at the same time that I am 'relaxing' my way up to a standing position? What do I move first, what do I move second; do I do it quickly, in one go, or slowly, or . . . ?"

Here, as the actors are moving back into the standing position, the teacher/director should clap once again, and repeat the side-coaching. Do this two or three times, then say, "You're more and more certain that it's no longer there—but you're not sure. So relax whatever you think you can relax without losing the edge of readi-ness. You are now looking for the minimal psychophysical organiza-tion that will keep you in a state of absolute readiness that will protect you in case you are wrong.

It's this sense of the "*minimal necessary sense of absolute readiness*" that we have been looking for in this entire sequence: the body is relaxed but the adrenalin level is very high, and all the senses are sharp and expectant.

Notes

1. Once the actors reach this last stage of the exercise—readiness in a state of physical ease—suggest to them that they should try to "imprint" this feeling in their system. It is the same feeling they should have before any entrance onstage—relaxed, razor sharp, and ready for anything. It is also a state of being that will be referred to frequently throughout the training.
2. *A suggestion*: Don't take a break after this exercise. Move from it right into the next exercise on your agenda. Just use it as a preparation and as a jump-start into readiness for the rest of the creative work at hand.

The WarmUp Sequence—A temporary structure

While an explanation of the inner logic of the WarmUp Sequence appears later in this book, here is a suggested structure for a workshop session using the exercises that have been introduced thus far:

- Arrival; Transformation (changing clothes).
- Crossing the Threshold (taking a private moment, then entering the work space; Exercise no. 1).
- NameBalls (Exercise 4).
- Staccato/Legato (Exercise 8).
- StickWork (up to whatever level has been reached).
- Mini–Maxi Pacing/Walking Variations/The Hunt and The Pounce (Exercises 13–15, this depends on the sidecoaching option that is chosen).
- Energy Circle (Exercise 7).

With a group of beginners, in the first stages of their training, these exercises and their many possible variations are enough to work on for an entire session. The following exercises are gradually added to the WarmUp Sequence until the entire Physical WarmUp is in place.

16. TOUCH AWARENESS

This exercise is a small, but crucial, detour that must be taken before moving into the next element of the Walking exercises, since it provides the actors with a palpable experience of what it means to "see" what they look like in space at all times. This can either be a one-time exercise to demonstrate the concept or a repeated exercise to provide the actors with a mechanism for physical awareness.

Setup

Actors take a partner and spread out at random in the entire space. The pairs face each other, and one of the two partners has his eyes closed.

Activity

This is an "exchange exercise" with partners changing roles at the end of the set.

To begin the exercise the "blind" partner must find a point of concentration somewhere inside (a "center"), and relax by using that point as a focus for all his energies. (NB: since the concept of *centering* has not been dealt with yet, don't stop to explain it here. Just let the actors do whatever they understand by the term.) Once the "blind" partner is concentrated, the seeing partner begins to touch the unseeing partner using only one hand (see Figure 15). The manner of touching should change from time to time—one finger or more, the whole palm, the back of the hand, a fist, and so on—and the point of contact should be held for a few seconds to give the unseeing partner time to "send his consciousness" to the point of contact and to "be" there briefly. The intervals between touches should gradually diminish so that when the touches come in rapid succession the unseeing partner has to "push" the activity of "sending his consciousness" to the point of contact. Needless to say, the actors should respect each other's bodies and refrain from touching any sensitive areas.

Figure 15 Touch awareness.

Notes

1. The points of contact should be as far away from each other as possible (e.g. one touch on the leg, the next one on the top of the shoulder; see Figure 15). This will help the actors avoid getting into clearly recognizable patterns, which make it easy for the "blind" partner to anticipate each touch.
2. The "blind" partner must use these points of contact to practice "sending out" his consciousness to different points in the body. He remains concentrated at that point for as long as there is pressure there. (The duration of each contact should be brief: just long enough for the unseeing partner to "get to" the point of contact, but not long enough for him to grow self-conscious about it.) As soon as the touching hand or fingers are lifted, the unseeing partner's consciousness should be "withdrawn" again into a Zero Point of anticipation.

NB

In Vladimir Nabokov's *Lolita* there is a wonderful description of Humbert Humbert sitting upstairs in his room like a large spider, waiting for the filaments of the web he has spun throughout the house to vibrate so that he can know by the various sounds and noises Lolita and her mother make exactly where each of them is. As soon as a noise is heard, Humbert immediately "goes there" along this filament in his imagination, and "sees" who is making which noise and how. This is a useful metaphor for this exercise: the unseeing partner is "sitting in his mind," or *center*, waiting for the touch of a hand or a finger to vibrate one of the filaments spread throughout his body. As soon as there is contact on any part of his body, he "goes there" and stays there, "analyzing" the touch until the pressure is taken away.

---

3. The seeing partner should constantly refer back to the unseeing partner's face to check on the level of concentration (see Figure 15). If the unseeing partner has lost his concentration (usually by twitching, smiling, or laughing outright), the seeing partner must stop and allow him time to regain composure.
4. As the exercise progresses and the pace of the touching grows—or the intervals between points of contact grow shorter and shorter—tell the actors that they can now use both hands but that there should always be only one point of contact. Sidecoach them to lift one hand before touching with the other.

Emphases

1. *Concentration.* This is, of course, a major issue in the concept of training, and will be dealt with extensively throughout the entire cycle. When it is introduced here, at this early stage, the actors should be coached to choose some point in their body, preferably low down in their abdomen, and use that as a point of concentration—a "center"—to help them overcome their self-consciousness and the sense of extreme vulnerability that comes with their "blindness" and the knowledge that they are going to be touched. The actors should be reminded to use the Actor's Catechism to follow this process of "draining away" their self-consciousness until the final point of relaxed readiness is reached. The seeing actors should be coached to pay attention to their partners' faces and body language and "watch" as their concentration goes down from their Head Center to their Abdomen Center (elaborated on later in the section on Centers).

2. *Concentration control.* The unseeing actor should use this exercise to discover his ability to control his concentration by concentrating on the point of contact exclusively—not letting the concentration wander—for as long as the touch lasts. The unseeing actor should concentrate all his energies only on the qualities he senses at the point of contact, and not on the partner doing the touching.

3. *Physical awareness.* This is the ultimate goal of this exercise—understanding the mechanism of "sending one's consciousness" to any and every part of the body in order to have some idea of the body's form in space.

4. *"Pushing".* This is a concept that will come into play later in the exercises on the imagination and is, in effect, a way of suggesting to the actors that they can develop a measure of control over their creative consciousness and their imagination. Here it is applied only to the concept of "sending one's consciousness" to a given point in the body.

5. *Readiness.* During the entire exercise, the "blind" partner has nothing to rely on except the knowledge that he is going to be touched somewhere. This generates a very strong sense of anticipation, a built-in readiness, between one touch and another, that the actors must explore through the Catechism.

6. *Feeling of Ease.* Being ready, in this sense, means being in a state of relaxed preparedness, and as a result not being surprised by any touch. This can only be achieved if the readiness is the result of maintaining a Feeling of Ease throughout.

7. *Trust.* A large part of this readiness depends on mutual trust, since the unseeing actors literally "entrust" their bodies to their partners, and must be certain that they can trust their partners to treat them with respect.

17. WALKING VARIATIONS—FASTWALK-FREEZE

The Touch Awareness exercise is a prerequisite for the next step, since an important part of all of the walking exercises as they are incorporated in the WarmUp Sequence is the *freeze*, during which the actors are asked to "see" what they look like without looking at—or touching—themselves. In a way, it's almost impossible to go on to the next part of the walking exercises without first practicing Touch Awareness.

The first two walking exercises—Mini-Maxi Pacing (Exercise 13) and Direction Changes (Exercise 14)—have their own intrinsic value, and should be used as often as necessary to get the technique down pat. However, like many of the platform exercises, they are only a basis for the more advanced—and ultimately more richly layered—versions of the exercise. The following variation is one of these more advanced exercises; it addresses a number of important acting techniques, depending on how the model of behavior is built up around it.

Setup

The actors spread out in the entire space.

Activity

Only the fast walking part of the walk cycle is used (and, for the sake of convenience—and workshop effectiveness—will be called from now on *FastWalk*). This exercise should follow directly after the end of a Mini-Maxi cycle of walking, with no drop of concentration in between. Standing at the same point where they ended the Mini-Maxi cycle—in a state of absolute readiness—the actors are now told to move directly into the FastWalk, following all the components of the walk—changes of direction, Soft Focus, The Hunt, and so on. At a clap, the actors freeze in place. A few seconds later, on a second clap, they go back into the FastWalk. These are rapid shifts of energies and physical adjustments—from forward-moving kinetic space, to freeze-stopped static space.

After this has been exercised for a while, the following element of physical awareness is introduced. The actors are asked to use the freeze to find out what they look like, to take an "inventory" of their form in space by "sending their consciousness" to their entire body. The actors should be asked, "What do you look like?" and encouraged to feel or sense this without moving or looking at themselves.

Notes

1. The freeze should be instant, and a good rule of thumb to follow is for the teacher/director to clap and, a second later, say "Freeze!" and to tell the actors that between the clap and the word "Freeze!" all movement should stop.
2. There are two distinct stages in the freeze. In order to stop instantly the actors will use virtually every muscle in their bodies. As soon as they stop, they should immediately relax from within—without changing their physical position—all those muscles that are not required in order to maintain the position they stopped in.

NB

This relaxation of "unnecessary" muscles should not be visible. It is an internal, *invisible* shift of energies so that the actor can (a) allow her consciousness to wander freely through the relaxed body to give her a sense of what she looks like, and (b) be ready to move back effort-lessly into the fast walk when the next clap is heard. The form of the body in space at the moment of freezing should be *precisely main-tained* after this inner relaxation. It is also a necessary physical state for the continuation of the exercise: a totally tensed-up body in the freeze will cause a "jerk into motion" when the clap is heard, instead of a smooth transition back to walking.

---

3. Sidecoaching for the freeze should include the emphasis on its two stages, and a callout: "What do you look like? Feel your body from within; *sense* its form in space. What is the angle of your head on your shoulders? Where is the little finger of your left hand? How is your foot touching the floor? What is the distance between your elbow and your side?" and so on.
4. As the exercise goes on, it is helpful to tell the actors to use the "Freeze!" call to throw themselves into an unusual physical position first and then freeze, and thus avoid working on more or less the same form of their bodies every time.

Emphases

All the *Emphases* from the basic walking exercises also apply here, but with the important addition of *physical awareness*: this is the object of the exer-cise—acquiring an inner mechanism for an ongoing awareness of the performing body in space.

Activity

Basically, the exercise involves walking backward through the space. Unlike the FastWalk–Freeze, where avoiding collisions elegantly is the name of the game, in this version, collisions are an integral part of what happens, and preparing for them is one of the objects of the exercise. The way to prepare for these collisions is by moving through the space using just enough muscular tension to hold the body erect and keep it moving, but no more than that, so that it offers no resistance when encountered. Actors move through the space like water—along the line of least resistance—barely upright, totally flexible, with no "weight" or momentum when coming into contact with other bodies in the space. When bodies do come into contact, the actors flow off each other and continue moving backward in the space.

In this exercise too, a "Freeze!" command is given every few minutes.

Notes

1. A convenient image for the resistance-free body is that of a marionette, with its wires held very loosely, barely up on its feet. Apart from the shift in physical focus (from the tension of the FastWalk to the relaxed body of the BackWalk), this looseness will guarantee no injuries or painful collisions.

NB

"Flowing off each other" does not mean taking action or making an effort. On the contrary, what is involved is *a total lack of effort*. Rather than tensing and recoiling from the contact—which is a defense mechanism—the actors should flow *into* the contact until they roll away.

---

2. This exercise occasionally produces massive traffic jams in the center of the space that defeat the purpose of the work. In order to prevent this from happening, tell the actors to make long crosses throughout the entire space rather than bunching up in the middle.

3. Here, the freeze requires a different organization of energies. Instead of shifting from the strong forward tension of the FastWalk to the static tension of the freeze, they now move from a kind of lassitude to the total

tension of the freeze. They should be made conscious of this difference through sidecoaching, and urged to examine the actions they must undertake in order to go into the freeze from their "watery" body in the BackWalk.

4. After the initial apprehension wears off, the actors should be told to speed up, to move through the space at a faster pace, trusting the flaccidity of their bodies and their readiness to roll off on contact to protect them from any kind of bump or knock.

Emphases

1. *Relaxation.* In this case, overriding natural protective instincts and remaining totally loose in the sure knowledge that collisions will take place is the key. This is a whole-body correlative of the Soft Focus technique.

2. *DangerWorks.* There is a real "danger" here—the inevitable collisions—and overriding our natural instincts always pushes us into an area of daring, or risk-taking, which is an important aspect of improvisation technique, and of the training as a whole. It is literally a Stepping into the Unknown—the actor knows for certain that he will collide with the others, but has no idea of how or when this will happen. Readiness, once again, is all.

23. EQUIDISTANCE

Strictly speaking, this is not a walking exercise since it is practiced on the run. Nevertheless, it shares many training qualities with the walking exercises, and it is also a very useful variation for the Mixing and Matching exercise (Exercise 24) that follows.

Setup

Ask the actors to spread out in the space so that there is an equal distance between them all.

Activity

Now the actors must move as rapidly as they can through the space, running, walking, jumping sideways, or what have you, as long as they keep an equal distance between them and everyone else in the space at all times.

Notes

1. An easy way to sidecoach this one is to suggest to the actors that they are all minus- or plus-pole magnets, with repelling magnetic fields between them and anyone or anything in the space.
2. *Everything* has to be taken into account in this effort at "equidistancing": the walls, the piano, even the teacher/director who may be walking around the workspace. The actors must always move midway between any two things, animate or inanimate, in the space.

Emphases

1. *Spatial awareness.* The need to move through the space rapidly and instinctively raises the level of awareness for the contours, limitations, and actual size of the space. There is also a natural element of Soft Focus at work here as the actors try to take in the entire space all at once on the run.
2. *Second-to-second decision making/readiness.* As we have already noted, this is a fundamental element in improvisation technique and, consequently, a prime factor in the creative moment—which is why it is being trained here in the first place. Moving through a chaotic space over which we have no control demands instantaneous, second-to-second decision making. Since nothing can be planned ahead, our only salvation is a total readiness to take instantaneous advantage of a developing pattern in space. Once again—as always—the actors should be urged to question themselves on the run, to try and find out what kind of psychophysical organization is necessary for this kind of readiness.

24. WALKING EXERCISES—MIXING AND MATCHING

Once the platform of the Walking exercise is in place, all the variations can be used in a cycle—variations in the form of the walk and variations in the activity during the freeze. A typical "set" might include a mix of the following: Equidistance, FastWalk–Freeze, the Zambrano BackWalk—all of which are announced by the teacher/director in no special order after every freeze, and with varying timeframes. In the freeze itself the actors might be told either just to "see what they look like," or go into a *mirror*.

This rapid changing of physical *Emphases* and points of concentration is a kind of "calisthenics" for the actors' concentration, readiness, Feeling of Ease, and all the other techniques that are part of these exercises.

There is more to come, but it is time to take stock and consider what we have been through thus far, and what is the desired structure for this part of the warm-up. The following may help set up a frame of reference.

Some more food for thought

Why use the word *danger* or any degree of actual danger in connection with a field of art, especially in relation to the budding, supposedly protected stages of primary training? The answer lies, among other places, in the basic concept of the actor's craft and in the concept of training for the theater that I outlined in the introduction.

The public presentation of the self in an artwork of any kind is inherently "dangerous" because it displays profoundly personal areas of the artist's psyche to total strangers, rendering the artist deeply vulnerable, regardless of how successfully he manages the neuroses (according to some theories of creativity) that fuel his artwork. How much more so, then, is this the case in theater, where the artist is his own artifact, when his chosen art form requires live contact between this self/artifact and an audience in real time? A successful sculptor can take in the sun on a blue-tiled terrace in Palma de Majorca with a piña colada in one hand, a copy of *Business Week* in the other, and a cream-colored Afghan hound at his feet, while the results—in marble—of his gut searching of twenty years earlier is eliciting a profound emotional response from observers in a museum in Bratislava. Actors have no such luxury: whatever gut searching they do is public, live, immediate, and can only take place in direct contact with the audience. Actors have to draw on their *own* profound emotional response, *repeatedly every evening*, in order to create their artwork and affect their audiences. In other words, a clear and present psychological "danger" is inherent in their work. Doing this well requires talent, but also a great deal of practice. This, among other things, is what the models of behavior in the DangerWorks warm-ups address.

Let's look at it from another angle. Teachers or directors often exhort actors to "take risks," to "go all the way," to "overcome inhibitions" (i.e. our natural psychological defenses). What is this if not "danger" terminology? Over the ages we have developed a vast array of defense mechanisms in order to prevent ourselves from doing such foolish things as revealing our innermost secrets to strangers in public places on a regular basis. Overcoming these inbred defense mechanisms in order to practice the art of theater requires training: a modeling, through repetition, of the kind of difficult psychological experiences that are an inseparable part of the actor's art. When we look at training in this way—as a modeling of performative behavior so that the actor can layer these experiences into a technique and learn how to call on them at will for the execution of his art form—then the "danger" in these DangerWorks exercises can, I believe, begin to make sense.

There is yet another aspect to DangerWorks training, which has to do with the fundamental asymmetry of the theatrical event: the repetitive nature of the performance as opposed to its single viewing by an audience. Making a dramatic moment recur on stage as if it were occurring for the first time, actors must be able to recreate, every evening, the physical and psychical structure that attends the moment of risk, the Zero Point before their characters make critical choices. This too is not totally a God-given ability. It is, rather, a skill that requires training so that actors can place themselves every evening—as a regular part of their craft—in the same thrilling, heart-pounding, first-time situation of their characters' fateful, destiny-determining, life-and-death choices. In other words, an actor needs to be able to recreate at will her own sense of danger, of jumping into the unknown, so that her character will live only once—*every time she performs its life onstage*. This provides one of the justifications for the repeated modeling of DangerWorks exercises.

If all this is true, then, one might be tempted to ask: Why not train actors in various forms of extreme sports? That should give them a good sense of risk-taking and danger, shouldn't it? Jumping out of a plane at 5,000 feet, with nothing between you and the desert floor but a small board, and a parachute that may or may not open when you finally pull the ripcord—that could provide you with a true experience of "Stepping into the Unknown" and give you a thrill of a lifetime that would be imprinted on your soul forever, no?

The only problem with that, of course, is that these life-threatening experiences really have nothing to do with the true nature of the actor's craft. In the theater there is no real equivalent to that kind of forced thrill. It is too outlandish an activity, which at best can feed into the actor's sense of physical daring or his fear of heights, and can give his ego a massive adrenal boost, but what it cannot do is teach him anything at all about his creative being. For all the "danger" involved, making theater is not a self-gratifying act of physical daring, but a cooperative creation that must connect with, and satisfy, an audience's ego. Remarking on the differences between an actor and a trapeze artist, Eugenio Barba draws a similar conclusion when he claims that the trapeze artist is a virtuoso with whom we cannot identify, since we cannot possibly imagine ourselves ever doing anything even remotely resembling his feat. All he can arouse in us is awe at his daring and fear for his safety.

The kind of "danger" suggested by the DangerWorks warm-ups is, I believe, a useful, applicable kind of danger, and not ever really dangerous. It is a way for the actor to learn how to fly on a metaphorical trapeze, a feat that does not involve manifest physical danger, and can teach actors something about the daily craft of acting, something about themselves as creative beings, and something about the very process of creativity—and not about themselves as physically daring people.

Finally, turned into a technique, this metaphorical flying act helps the actor reach out to the audience, and *together* they can touch on personal fears, anxieties, and trepidations in the communal space of the theatrical performance.

The list of DangerWorks exercises described here is by no means exhaustive. Rather, it is representative, and many more similar exercises can be added—either invented, adapted from these, or culled from other sources. As long as the basic concept of "danger" outlined above and the fundamental nature of training as I have explained it thus far are clear, it will be fairly easy to make the choices.

The next step in the WarmUp Sequences—the Partner Exercises—belongs in this area of pure physicality and preliminary improvisation technique, all of which gives us a stepping-stone into the creativity training that follows.

Partner exercises

The logic of the exercises outlined above leads into the partner work along a work-shop trajectory that I believe to be pedagogically important: beginning with the actors alone in their "private moment," then moving, in sequence, from group exercises to alone-in-a-group exercises and then to Partner Exercises.

The most important aspect of the Partner Exercises is the modeling of *initiating/yielding*, or the balance between initiating and giving way. This belongs to the area of *creative cooperation*, which I noted in the introduction as one of the actor's five basic tools. Recognizing the moment of yielding or conceding is the beginning of the understanding of what initiating and yielding between fellow artists really is, what creative cooperation in the theater really means. What is more, recognizing the moment of concession is also a way of understanding the moment of initiative, as though by seeing the negative (giving way) we also learn about the positive (taking the initiative).

In some of these exercises, an important element of improvisation technique is introduced for the first time: the idea of "offers" and "counteroffers," which are the basic dynamic of any improvisational dialogue: the offers are gestures, sounds, or words given to one partner (or to oneself), and the counteroffers are both the response to that offer, and new offers in their own right.

25. THREE-WAY BLIND

This is a fairly basic trust exercise, which helps develop a number of elementary sensibilities in the Logic of Training.

Setup

Actors pair off in the entire space, one with eyes closed, the other leading with eyes open.

Activity

This is a three-step exchange exercise with the two partners exchanging "blind" and "leader" roles at the end of the three-part set. The steps are as follows:

Step 1—Hand in Hand: The seeing actor leads the "blind" actor by the hand around the room (Figure 16).

Step 2—Hands on Palms: Facing each other, palms barely touching, the seeing actor now leads the "blind" actor through the space (Figures 17 and 18).

Step 3—Voice Leading: The "blind" partner moves through the space with no physical contact, following only the sound of his name as it is called out by his seeing partners (Figure 19).

NB

This is a continuous exercise with no relaxation or opening of eyes during the transitions. Each time a change of organization is made—from leading by the hand, to leading by the palms, to leading by voice alone—the "blind" partners keep their eyes closed. The actors do not talk among themselves, and every effort is made to ensure that the exercise flows from one form to the next with no drop in energy or concentration. To enhance the continuity of the exercise, all of the instructions and demonstrations should be given before the exercise begins.

Notes for Steps 1 and 2

1. In all of these variations it is important to stress the "blind" partner's active acceptance of her guide's leadership as a trust-building factor. Active acceptance means that the "blind" actor should move effortlessly through the space—as though she can see—and in so doing force the seeing partner to take responsibility for her safety while negotiating the room. If the "blind" actors try to protect themselves by holding back, or

Figure 16 Three-Way Blind: Hand in hand.

Figure 17 Three-Way Blind: Hand on palms: The feather-light touch.

Figure 18 Three-Way Blind: Hand on palms.

Figure 19 Three-Way Blind: Voice leading.

waving their arms about in front of themselves to feel their way through the space, the seeing partners will expend most of their energy just trying to overcome their blocking tactics—and the point of the exercise will be lost.

2. The pairs of actors should be encouraged, through sidecoaching, to explore the limits of their trust by crawling, skipping, jumping, or even running. This can only happen if the "blind" actor takes up the challenge of active acceptance with a true Feeling of Ease.

3. This is a good place to point out that Partner Exercises are *never* one-sided—including this one, which seems on the face of it to be a "leader" exercise. Tell the actors that the "blind" actors can also initiate changes of pace, direction, or forms of movement, and it is up to their seeing partners to respond immediately, and lead them safely in the direction they want to go. When two actors reach a high level of proficiency in this exercise, no leader is necessary. (See "Initiating/Yielding" in *Emphases* below.)

4. In step 2 contact between the palms must be very light and holding should be avoided at all costs. It is the lightness of the touch that determines the difficulty of the exercise—and its effectiveness (see Figure 17).

Notes for step 3—Voice leading

1. In order to lead their "blind" partners effectively, the seeing actors should say their partners' names *repeatedly* and *continuously*. It is the only thing the "blind" actors have to go by, and they must not be left hanging in the space, waiting to hear their name called to get a "fix" on their seeing partners. Inexperienced groups or young acting students should be cautioned not to play tricks on their partners, like surprising them by moving away silently and then calling out from across the room or right behind their ears. The challenge, of course, is to keep up a constant flow of movement throughout the space, with a great deal of initiating/yielding and trust. Therefore, the names must be called out continuously, for virtually every step the "blind" partner makes.

2. Imminent collisions or changes of direction can be indicated by saying the name with a different intonation.

3. In this variation, the "blind" partners following vocal leads obviously cannot initiate changes of direction, as they can in steps 1 and 2. However, they can—and should—develop the "danger" factor of this part of the exercise by responding *instantly* to any vocal command. As soon as a "blind" partner hears her name called out, she should move swiftly and confidently in that direction until her name is called again. This will force the seeing partners to be on their toes at all times.

Emphases

1. *Trust.* The "blind" actor has no choice but to trust her "seeing eye," and should follow him with complete confidence. But trust goes both ways, and the blind partner must demand or enforce this trust by moving easily and confidently after the leader in all the variations; the leader must justify this trust by working with his "blind" partner to move safely through the space.

2. *Feeling of Ease.* To overcome the enforced "blindness," the "blind" partner must remain loose, relaxed, and totally amenable to being led anywhere in the space—as if she can see. The seeing partner's Feeling of Ease is no less a part of the challenge: too much—or too little— concern for the "blind" partner's welfare yields few training benefits.

3. *Initiating/yielding.* Done properly, all the versions of this exercise involve absolutely no physical tension between the two partners—and that is one of the main purposes of the exercise. Either one of the partners— the seeing or the "blind"—can initiate a change of direction, to which the other partner must immediately concede. The moment of initiating a move is also, at the very same time, the moment of giving way to the other partner's initiative—the most basic concept of initiating and yielding.

4. *Danger/control/readiness.* As in any "blind" exercise, there is always the potential danger of collisions. The "blind" actor must be ready to deal with any such encounters by using the skills acquired in the preceding walking exercises: expansion of sensual awareness, loosely held body, danger readiness, overriding defense-mechanism reactions, and so on. The seeing actor must use Soft Focus to take in the shifting movement patterns of the other couples in the space on the move, so that he can prepare for the unexpected and respond instantly to any changes in the space.

26. PARTNER MOVING

This is similar to the previous exercise but requires much higher levels of Soft Focus, spatial awareness, readiness and Initiating/Yielding.

Setup

The actors pair off, everyone with eyes open, using the entire space.

Activity

The pairs are now asked to move through the space side-by-side, *without* holding on to each other in any way, without looking at each other, and, as far as possible, without touching each other in any way. The object of the exercise is to respond instantly to random shifts of direction initiated by either of the partners. Pace, direction, and level (e.g. crawling, or walking in a squat or on tiptoe) can be mixed-and-matched at will by either actor at any moment.

Notes

1. Throughout the exercise, the two partners should be as close as they can to each other without actually touching. Breaking away or creating large distances between them defeats the purpose.
2. This is a free-for-all in which there is no leader and either one of the two can take the initiative at any second. The instant one of the two makes the slightest shift of direction, the other follows.

Emphases

1. *Readiness.* Goes without saying.
2. *Initiating/yielding.* Goes without saying, and leads into instant responsiveness.
3. *Soft Focus/spatial awareness.* Clearly this exercise works best with Soft Focus. It is the only way the two actors can keep track of each other while moving quickly through a space filled with other moving bodies.

27. ENERGY EXCHANGE

Even though this is, in some ways, an advanced exercise in improvisation technique, and is best "played" by experienced actors, nevertheless it belongs to this series and can be introduced at regular intervals as the actors' skills improve. It is also a useful introduction to the concept of *Abstract Movement*, which is an important element in the *Creative WarmUp below*.

Setup

The actors pair off, everyone with eyes open, using the entire space.

Activity

In Viola Spolin's *Improvisation for the Theater* there is an exercise called Space Substance that involves actors imagining that the space they are moving in is gradually thickening around them. Using this metaphor, the pairs of actors enter into physical relationships within an imaginary gel-like "space substance" that totally surrounds them. Any movement—even the tiniest twitch of the nose—by one actor changes the entire space and creates a ripple effect that moves the other actor. His reaction changes the space again, and moves the first actor, and so on in a never-ending continuum of mutually-influenced movement.

As the exercise develops, the teacher/director can create groupings of four or six, or even the entire group, all of whom respond as best they can to everything that is happening around them. This variation multiplies the main *Emphases* of the exercise set out below virtually to the *n*th degree.

Notes

1. The physical exchange between the partners or the groupings should remain completely abstract throughout. If a couple slide into a "plot" or a "story," with characters and conflicts, they will lose their improvisational freedom as the story line begins to dictate itself.
2. There is, of course, no right or wrong way of doing this exercise, nor can there be any objective criteria for measuring the actors' relative "success" in doing it. Actors doing this well will emanate a kind of palpable joy and intensity, which clearly shows that they got the idea.
3. In the early stages of the training, the actors should be encouraged to think of this as a physical dialogue, a Give-and-Take of gestures. As the training progresses and more and more improvisational skills are acquired, this exercise can turn into an extraordinarily beautiful dance of impulses, where "offer" and "reaction" turn into a seamless physical dialogue.

Emphases

1. *Offer/counteroffer*. As mentioned above, this is the basic dynamic of an improvisation. Later we will be discussing what makes a "good" offer as opposed to a "bad" or "uninteresting" offer, but at this early point in the training it is sufficient to point out the basics.

2. *Remaining in the abstract/creative freedom.* In the early stages of this training, when the work is still totally physical and nonvocal, it is very important to emphasize the freedom and the realm of all possibilities that comes with avoiding storytelling and remaining in the abstract. This is not easy, since human beings have an inbred fear of anything that is unformed or inherently chaotic—and playing out a totally abstract improvisation sometimes feels like walking on a high wire with no wire. But setting up a plot-oriented safety net—a story line—deprives them of a crucially important element of training: the breathtaking exhilaration and sheer joy of absolute, unlimited creative freedom.

NB

Since inculcating in actors a fundamental, experiential understanding of creative freedom is one of the most important elements in the entire Logic of Training, I can hardly emphasize it strongly enough. That is why these exercises in abstract improvisations are so important and should be used in the training over and over again, until the habit is acquired.

---

28. THE NAME OF THE GAME

This exercise, too, is based on advanced improvisation technique, but it can—and should—be introduced very early in the training. Basically, it too enables the actors to experience the joy of creative freedom through totally abstract physical improvisation. As the name suggests, this is very much a "game" because of the way it makes use of rules, but watch out—this is no ordinary hop, skip, and jump!

Setup

Initially, one or two pairs of actors should try this out in front of the group for demonstration purposes; then, the entire group works in pairs in the space.

Activity

Two actors facing each other are told that the exercise will begin as soon as the teacher/director says "Now!" From that point on, anything that happens between them—*anything at all*—is an improvisational "offer" that has to be worked with. And it goes roughly like this: one actor makes a move (e.g. scratches the top of his head with his fingers outstretched) and his partner responds in some way with a physical gesture that need not be the same as the offer (e.g. scratches her stomach with fingers similarly outstretched). This initial exchange should be enough to establish a basic pattern for the "game" of *I Scratch, You Scratch—with Outstretched Fingers*. The two actors must now try to discover the rules of their new game as they go along. For example, one of the actors might start scratching the other—and the game eventually turns into a frantic four-handed affair worthy of chimpanzees under attack by killer ants as it evolves into *I Scratch You, You Scratch Me—Frantically!*

NB

The actors do not have to say the name of their game out loud or stop to think about it. If the game is a good one it will define itself as the two partners follow the rules that evolve out of their playing.

This goes on as long as the couples manage to invent variations that keep them interested in any given game. When they tire of that game, like children, they begin looking for another one. All they need is for one of the actors to pick up on the slightest physical offer from the other, and they're off!

NB

This exercise should be done without voice, but if actors break into laughter when they discover a particularly exhilarating game, or if they find themselves naturally adding a voice to a movement that's okay, but there should be no verbal dialogue or gibberish. One good way of limiting this is by emphasizing that (a) there should be no voice, and (b) if voice comes that's okay, but there should then be no words.

The need to remain in the abstract through concentrating solely on qualities of movement is paramount here, and sidecoaching can help the actors stay away from plot-oriented stories.

Example

Here is a blow-by-blow account of an encounter between two of my nephews—Shai and Matan, aged three and two, respectively, at the time of this writing—that is an excellent example of this exercise.

Coming through our front door, Shai caught sight of his cousin, Matan, and began running toward him. As he did so, he inadvertently tripped on the carpet, fell to the floor, and rolled over. Matan understood this immediately as an offer—an invitation to a game—and instantly followed suit, throwing himself down on the ground and rolling over, and launching—without saying a word—what they both knew was a new game called *Falling Down and Rolling Over*. But games have to be made interesting, so Shai got up and did it again. He threw himself down on the ground and rolled over, but this time added a new twist: after rolling one way, he then rolled right back the other way. Matan had no trouble incorporating this one, and responded with a variation of his own, rolling one way and then the other, but screaming delightedly on the roll. Without a word being exchanged between them, these toddlers went joyfully from Falling Down and Rolling Over, into an even better game: *Falling Down, Rolling Over This Way and That Way*, and then transformed this into a vastly improved version, *Falling Down, Rolling Over This Way and That Way and Screaming*.

This went on for a few minutes, until Matan got bored, raced off down the corridor, coming to a sliding stop at the end. Shai needed no prodding—clearly this was a new, much more exciting game—and off he went, racing down the corridor himself and sliding to a halt at the end. As he was doing this, Matan was already making his way back to the starting point at the entrance to the corridor, and—*voilà!*—before any of us even had a chance to think about what was happening, the two youngsters were deeply absorbed in a new game, *Racing Down the Corridor and Sliding to a Stop*, which filled their lives for the next few minutes—until a new game emerged.

Notes

1. The emphasis in this exercise is on *qualities of movement*. It's all right if the actors go into conflicts—mock battles of some kind—or competitions, as long as the abstract "rules of engagement" are retained. For example, they may play a game called *You Tap Me Three Times/I Tap You Three Times* that develops into in *Different Places Each Time*, and then slides into *With Backsides Only*, which may then turn into *With Torso Only*, or *Five Times*, but they should avoid turning them into plotted battles with heroes and bad guys.

2. *Anything* that happens between the actors in the course of one game can be taken up by one of the partners as an offer marking the beginning of a new game—even if it was not *intended* as an offer. This encourages a very high level of attention, because there is no knowing when a

new game might suddenly appear out of an unintentional movement or gesture.

3. Suggest to the actors that there is more to these games than conflicts. Some of them can be noncompetitive, cooperative games. For example, two actors playing a game called *Crossing the Space with the Fewest Possible Steps* may end up helping each other take enormous steps or jumps to cross the studio in three giant leaps *together* rather than competing with each other over who gets there first.

4. Suggest to the actors that they avoid the temptation to go into a mirror exercise. This is a game in which the differences between the two participants are more important than the similarities.

5. A suggestion. This exercise naturally releases a great deal of playful energy; therefore its place in the overall structure of a workshop session must be carefully chosen. One possibility is to use it after the WarmUp Sequence and just before taking a break, or before moving out of the WarmUps into the specific content of a particular workshop or class session.

Emphases

1. *Play*. As Steven Nachmanovitch notes in his book *Free Play*, "Improvisation, composition, writing, painting, theater, invention, all creative acts are forms of play, the starting place of creativity in the human growth cycle, and one of the great primal life functions. Without play, learning and evolution are impossible. Play is the taproot from which original art springs" (42) 'Nuff said!

2. *Readiness*. Since the rules can evolve or change at any moment, even "mistakenly" as the result of a response to a gesture not intended as an offer, the game provides an intense experience of readiness.

3. *"Danger"/first-time sensibility*. The behavior "modeled" in this exercise is twofold. There is the sensation first that anything can happen at any time, and second, that any stimulus—visual or aural—must be responded to instantly. Repeated training in The Name of the Game helps actors acquire the habit of regarding *everything* that happens onstage as a new offer, with the result that every performance—the tenth or the hundred and tenth—retains the excitement and "danger" of the first.

4. *Improvisation technique/exhausting the moment*. In the creative cycle, after recognizing and seizing the creative moment, the next step is to "manage" it—make it last as long as possible. This is modeled here by the challenge to make each game last as long as possible with the help of endless innovations or the invention of new rules and variations. This

concept of *exhausting the moment* is a crucially important element in the training and appears in many of the following exercises.

5. *Remaining in the abstract.* If two actors each find themselves hopping on one foot to a complex rhythm, then the name of the game might be *How Complicated Can We Make It without Losing It?*—and there is no need to turn it into a story about two skiers commiserating about nasty falls on the piste. If two actors find themselves bent in half and making contact with the tops of their heads, the name of the game might be *Stepping Backward As Far As We Can without Losing Head Contact before Falling*—not the fate of two Siamese twins trying to get a job interview. Or, if two actors find themselves jumping up with one hand stretched high in the air, then the name of the game might be *How High Can We Jump, How Softly Can We Land?*—not the story of two dwarf basketball hopefuls trying out for the NBA. Whenever a new move is detected (or injected) a movement quality—*not a story*—must be immediately looked for, then "seized" and "managed" through the invention of rules pertaining only to the physical aspects of their relationship.

A note on Contact Improvisation

Those of you who are familiar with Contact Improvisation (see Figure 20) will probably recognize its obvious affinities to the Energy Exchange and The Name of the

Figure 20 Contact Improvisation.

Game, particularly in the all-important area of abstract movement and Initiating/ Yielding. And indeed, following the introduction of these exercises, I often go into brief sessions of Contact Improvisation in the warm-up sequence. "Contact Impro," as it is affectionately known, is pure abstract improvisation based on a continuous, totally contentless sharing and exchange of body weight and tension ("an endless flow of accidents," according to one definition). I believe that Contact Improvisation is a *must* for anyone interested in any aspect of the physical approach to theater, and it is well worth looking into. The only drawback I have found, admittedly from my particular bias, is that in most forms of Contact Impro there is rarely any attempt at repetition (i.e. no attempt to "exhaust the moment"). Other than that it is one of the best ways I know of for actors to keep up improvisation/creative skills outside of rehearsals or training, and one that I heartily recommend to all my actors and students.

29. STICKTALK

Every so often in the preparation of this book, I came across an exercise that absolutely defied categorization, and the following is one of them. On the one hand, it uses sticks but doesn't belong in the StickWork sequence. It is also a Partner Exercise, but one that is brought in much later in the Logic of Training as an aide to the concept of the Feeling of the Whole in the Creative WarmUp Sequence (which appears later in this book). One of the reasons for this is that this simple exercise—more of a "theater game" improvisation than a bona fide training exercise—is no less "seminal" than some of the major training exercises. It is seminal in the sense of its being applicable to many different aspects of the training, depending on where it is brought in and how it is angled through sidecoaching. Having said all of that, here it is—the last in the present series of Partner Exercises. Use it as you will.

Setup

The group arranges itself in a loose, large circle, equipped with two sticks of the kind described earlier in the stick exercises.

Activity

The teacher/director throws sticks simultaneously to two actors, who catch the sticks and approach each other on the run, and create a brief physical, nonverbal improvisation with the sticks, leading to a clear "punch line" at the end. Improvisational offers flying, they relate to each other physically through the sticks, and look for the closing moment. When they feel that the impulse—or their mutual inventive-ness—is over, they freeze (see Figure 21). This is not unlike The Name of the Game (Exercise 28), but it involves two basically unwieldy sticks, and the emphasis is on an abstract improvisation and not qualities of movement.

Example

A comes rushing into the circle, holding her stick with both hands, and taps one end of it in a rapid staccato rhythm on the floor. *B* responds by holding his stick horizontally just above *A*'s stick so that *A*'s stick taps on the floor on the down swing and on *B*'s stick on the upswing. *A* responds by sliding her stick through *B*'s open legs, running around to catch it on the other side. As she does so, *B* jumps up and turns around in the air, still holding his stick horizontally, but when he lands he slaps the stick onto *A*'s stick, making it impossible for *A* to draw it away. This might be the end of the improvisation, unless *A* can come up with something really surprising—like wrapping herself around *B*'s stick or dropping her stick and walking out of the space.

Figure 21 StickTalk:
The punchline.

Note

It is very important to emphasize that as the actors rush in to meet each other and begin the improvisational exchange, they must split their concentration between the second-to-second responses to their partner's offers and their search for closure—the physical punch line. The idea of closure that they are seeking should be kept in what Viola Spolin refers to as "No Motion"—in the back of the head—as they play the improvisational game. It's as though they have two different clocks running simultaneously in their bodies: one showing the seconds of improvisational play, and the other ticking away the seconds until closure. Training with this exercise repeatedly helps the actors develop their instinctive sense of one of the more important of Chekhov's "Four Brothers" mentioned earlier—the Feeling of the Whole. Practiced over an extended period of training, the actors acquire the ability to simply enjoy the fun of the game, confident that their "closure clock" will sound the alarm in good time.

Emphases

Part of this exercise's usefulness derives from the numerous elements of improvisation technique that inform it. Since these will become part of the daily vocabulary of the entire training, the exercise has important training benefits.

1. *Offers/counteroffers*. These are mentioned in the introduction to this section and in relation to the Energy Exchange and The Name of the Game. In this exercise, offers begin to fly the moment the two actors rush into the circle. Anything that one actor does there, with the stick or without it, is an offer that the other actor must accept and respond to with a counteroffer. In other words, this is the basic improvisational dialogue.
2. *The Feeling of the Whole*. See note above. This aspect of the training will be dealt with at some length in the section on the Creative WarmUp.
3. *Interesting/uninteresting offers*. The lifeblood of the improvisational dialogue is the quality of the offer. Given an interesting offer an impro-viser can "fly"; given a drab, uninspiring offer, the same improviser, no matter how good she is at the technique, will "die." This is demonstrated at great length in the Random Talk exercises (nos 59 and 60).

The mirror exercises

This is one of the most unfairly maligned group of exercises in the literature of actor training, since it is regarded as the most basic exercise in partner work, one best done in the first few lessons of "Acting 101" and then forgotten. Over the years I have found the "family" of mirror exercises to be extraordinarily flexible training tools that, with all of the many possible variations, provide actors with a highly effective modeling of a number of vitally important aspects of their craft: the ability to send out a powerful, emotionally charged "emanation" of presence for a relatively long period of time, over a relatively large distance, and to connect with someone else at the other end. This allows the actors to learn, through repetition, an important lesson about what happens at all times between the actor radiating from the performance space and the spectators receiving this radiation in the audience. That alone—not to mention all the other training benefits that are elaborated below—is reason enough to spend a substantial amount of time working through all of the mirror exercises, detailed here and any other variations you may come up with.

NB

For reasons of convenience, the following section on mirror work includes *all* the variations, right up to the most complex and sophisticated versions. Clearly, in training, these forms of the mirror are introduced gradually, at the same time as the work being done on other sections of the WarmUp Sequence. Like all of the exercises in the Logic of Training, the mirror family has to be used in training over a significant period of time for its benefits to be fully incorporated in the actor's growing body of skills.

---

30. THE BASIC MIRROR EXERCISE (see Figure 22)

Setup

The group split up into pairs, and spreads out, using the entire space.

Activity

There are a number of steps to the exercise:

- The pairs decide among themselves who is going to be the "mover" and who is going to be the "mirror" reflection.
- The two stand facing each other, and the mirror tries to create a true reflection of the person facing her. The instructions to the mirror are, "Take on as many of the physical characteristics of your

partner as you can"; the instructions to the moving partner are, "When you see yourself in the mirror, start moving." The mover begins to move, and the mirror reflects her movements as closely as possible.

- After a while, the teacher/director stops the exercise and asks the actors to switch—the mover becomes the mirror, and vice versa.
- As this initial phase of the exercise goes on, a number of variations should be introduced. The first is to vary the distance between pairs so that the actors (who in the beginning tend naturally to work quite close to each other) work with each other from opposite ends of the work space, or at least a significant distance away from each other. This changes their perspective and demands a different kind of concentration and a different level of *radiation*. The second variation involves changing functions from mirror to mover without a break in the flow of physical actions.

NB

Once the exercise moves into the changeover without a break in the flow, sidecoach the actors to use the Actor's Catechism to notice the differences that occur in their psychophysical tensions and resonance when they change functions on the go from mirror to mover or vice versa.

Figure 22 The basic mirror exercise.

Notes

1. The movements of both mover and mirror should remain abstract at all times. The use of either realism (e.g. waving goodbye or flicking away an imaginary speck of dust) or imaginary objects (e.g. combing hair, smoking a cigarette, putting on lipstick) turns the exercise into a "scripted" event and removes the element of readiness because the mirror knows what the next move is going to be (e.g. after lighting a cigarette the usual sequence involves shaking out the match, throwing it away, taking a deep drag on the cigarette, then flicking the ash from the tip).

2. The enforced intimacy or physical proximity of this exercise will occasionally cause some embarrassment and nervous laughter in inexperienced actors. You can preempt this by talking about it before beginning the exercise, or you can discuss it if and when it occurs. Tell your actors that this kind of nervous laughter (unlike the playful laughter that may occur in The Name of the Game) is a defense mechanism that prevents them from committing themselves to the kind of openness and vulnerability that is a fundamental part of their craft. Laughter is infectious, so when you hear one laugh you can expect to hear more!

3. In the very early stages of the work, actors will tend to work solely with their hands and arms, ignoring the rest of their bodies. Point this out to them through sidecoaching, and remind them that they are working with a full-length mirror so they should work with the entire body.

4. Remind the actors that there is a mirror *between* them, so they cannot move any part of their bodies into their partner's space. Whatever they do has to remain on their "side" of the mirror.

5. Early on in this training, the mirrors will tend to look at whatever part of the movers' bodies they are mirroring. Suggest to them that it is in fact much easier—and the contact is much deeper—when they do the exercise while maintaining eye contact only with their partner. Soft Focus peripheral vision is handy here too. Watch out for actors who *think* mirror instead of *doing* it. For example, if I raise my right hand to scratch my head, and my partner raises *her* right hand to her head, we will be cross-mirroring. Remind the actors to reflect exactly what they see opposite them—in this case it will be the right hand on one side mirrored by the left hand on the other.

6. Suggest to the actors that their work should be so precise that someone coming into the room from outside will not be able to tell who is the mover and who is the mirror.

7. As the training in this exercise proceeds, the actors should work with someone else each time. This enhances the level of trust at the beginner

level, develops the sense of ensemble as the actors get to know each other one-on-one, and sets up a standard that will later be deliberately contravened for more advanced work as this exercise platform develops.

Sidecoaching

Here are some suggestions for sidecoaching this exercise:

- Don't begin to move until you see your "reflection" in the mirror.
- Keep all your moves abstract, stay away from any kind of realism.
- Tricking the mirror is too easy, so stick to the challenge: achieving total physical precision in the mirroring.
- This is an exercise in rhythm, so look for a shared rhythm.
- Don't watch each other moving; maintain direct eye contact at all times and you will see everything you need to see—including your partner's intentions.
- Work with your whole body, not just with your hands.

Emphases

1. *Initiating/yielding*. Despite the initial division between mirror and mover, this is not a one-sided exercise and *both* partners have to yield at all times. The mirror yields by reflecting his/her partner's movements and not initiating any of his/her own; the mover yields by adapting the rhythm of her movements to the capabilities of her mirror.
2. *Openness/availability*. Looking closely into each other's eyes, following the other's body movements in great detail, and copying physical movements precisely—all these require and develop a great openness and trust.
3. *Radiation*. In order to reach a high level of precision, particularly in the more advanced stages of this exercise, it's not enough for the movers just to move. They must also try to radiate their intentions to their partners. This is effective only if it is done through deeply connected eye contact (NB: *this is not a call for telepathy or any other kind of mysticospiritual process!* It is merely a way of giving the actors a model of behavior that can teach them something about one of the basic requirements of theater: that an actor must send out over a distance—*radiate*—whatever is happening inside her to her partners, director, or audience.)
4. *Readiness*. In this version of the exercise, *Readiness* is different for each of the partners: for the mirror it means being ready to go with whatever the mover does the instant she does it; for the mover it means being

ready at all times to read the level of precision in the mirror's body, and develop the range and pace of the exercise according to what the mirror can or cannot do.

31. FREE MIRROR

Once you move into this form of mirror exercise it becomes the standard, and, in all the subsequent variations, there is no need to revert to the earlier designations of mirror and mover. The time to introduce this variation will almost invariably present itself when, after a sequence of Basic Mirror Exercises with different partners, the actors start talking about not knowing who was moving and who was mirroring, or not knowing who was initiating and who was following. Don't be tempted to move into this too quickly. The Basic Mirror Exercise is not just a preparatory exercise for the next stage; it has its own value as an exercise, as its *Emphases* point out.

Setup

As in the Basic Mirror Exercise, the actors are paired off in the space.

Activity

At a certain point in a Basic Mirror Exercise, the actors are told there is no longer any distinction between mirror or mover—both partners can initiate and/or reflect at all times, so they are in fact simultaneously and constantly mirroring each other. Bringing this into the workshop when it is in fact already happening between the pairs anyway makes the shift surprisingly effortless.

Notes

1. In this version, more emphatically than in the previous one, the actors should maintain constant eye contact and Soft Focus rather than following the moving parts of their partner's body.
2. Remind them again to stay in the abstract and not to get into any kind of miming of realistic actions.
3. When a fair degree of technical competence is achieved, suggest to the actors that meanings—a kind of unintentional "subtext"—may emerge and take the form of an interior (nonverbal, nonlinear) dialogue that may lead them into a "relationship." This is okay, and in fact enhances the depth of the contact. The only thing to watch out for is any possible descent into storytelling realism.

4. Suggest to the actors that the greater their physical precision, the greater the flexibility and variety of their physical dialogue.

Emphases

The same emphases apply as for the Basic Mirror Exercise, except for the following:

1. *Advanced readiness.* Moving from the simplicity of designated mover and mirror into the complexity of no designated functions multiplies the need for readiness tenfold.
2. *Freedom and limits.* An early modeling of one of the most fundamental elements of performance "behaviors": seeking the greatest possible freedom within the strict limitation imposed by the requirement for absolute physical precision in the mirror.

32. CHANGING MIRRORS

The next member of this "family" moves the actors into a new kind of flexibility, modeling the ability they must develop to adapt their techniques to ever-changing circumstances.

Activity

1. Start the actors working in Free Mirror, then tell them that at your handclap they are to break eye contact with their partners, and, from wherever they are, look for new partners.
2. Once each has "locked on" to a new partner's eyes, the new pair should make minimal adjustments until they reach a precise physical mirror, and then get to work.
3. These changes of partners are repeated a number of times, until the teacher/director sidecoaches them back to their first partner and ends the exercise.

Notes

1. After the handclap, the actors should try to continue radiating energy outward—just as they did with their partners a moment ago—until they find their new partner.
2. New partners should start working the instant they make eye contact.
3. Sidecoach the actors to pay attention to the psychophysical organization they need during the four different parts of the exercise: (1) when

they are deeply involved in a mirror; (2) when they hear the clap and have to cut their connection with their partner; (3) when they are in limbo after the clap, looking for someone else to lock on to; and (4) the first few seconds after they lock on to a new partner's eyes.

4. If there is an uneven number in the group, the unpartnered "free agent" should be told by the teacher/director to wait a while until the next change, and then move in, leaving someone else waiting for the next change (see also Exercise 35 for more on "free agents").

5. In the initial stages of this exercise, it is often a good idea to let the actors work with their first partners for an extended period of time before making the first change. This sets a standard of connection against which they can measure the depth of their work with their subsequent partners. This also generates some wonderful mirror "reunions" when they meet their first partner again on the last change.

6. In the critique session it is important for the actors to talk about the differences they felt between their first partners and all the others in terms of the depth of the exchange and the nature of their "conversation."

Emphasis

Technique—A movable feast. While working in the Basic Mirror Exercise with only one partner, actors often develop a deep relationship with that partner. Changing Mirrors models the idea that this level of concentration and exchange does not—and should not—depend on the coincidence of having one particular partner and not another. It should be an inner technique, one that the actor carries with her into any period of joint creativity with other actors. This is a fact of the professional life of an actor that should be pointed out here.

Ending the mirror exercise

When this exercise is done well, it can reach an extraordinarily high level of intensity as the actors lose themselves in their relationships with their partners and body expression flows. In order to ensure that this will be a viable training experience, one that they will be able to articulate and then layer into their accumulating self-knowledge, "stepping out" of this intensity must be done slowly and gradually. Shifting out of this deep connection too abruptly is almost like coming out of a dream too quickly—everything is lost. The most effective method of doing this involves a few key steps:

- Sidecoach the actors to keep working in the mirror but to begin making their way back to a basic standing position.
- While they are doing so, they should also gradually reduce their move-

ments until they are standing still with only mirror bodies and eye contact.

- After a moment, when all there is between the partners is deep mutual resonance, you can tell them to "step out" and end the connection. A soft handclap helps facilitate this.

33. THE MIRROR CIRCLE

This is a follow-on from Changing Mirrors, and is introduced at the end, when you bring the original pairs back together again.

Activity

Tell the actors to work their way up to a standing position while reducing their physical movements, and at the same time to begin backing away from each other. They should be sidecoached to move as far away from each other as the space permits. Mention also that as they move backward through the space each actor is responsible for the space *behind* her partner, so that no one steps on, or collides with, anybody on the way. Adjustments to avoid stepping on someone should be made without "breaking" the mirror.

When they have all moved back as far as they can, and have reduced their physical movements to zero, tell them that you are going to make some physical adjustments to their placement in space, but that they are *to maintain their concentration and mirror eye contact no matter what*. Taking care not to break their eye contacts, the teacher/director should now arrange the actors in a loose circle, around the periphery of the space, moving them gently into position if necessary—by holding them from behind—until they form a *mirror circle*: each actor connected to his or her partner across the entire width of the work space.

Now tell them that when you clap your hands they are to break their connection with their partner and look for eye contact with someone else—without moving out of the circle and without initiating any physical movement, only eye contact.

Do this a number of times, suggesting to the actors that they examine the moments of transition: the clap, the "limbo" until a new pair of eyes is locked into, and the moment of relief when a pair of eyes is in fact engaged.

Notes

1. The explanation of this exercise, which is the only way the actors can be led into experiencing its training benefits, should be given as side-coaching—as the actors are working. When they form the circle, working with their partners through eye contact only, suggest to them that the connection between them now is like a muscle—something palpable, sinewy, flexible, and strong. This image will help them define the relative strength of the connection they have with any given partner.

2. This is a very intense exercise that requires an enormous amount of concentration. If it comes after a fairly long Basic Mirror Exercise, too much of the Mirror Circle can cause the eyes to dry out, resulting in a slight stinging and some tears. Bear this in mind when you move into the Mirror Circle exercise.

Emphasis

Radiation. Through the intensity of any mirror exercise the actors reach a very high level of radiation. As they reduce the physical part of the mirror work to zero and remain only with eye contact, they should have a palpable sensation of the radiating connection between them and their partners, a connection that is achieved through some kind of internal organization of their energies. Using the Actor's Catechism may help them begin to understand what they are doing when they are radiating.

34. MIRROR CIRCLE VARIATIONS

Free-for-All: In the mirror circle, when one of the partners in a mirror feels that the "muscle" between the two of them has become flabby, or when they begin to become self-conscious and lose the tonus of the connection, they can *unilaterally* break the connection, "turn it off": turn their heads away and look for someone else.

Technically what happens here is that one actor will end a mirror relationship and begin searching the circle for someone else who is similarly looking for a new partner. The actors must be told that part of this variation involves maintaining a state of *Readiness* and *radiation* for as long as it takes until someone else in the circle becomes available.

The Radiation Circle I: This variation creates a new standard of difficulty that should be introduced after a number of sessions of the basic Mirror Circle. Ask the actors to maintain eye contact with their partners across the circle, but when you snap your fingers, they are to "turn off" the connection *without breaking eye contact.* At that point they are "there" for their partner in a kind of formal eye contact, but mostly "not-there" because they they are no longer radiating anything; they have taken away the "muscle" that connects them. At the next finger-snap they are to turn the radiation on again—and note the difference.

NB

There is no need to explain to the actors how to "turn on" or "turn off" radiation—you probably can't explain it anyway—and don't field any questions about it while the exercise is in progress. Just tell them to do whatever they feel they have to in order to radiate or stop radiating. Clearly, the Actor's Catechism comes into play here with questions like: "What am I doing when I turn off or on?" "What psychophysical organization is necessary in order for me to radiate a presence?"

The Radiation Circle 2:   The next stage of this variation is simply a further difficulty: the same turning on and off takes place, and eye contact is maintained no matter what, but there is no external indication of when to do it—no finger-snap.

Notes

1. The emphasis here is on a clear sense of when you are "on" and radiating and when you are "off" and not radiating, what the difference is between them—experientially—and how you do it. What exactly is it that one does to "radiate" a presence over a distance? What do I stop doing when I "turn off" and am no longer in the space as a presence?

2. The form of this exercise introduces an important difference into mirror exercises: the need to maintain a high level of "content" in the eye-contact relationship. It is important to impress upon the actors that the only way to keep one's partner is by enriching the "dialogue." When there is nothing more to "say" to your partner, chances are he will leave you. Set that as a challenge.

3. The level of intensity here is very high, so this exercise has a limited time span. The sheer psychophysical effort involved in radiating over a distance (the diameter of the circle) for a long time soon causes the actors to lose their edge of alertness and concentration. You should sidecoach them about this during the exercise. Tell them that they do not have a great deal of time to examine this particular model of behavior, so they must ask themselves all the appropriate questions—the Actor's Catechism—immediately.

Figure 23 The Free Agent in Changing Mirrors: Taking over a partner at one end of the mirror—not in the middle.

3. The frantic pace of this exercise, when it gets going, means that any one of the couples may be split up at any moment, so you should suggest to the actors that if they want to finish what they are "saying" to each other, or go as far as possible into this mirror relationship, they had better get focused and do it soon—before they are separated! The dynamic here is similar to what happens in One Moves—All Move (Exercise 19).

Emphases

Apart from all the *Emphases* mentioned earlier in relation to mirror exercises in general, there are a few more that are very important here:

1. *Concentration/radiation—Even more of a movable feast*. The rapid-fire changes that occur in this exercise bring this idea home in a very powerful way. Concentration and radiation cannot be dependent on any accident of casting; they must be personal techniques that do not depend on anyone or anything except the actor's own decision and ability.

2. *"Pushing" availability*. In this version of the mirror exercises, there is no time for careful, lengthy explorations of a relationship. The speed of the changes generates a need for the actors to instantly "be there" for their partners, so the challenge is to make even the briefest connection as

deeply meaningful as a long, highly detailed mirror exercise. This means learning how to push their availability and their radiation, have it "on tap" at full force at all times, no matter what—or who—comes into their field of vision. This modeling makes availability/openness a craft tool of the first order.

3. *The creative moment.* Every time an actor loses his partner, he moves into a "limbo" or Zero Point sensibility. This moment of transition between one form of psychophysical organization to another, between one partner and another, is a pure instance of the creative moment: unlimited potential is about to become focused into a choice. This should be pointed out to the actors so that they begin to acquire an active understanding of the elements of their creativity, and the organization of all these into a form through creative choices.

36. MIRROR IN THE FASTWALK (*see also* FREEZE-MIRROR, EXERCISE 21)

In the walking exercises section, I mentioned that this variation can be used there if the mirror exercises are taught concurrently with the walking exercises. So, bowing once again to the linear logic of a book, here is the full explanation of how a mirror exercise is incorporated into the walking exercise.

While working through the Fast Walk–Freeze (Exercise 17), tell the actors that at the handclap, instead of going into a freeze, they are now going to go into a mirror. As soon as they hear the clap, they should freeze out of the walk, look around until they lock onto someone's eyes, and then begin a mirror from wherever they are. At the next handclap, they should continue the Fast Walk. Since this is part of a walking exercise, these "mirror moments" should be fairly short, and the actors should be told that, as in the free agent version, each mirror-connection will be very brief, so whatever it is they want to "say" to each other should be said very quickly. As the group's proficiency grows, these mirror moments should be made shorter and shorter—eventually no more than a few seconds at a time, during which the actors have to try and develop a deep, complex mirror relationship.

All the rules of the mirror exercises apply here, so despite the apparent rush to "results" the contact should be deep and inventive. If the group is an uneven number, in this exercise too the free agent version kicks in immediately.

37. FREE CHANGE

This is an exercise that grows naturally out of Changing Mirrors.

Setup

A slightly limited space should be used so that throughout the exercise pairs of actors will be moving within each other's fields of vision. One possibly is to set up mirror-pairs in a tight square.

Activity

While in the mirror relationship, tell the actors to keep a Soft Focus lookout for the other actors in the tight space. If as they do so they catch the eye of someone working in their space, they can leave their partners at any time. The actor who has been left will now try—without moving from his place—to catch the eye of someone else and create a new mirror relationship. Spatial awareness expands here and the entire group enters into a fascinating kaleidoscopic flow as partnerships dissolve and grow in and out of each other.

Note

The sense of aggression that initially accompanied the free agent intrusions is replaced here, at least in the beginning, by a sense of abandonment or betrayal as the partner you thought you were so deeply involved with in the exercise suddenly leaves you for no apparent reason. When the actors are reminded that their concentration does not depend on whom they are working with but only on the level of their own Radiation and Availability, this sense of betrayal abates and is replaced by an enjoyment of the flow and constant renewal that results from the seamless shifting of relationships.

38. VOICE MIRROR

The longer you work with the many variations of the mirror exercises, the closer you will get to that point when you can no longer hold back the actors' voices. The more deeply they connect through the mirrors, the more likely they are to move naturally into a more complex, multilayered level of expression. When this point comes—and it will be unmistakable when it does—you must allow the voices to emerge, even if you have not reached the voice work section of the training. Also—as is the case with the natural move into free mirror—once you introduce this possibility and discover its potential it becomes the norm.

Activity

Start the mirror exercise (by now, the standard Free Mirror) and do not change partners. When the actors have worked up to deep connections, tell them to add a voice to their movements—without breaking their concentration—and continue the mirror with voice *and* gesture. (NB: no actual words should be used. Anything vaguely resembling words adds an element of conversational meaning and sends the actors into "scripted" relationships or stereotypes; suggest to them that they use sounds, preferably with no consonants, to help them avoid falling into gibberish.)

Notes

1. The addition of voice to the mirror often provides an excellent example of the need to follow the *physical* to *physical/vocal* to *physical/vocal/ verbal* trajectory mentioned in Chapter 1. In most cases, the instant the actors try to open up their voices their physical commitment goes down by as much as 75 percent—as though they can't move and "sound" at the same time! Pairs who have engaged in the most extravagant physical mirroring suddenly turn timid, and—in order to use their voices— revert to extremely simple gestures. This should be pointed out, either before or during the exercise, so that the actors will be aware of the problem and try to address it immediately. Eventually, as this exercise is repeated in the training, this constraint falls away; body and voice become one and the mirror exercise takes off into a new dimension.

2. The actors should be told not to think of or choose a voice, but to just "open up" their vocal passages, almost as if they were opening a tap. Until now they have been breathing normally but not strongly enough to vibrate their vocal cords. Now they simply have to use more breath to vibrate them and produce a sound.

3. The sound should be a "mirror sound" just like their physical work, with both partners mirroring the same vocal quality. In time, as they gain more experience in the exercise, this becomes second nature. After all, they should be moving in virtually the "same body," so without thinking about it at all they should be producing the same sound.

4. When you take this into Changing Mirrors, the progression from the

hand-clap is as follows: eye contact with the new partner first, then physical adjustments to create the initial mirror, then movement, and then—only then—sound.

5. In the Free Agents exercise (no. 35), the use of the voice is instant. As the free agent moves in, without a second's thought he instantly takes up both the physical position and the voice.

Emphases

1. *Depth and variety.* The addition of the voice gives the actors a much more varied and complex instrument for creating a nonverbal, "abstract" dialogue within the limitation stemming from the need for physical precision in the mirror.

2. *Body/voice connections.* This is also a first experience—long before getting into voice work—with the concept of body/voice connections. Actors concentrating on the mirror connection will not be actively thinking about their voices, and as a result their bodies will naturally produce deeply "connected" voices. This should be pointed out here as a prelude to the subsequent voice work.

Mirror exercises—Conclusions

The basic mirror exercise is indeed a simple exercise, but, as I hope I have managed to show here, with inventive teaching or directing it is also an enormously powerful training tool, and one of the most fertile exercises in the training canon. Apart from using it in training, I have, on many occasions, included it in rehearsal procedures or even in performances. Depending on the way it is side-coached, the mirror exercise can be tailored to almost any aspect of training: improvisation/creativity, the creative moment, readiness, Stepping into the Unknown, Initiating/Yielding, radiation, openness/availability, and freedom and limits, to mention but a few.

Actors who keep to the simple rules of avoiding "realism," remaining in the abstract, and seeking a shared rhythm often find themselves spending twenty minutes to an hour—if I let them have that much time—in a state of pure creativity in which they have no need to make any conscious physical choices; they simply let the back-and-forth radiation between them dictate their movements. All they need to do is maintain their eye contact, remain *disponible*, and leave the rest up to their Soft-Focus consciousness. With constant use of the Actor's Catechism technique, this is a vitally important model of behavior that provides actors with a virtually unmediated experience of their own creativity. And wherever a "model of behavior" turns into a professional habit through questioning and repetition, that's where technique is born.

The Physical WarmUp—The Logic of Training

For all my emphasis on structure, the specific makeup of the *WarmUp Sequence* is very far from dogmatic. It is determined to a great extent by the nature of the group and the time frame of the workshop session or rehearsal period. The following, then, is a skeletal structure of a typical workshop session at this point in the training, with no time divisions:

- Arrival; transformation (changing clothes).
- Crossing the Threshold (taking a private moment, then entering the work space; Exercise 1).
- NameBalls (Exercise 4).
- Staccato/Legato (Exercise 8).
- StickWork (Exercises 9–12; up to whatever level has been reached).
- Mini–Maxi/Walking Variations/Hunt and Pounce (Exercises 13–15).
- Mixing and Matching (Exercise 24).
- Partner Exercises—a selection from Partner Moving (Exercise 26), Energy Exchange (Exercise 27), The Name of the Game (Exercise 28), and Contact Improvisation.
- Mirror Exercises (Exercises 30–38; up to whatever level has been reached).
- Energy Circle (Exercise 7).
- End.

The logic of this order of the training is as follows:

Arrival and Transformation: Preparing for the move into the extradaily self and the work space.

Crossing the Threshold: a commitment to the work at hand by stepping into the work space and into the extradaily self.

NameBalls: Opening the session with a reacquaintance with self and others: Who am I today, who are you for me today and—most importantly—who are we, as a group, today?

Staccato/Legato: Introducing the element of pure physicality through a controlled but extravagant expenditure of energy—a very positive way to begin the day. It also emphasizes three important training elements: Sustaining, Radiating, and the Zero Point.

StickWork: More of the pure physicality, this time emphasizing precision and control and leading into a heightened concentration for the rest of the session.

(NB: this exercise should begin *every time* with one stick and work up to the level of complexity that the group has reached.) This exercise activates Soft Focus for the first time in the session and brings the actors into direct contact with a palpable criteria for measuring their development—their growing ease and proficiency in a physically demanding exercise. Ending this sequence with the sheer fun of Sticks in Space is an energizer of the first order.

Mini–Maxi Pacing/Walking Variations/Hunt and Pounce: From the freedom and exhilaration of Sticks in Space back into an exercise that demands a high degree of control, the object being to bring the fun and freedom of the previous exercise into the strict limitations of this one. The walking cycle helps the actors "spiral in" on themselves, their bodies, and their energies in space, enhances their sense of readiness and zero-point sensibility, and brings the ideas of freedom within limitations and Stepping into the Unknown into any given training session for the first time. The end of the walk cycle, and pounce at the end of Hunt and Pounce gives the actors a very powerful sense of readiness incarnate—an excellent way to start a training session, a rehearsal, or a performance.

Walking Exercises—Mixing and Matching: Moving into a major element of the WarmUp Sequence: physical awareness (the actors "seeing what they look like" in the freeze). The different emphases of the exercises used in mixing and matching address basic aspects of the actors' spatial awareness, physical awareness, coordination, concentration, and control.

Partner Exercises: Changing the actors' focus now to another major emphasis: Initiating/Yielding.

Mirror Exercises: Having "warmed up" so many different elements of the training, the mirror exercises are now introduced as the main learning section at this point in the training. Because of the wide-ranging applications of these exercises and the flexibility of their variations, and training benefits, time should be spent on them.

Energy Circle: Back into the circle for closure. A simple DangerWorks exercise based on pace, energy, readiness, and group work, leading the workshop session to a high-energy ending that usually leaves everyone smiling and eager for more.

Having come this far, nominally, about halfway through the training, let's have a look at the elements of the actor's performative expressivity—more or less in the order of their importance—that by now have become part of the group's daily training sessions:

The elements in training

Improvisation/creativity

Concentration/controlled concentration

Feeling of Ease

Sustaining/radiating

Zero Point

Soft Focus

Remaining in the abstract/creative freedom

Play/creative excitement

The improvisational dynamic—Offers and counteroffers

Readiness/Alertness

Stepping into the Unknown

Second-to-second decision making

Repetition

Freedom in limits

First-time sensibility

Exhausting the moment

Initiating/Yielding

Spatial awareness

Physical awareness/control/coordination

Timing

Rhythm

Trust

Ensemble training

Technique—A movable feast

Body/voice connections (in the mirror exercises)

Each of these elements represents a wealth of training disciplines and many hours of workshop sessions, yet in fact we have only scratched the surface of the training. All we have done so far is introduced these absolutely basic elements of the actors' creative instruments and raised their collective consciousness about their importance to their performative skills. Some of these exercises have been described in their entirety, together with all their more advanced variations, and the actual process of working through them all to average levels of proficiency takes weeks. Finally, the sheer variety and length of this list is merely an affirmation of the seminality I have been talking about. Every single exercise detailed here can feed into one or all of these creative qualities, depending on how it is presented or sidecoached, or where it appears in the sequence. In this way, each one of these exercises can serve many different purposes, and the mix of exercises can be configured to suit the abilities and requirements of almost any group.

Having set in place so many training procedures for the basic elements of the actor's creative instrument, we can now move into the second phase: the Creative WarmUp. This part of the Logic of Training addresses itself more directly to the development—and awareness—of the actor's creative instrument, his or her ability to radiate a presence into the performance space, and to the all-important aspect of Connecting—the psychophysical "oneness" of body, voice, and imagination that is the doorway to transformation.

The Creative WarmUp

The preceding list of elements in training includes a number of direct references to the actor's creativity, so a brief explanation is in order about the differentiation of this WarmUp Sequence as being *creative*, as opposed to the *physical* nature of the first WarmUp Sequence. Basically, the distinction derives from the fact that this second sequence moves into the realm of body/imagination connections, concentrating on complex techniques that, still within the concept of "instrument training," move the actor closer to an approximation of performance. Indeed, many of the exercises in this section are initially demonstrated in a performance format: one or two actors going through a training exercise in front of the rest of the group and getting immediate feedback on their work.

Like in the Physical WarmUp, the exercises that constitute the Creative WarmUp are repeated at every session throughout the workshop or training period. However, there is this important difference: while in the Physical WarmUp there is very little personal expression, the Creative WarmUp it is all about personal expression. Despite the fact that the exercises are worked, for the most part, with the entire group in the space, the work itself is highly individual, and therefore becomes a prime source of information on the actors' development.

A word about the body/imagination connections mentioned above. In Chapter 1 I advocated leaving the imagination for last, mainly because of the sheer seductive power of the imagination, and the difficulty of dealing with its essential ephemerality. And, indeed, we are not going into imagination training yet. As we shall see, the imagination is engaged—unavoidably—for these exercises, but the point to remember is that imagination as such is not the subject matter of the training at this point. It is only an aide for other aspects of the training.

Apart from these two important aspects of "performers" and "observers," and body/imagination connections, this part of the Logic of Training also addresses itself to an extensive area of actor training: centers, physical awareness, The Feeling of Form, The Feeling of the Whole, timing, and repetition, and also includes techniques such as Body Memory and many additional aspects of improvisation techniques. So, before plunging into the exercises, some groundwork is required to place all of these training elements in the overall perspective of the Logic of Training.

Observation

Since this part of the training involves—for the first time—individual work in front of the group a word first about observation. There is a rule of conduct that I apply in my workshops, which may sound unusual, but is, in fact, highly effective in training terms. Simply put, observers watching an actor at work are asked *not to respond audibly*—with laughter, gasps, cries, or sighs—to anything their colleagues do on the floor in the course of the exercise, even if the performer does something that is inherently comic, sad, amazing, or dangerous. Exercises like these are part of a training session, not a public performance, and need to be treated accordingly. The problem is that as soon as an actor—particularly, but not exclusively, an inexperienced actor—hears audible laughter from observing colleagues, he will immediately (and quite naturally) seek further gratification and support by consciously trying to elicit the next laugh, and thus will begin to perform insincerely. Consequently, the actors in the group are asked to watch intently—to "radiate" their attention, if you will—but to hold in their responses. Their silence and concentration will provide the actor in the performance space with the best kind of support—committed, *professional* attention. This is not the overzealous caprice of a purist; it really works, and truly changes the quality of the actor's work.

NB

Having insisted on this form of observation in training for many years, it was particularly gratifying for me to learn (at the Centre for Performance Research's 1999 "Past Masters" Symposium on Grotowski) that Grotowski set the same ground rules of observation for his actors in training sessions.

However, observation is only part of the performative process we are now entering—*evaluation* is its indispensable flip side.

Evaluations

Over the years I have developed a pattern for critiquing this part of the training, which, I believe, helps address the issue in an effective and positive manner. So

closure—a *Feeling of the Whole* that retroactively bestows entirety upon all the component parts. In any form of art, this sensitivity to wholeness is a natural part of the artist's talent—but only a *part*. The well-worn commonplace of artistic creation, that it is "5 percent inspiration and 95 percent perspiration," tells it all: these crucial elements of the actor's tools, the *Feeling of Form* and the *Feeling of the Whole*, are sensibilities that must be trained in order to be incorporated into the creative body as a technique.

But there is more. Beyond those two all-important elements, there is another element that derives from the particular nature of the performing arts. Unlike the graphic or plastic arts, where the artifact is timeless and *space* is the most important dimension, in the performing arts the artifact is essentially perishable, and therefore *time* is the most important dimension, playing a crucial part both in the creation and in the overall perception of a work of art. This has two important consequences. First of all, the creation of a work of performed art requires a finely tuned sensitivity to the time-beat of each component; its duration and trajectory, its rise and fall—in short, *its form in time*. Second, theater is live performance, which means that there is no such thing as a "draft"; whatever is shown to the audience in the real time and space of the performance has to be as perfect as humanly possible *as it is being created*. This places a premium on the *constant* perception of form and wholeness unfolding in the time/space of the creative act. Like the Feeling of Form and the Feeling of the Whole, *timing/duration* is also an integral part of talent, but it, too, requires practice before it can become an incorporated technique for the creative actor.

NB

It is important to point out to the actors the importance of these two concepts of form and the whole, and their application to almost anything they will ever do in the theater, from playing out a beat in the action of a play to finding the entire trajectory of a character. Modeling these concepts in simple physical exercises will, over a period of time, enhance the actors' critically important sense of timing, form, and closure.

From the physical to the creative

As in the Physical WarmUp that precedes it, in the Creative WarmUp each element is introduced and trained separately. Only afterwards are all the elements put together into a sequence, and repeated fully at every session. The Creative WarmUp also has a similar, built-in element of repetition training, since, once it is trained, the sequence is repeated in more or less the same order at every workshop session. As you will see, the order of the exercises follows a clear trajectory, from the total freedom of abstract movement, through a series of increasing limitations, to the creation and repetition of definite forms.

The exercises

As is the case in the Physical WarmUp, the individual exercises that comprise the Creative WarmUp are the subject matter of the workshop sessions. The structure of the warm-up itself sets up training parameters for these five elements:

1. Creative freedom
2. Physical awareness
3. Feeling of Form and Feeling of the Whole
4. Body Memory
5. Timing/duration.

There is a sixth element—the *Plastiques*—that has not been described in the groundwork above because it requires a separate explanation and will be elaborated on below.

The ultimate effectiveness of these elements as a warm-up depends on the daily repetition of the Physical WarmUp before the Creative WarmUp. Run in a much more compact form, the Physical WarmUp now becomes just that: a warm-up. The same thing will occur at the end of the learning section of the Creative WarmUp: the learning exercises will be run in sequence, and will turn into a warm-up, preparing the actors' instruments for the rest of the training session.

NB

All of the following exercises have the same setup (unless otherwise indicated): an individual demonstration, followed by "alone-in-a-group" training by the entire group in the space.

---

39. THE BASIC CENTER EXERCISE

When you start working with something called a *center of energy* there should be no beating around the proverbial bush: working with a center is an act of the imagination, and this should be pointed out to the actors from the outset—with the proviso that the imagination is not the subject of the training. Eugenio Barba's concept of "preexpressivity"—a concentration of performative energies before getting into character or scene work—should be sufficient to explain the idea of the centers in purely practical terms without waxing overly mystical.

Activity

Explain to actors the idea of the three centers—*head*, *chest*, and *abdomen*. Ask them to find a space for themselves and to stand quietly, in a state of readiness (NB: suggest to them again to recreate in their bodies the "readiness incarnate" state at the end of Mini–Maxi Pacing (Exercise 13) or before the pounce in The Hunt and The Pounce (Exercise 15)).

Inform them that you are going to call out the name of one of the three centers. When they hear that name, they needn't do anything except concentrate on that area of the body (just as they did in Touch Awareness (Exercise 16)), and imagine a "center of energy" there. After a short while of getting used to the idea, they are to begin walking through the space on their own, concentrating on the center that has been named. (NB: it is helpful to tell them that they can use an image if one appears, but don't suggest any.)

The actors should be told to examine the sensation of being centered in that area of the body by bringing in the Actor's Catechism again, asking themselves—as they are working, and without stopping—how this center affects their posture, their gait, their sense of space, and their general sense of movement and physical awareness.

After a while, tell the actors to stop moving and to remain concentrated in the chosen center—say, the head center. Then call out another center—chest or abdomen—and ask them to "move" their center to that new "location," and when they sense it there, to begin walking again in the space, and to examine the experience of that center of energy in the same way.

Sidecoaching

Any new element in the training requires extensive sidecoaching, and this exercise is no exception. Here are suggestions for what to say in sidecoaching:

- "Imagine you have a highly compact source of energy in your abdomen—a center—which provides you with all your energy for walking. You can imagine it any way you like, as long as you have the clear sensation that it is the only source of your movements."
- "As you walk through the space with this center, do not make eye contact with anyone, do not come into physical contact with anyone,

and don't make up any stories to justify the walk—it's a simple walk through the space."

- "Now, stop in place easily, not in a freeze. Take this center of energy and 'move' it up slowly to your head, and as soon as you 'feel' it there, begin walking again with your source of energy in this new location. Don't make any conscious adjustments to your body or motion—just imagine the center of energy in your head and let it move you."
- "Just let the body work with the center; let the center move the body, don't think in stereotypes about what a head-center should do to you."
- "Stop. Now move the center again slowly, down from your head into your chest, and let that be the source of energy for your walk." (NB: you might suggest at this point—but not earlier, so as not to burden the actors with too many issues—that as they are walking and concentrating on the various centers, they should try to discover with which center they feel the most comfortable, the most at home.)
- (*After a while*) "Stop. Take the center and move it slowly back down into the abdomen."

When you have taken the actors through all the centers, you can repeat the exercise, this time directing them to different centers at random, and suggest to them that they try out other movements. Despite the very strong emphasis that I have placed on remaining in the abstract, this is an easy exception; just ask the actors to do simple, everyday actions with the various centers: sitting down, lying down, touching the wall, opening a window, picking up a sweatshirt, or taking it off, and so on.

Generally, after this demonstration exercise, I sit down and discuss with the actors how they felt in the various centers, and which one was the most comfortable for them. I tell them right from the beginning that there is no right or wrong in this exercise, and that we will not draw any dramatic conclusions from what they did. It is merely a demonstration of a concept that will be dealt with extensively in their subsequent training. All it is meant to do is to suggest the idea to them, show them how it works, and prepare them for the next step.

40. MOVING WITH A CENTER (PHYSICAL AWARENESS)

This exercise deals directly with the first element of the Creative WarmUp: creative freedom, physical awareness, and expanding physical expression. It also serves as a basic platform for most of the other elements in this warm-up.

NB

Once again, working with a center of energy involves an act of the imagination, and this should be pointed out to the actors before they begin this exercise, together with the rider that the imagination is just a passive tool here and not the subject of the training at this point.

Activity

Ask the actors to find a space for themselves and to stand quietly, in a state of readiness, concentrating on the *hara* (the Working Center). Tell them that they are about to begin moving, but that in order to move any part of their body they must draw energy from that center. (NB: it is useful once again to remind them of the psychophysical state of readiness before the pounce in The Hunt.)

Once they have "connected" in this way to their center, they are to begin moving the different parts of their body that they have "wired up."

Sidecoaching

Here are some suggestions for sidecoaching:

- "Think of connecting up a marionette—but from inside. Connecting to the center means 'wiring up' your expressive system into its central energy source."
- "Every move you make starts in the center, not in the muscles."
- "The center is an endless source of energy; the more you draw on it the more you will have."
- "Every move you make radiates far beyond your body into the space around you."
- "Keep all the movements abstract; don't get involved in situations, and don't start using imaginary objects."
- "Avoid symmetry. Don't work the same gesture with both hands or both legs simultaneously. Every part of your body has its own independent form of expression." (NB: working asymmetrically ensures a higher awareness of each individual part of the body, and challenges the actors to achieve a higher degree of precision and concentration.)
- "Since every move originates in the center, nothing you do is accidental. Every move is the result of a choice and is monitored as it is unfolding."

- "Once you are 'wired,' you are constantly aware of every detail of your physical expression in space. Having moved one part of the body with energy from the center, it is now 'on' and cannot be ignored. Concentrating on moving your upper body does not mean that you can forget—or not know—what your left ankle is doing or how it is arrayed in space."

NB

This is a good time to remind the actors of Chekhov's exhortation, "Everything you do is a little work of art." Suggest to the actors that this applies even to the most minute, incidental action. So even if they are only moving a finger, or tilting their heads, they should think of it as an action imbued with beauty—a work of art.

Notes

1. In the initial stages of this exercise, the actors will tend to remain more or less in one spot or in a small area of the work space, and their movements will generally be limited to the hands and arms. This is fine for the first time, or for the first few minutes of this connecting procedure. In succeeding sessions, however, they should be urged (a) to move into more complex movements and "take space" as soon as they feel connected to the center, and (b) to try out as many unusual combinations of movements as they can, using every part of their bodies.

2. A key element in this exercise is to avoid repetition. This is also what makes the exercise a difficult one: urge the actors—and sidecoach them individually, if necessary—to maintain the flow of movements but refrain from any kind of physical repetition. For example, having taken a step in a given direction, the next move should not be a step, or even in the area of the leg at all. This can be expanded over a period of time to avoid *any* kind of repetition, in other words to look for absolutely new forms of physical expression in every workshop session, and to avoid repeating physical forms from any previous session.

3. Keep up a steady stream of sidecoaching to expand the actors' experience of the exercise. Stress the limitless nature of the energy at their disposal; the radiating of energy beyond the body; the fact that even though the movements of the body are abstract and totally improvised still they are not accidental—they are, rather, a product of choice that requires a drawing of energy from the center.

4. Remind the actors to be constantly aware of every part of their body

simultaneously, and not to "forget" one part of their body as they are working on another.

5. Remind the actors to work alone in the space and not make any kind of contact with the others.

6. Remind them repeatedly that despite the connection to a center and the need for concentration on sensing the body, everything they do should be done with a Feeling of Ease. There should be no tension, even if the movements themselves require a great physical effort.

7. As the training sessions go on, the actors will find it increasingly difficult to create totally new forms of physical expression. At some point, give them the example of the marathon runner's "wall"—that moment in the long run, which, once they have passed through it successfully, they can go on forever. When an actor complains that she can't find any new movements, sidecoach her to "break through the wall."

NB

As the actors' proficiency in this exercise grows you should provide them with an incentive for improvement by suggesting to them that of all the elements in the Creative WarmUp this one is the most difficult. The requirement to create an endless series of different moves without repeating any one of them on the way, either in an individual session or an entire workshop sequence of sessions, is a major challenge to their creativity. One of the ways to help actors overcome the limitations of their physical expression is to emphasize the need for variety and suggest to them that during this exercise they explore different elements of movement such as *direction*, *level*, *pace*, *rhythm*, *amplitude*, as well as overall qualities such as *staccato* and *legato*, or *molding*, *flowing*, *flying* and *radiating*. In advanced work, the actors can also be sidecoached to experiment with "themes and variations," i.e. working with an initial "theme"—say, a circular movement of the arm—and finding as many different variations as possible on that basic move before going on to another movement/theme.

---

8. This is an excellent platform for the teacher/director to discover the actors' habits of physical expression. These should be pointed out to the actors as they are working so that they can go beyond these "areas of comfort" into totally new forms of physical expression and thus expand their physical expressiveness. An actor who tends toward an angular quality of movement, for example, can be told to work on soft, round movements for two or three sessions.

Emphases

1. *Physical awareness.* This is the object of this exercise. The static technique of physical awareness used in Touch Awareness (Exercise 16), or in the freeze of the Mixing and Matching walking exercises (Exercise 24) is now employed dynamically in movement. Using the center as the source for every movement creates an entirely new sense of movement, which, with sufficient training, can provide the actor with an enormous amount of control over his performative expressivity. This in turn will greatly enhance the actor's control over the effects the various elements of his acting has on the spectators. With every repetition of this exercise during the workshop or rehearsal period, the actor should try to achieve ever more minutely detailed awareness of different parts of his body.

2. *Expanding physical expressiveness.* The emphasis on no repetition and pointing out habits of physical expression move the actors into explorations of new and unusual areas of physical expression.

3. *Freedom and control.* The kind of control suggested here does not mean limitations—on the contrary. Working from a center, being totally aware of their physical movements and understanding that no move is accidental, the actors should nevertheless strive to work as freely as possible without any planning or forethought, by just letting the body move in response to energy drawn from the center.

4. *Remaining in the abstract/creative flow.* If the sequence of movements remains abstract and no movement is repeated, the actors will experience an exhilarating sense of discovery and innovation as the flow of their physical inventiveness takes off.

5. *Connecting.* This exercise relates directly to one of the basic elements underlying the entire logic of training—*connecting*—and begins here with the actor "wiring" his body for the business of creating art. *Connecting* is a term that will reappear many times in the following sessions, relating to the striving for oneness, for a seamless whole of the actor's entire expressive organism.

6. *Feeling of Beauty.* In his address to the students on the opening day of the Chekhov Theater Studio at Dartington Hall, on October 1, 1936, Michael Chekhov said, "It is very important that during the whole lesson you must be very active at all times. Your figure (body) must be beautiful during the whole lesson. In whatever you are doing, you must feel yourself full of power, full of energy." This is not only a wonderful concept on its own merits, but it is also an important one in terms of training the performer. The three crucial elements here are: (a) accepting the idea of living the life of a performing artist, whose body is his artifact, and therefore must at all times be beautiful; (b) understanding that every

gesture, every move the actor makes, in workshop, rehearsal, or performance, is an integral part of his craft, and should—through the conscious effort of the actor—be imbued with a Feeling of Beauty, as it aspires to the condition of art; and (c) taking the greatest possible pleasure in having a body that moves and creates aesthetic forms in space.

7. *The Feeling of Ease*. This is the companion concept to the Feeling of Beauty. However strenuous the movement, it should be informed at all times by a Feeling of Ease.

41. MOVE TO FORM (THE FEELING OF THE WHOLE)

The totally abstract, free-flowing nature of the Basic Center Exercise provides the freedom to move without any conscious effort at creating a meaningful form. Now we have to test this sense of freedom and to expand it—paradoxically—by imposing limits. As Stephen Nachmanovitch points out in *Free Play*, "Improvisation is not breaking with forms and limitations just to be 'free,' but using them as the very means of transcending ourselves" (84). Since this is such a crucial element of improvisation technique, it should be stressed whenever the opportunity arises.

Setup

As noted earlier, individual demonstration followed by group work.

Activity

Starting from her Working Center, an actor "sends out" some part of her body at random—a hand, an arm, the chest—then follows this single impulse with the rest of the body, in a sequence of movements, until the initial impulse is exhausted. This sequence is the movement/ phrase that is the basic unit of this exercise.

The process is as follows:

1. Choose one actor, and explain to her that she is about to begin moving using the Working Center. Say to the actor, "Go to your Center," and explain that this means bringing her concentration down from the self-conscious head center to the Zero Point readiness of the Working Center.

2. Once she is there (and the visible aspect of being "centered" will be discussed later in the training), she should be told to give herself

---

an "offer" for the beginning of the movement/phrase by simply sending out a part of the body into space and following the impulse to its end. (NB: the movement/phrase should be the expression of a *single* impulse and no more.)

3. Now, instead of moving in the formless abstractions of the previous exercise, the actor must try to move from the catalyst, the initial gesture/offer, into a complete form—a movement/phrase with a beginning, a middle, and a clear ending. This is the "placing of the grid" and the "closure" I mentioned in the introduction to Chapter 4 (in the section on The Feeling of Form, the Feeling of the Whole and Timing): a sequence of abstract movements that has a beginning, a middle, and a clear ending.

Note

Before we move into the exercise itself, a word or two about how we know when a movement has this *Feeling of the Whole* or not. And for that we resort to three somewhat bizarre categories: the "Smile Factor," the "Nod Factor," and the "Uh-Huh Factor."

Generally speaking, most human beings have an inbred sense of "the whole." This is an integral part of our aesthetic sensibilities. When we sense this property of "wholeness"—consciously or subliminally—in a statue, a beautiful building, or even a well-designed car it is immensely satisfying, and generally raises a smile. This, then, is the Smile Factor, which is the outward indication of the pleasure we derive from seeing a manifestation of our Feeling of the Whole. Using this idea as a benchmark, we can then conceive of a descending order of responses, which correspond to a diminishing degree of "wholeness:" the encouraging "nod," or the noncommittal "Uh-huh."

Here's how it works. Ask the actors to watch carefully as one of their colleagues executes a complete movement/phrase; suggest to them that if they find themselves involuntarily breaking out into big smiles and saying "Yeah!" when the actor ends the phrase it is because the abstract movement/phrase was *just right*, neither too long nor too short, and the actor displayed a good Feeling of the Whole. This irrepressible Smile Factor will be a clear, instinctive indication that the movement/phrase satisfied their desire for closure—for form and wholeness. If, instead of a smile and the satisfying "Yeah!" there are vague smiles and uncertain nods of approval— the Nod Factor—then apparently the movement was complete, had an element of closure, but was not totally satisfying. There was a strong enough sense of wholeness to warrant our approval, but either the move-ment went on just a bit too long—leading to loss of concentration or boredom—or it ended a bit too soon, leaving us with an unfinished reso-nance that we would have liked to have seen completed. Finally, if the movement only elicits quizzical looks, apologetic glances, or silence—the Uh-Huh Factor—then there is something missing. The movement/phrase ended far too soon, leaving large chunks of unresolved physical reso-nance hanging in the air, or came to a stop long after the initial impulse had drained away, or simply did not "hang together."

These exercise/demonstrations in front of the entire group should be done individually by each of the participants so that they can be given multiple feedbacks. Each demonstration by every actor should be discussed briefly in the group to try and gauge which of these factors was most prominent, and to discuss the details of what made the movement/phrase achieve—or fall short of, as the case may be—the wholeness we are looking for.

NB

The fact that there is no mathematical formula for judging "whole-ness" also means that there is no premium on long or short move-ment/phrases. A quick jab of one arm in the air and a collapse into a tight ball on the floor could easily be just as complete and whole as a long undulating slither/roll across half the room, ending up with a slow rising on to tiptoe, arms outstretched, along the wall in one corner.

In the evaluations, there will be, at best, only a consensus about the Feeling of the Whole of any given exercise. Given our subjective natures, this is absolutely natural. Don't argue this point, and avoid categorical judg-ments! Almost invariably, when a movement/phrase is really perfectly timed at its closure, there will be more or less universal agreement on it.

Finally, a word about using this exercise on a daily or regular basis in an extended period of training. Here too, repetition should be avoided, and the actors should be sidecoached to use the elements of variety—direc-tion, level, pace, rhythm, amplitude, and qualities of movement—to continue to expand their physical expressiveness.

Emphases

1. *The Feeling of Form, the Feeling of the Whole.* These are the objects of the exercise.
2. *Improvisation technique/No Mistakes.* As I mentioned in Chapter 1, improvisation technique is nothing less than the vehicle for the entire

Logic of Training, and since it appears everywhere in the training, it is not dealt with under a separate heading. Therefore, as was the case in the Physical WarmUp, when "nameable" elements of improvisation technique come up in the training, these elements should be pointed out. In this case, we are talking about another fundamental rule of improvisation: *No Mistakes*. Since improvisation (= creativity) is, by definition, a "jumping into the unknown," there can be no such thing as a mistake. Anything that happens in the performance space is valid material, and *everything*—even a slip or a fall—is "right" and should be *incorporated*, not "corrected." A good improviser tripping on the set and falling flat on his face will always make us believe that it was a preplanned, beautifully executed part of the original blocking, simply by "taking responsibility" for it after the fact. In the same way, no part of any individual movement/phrase should be "corrected," and when a "correction" like this occurs—as it almost invariably will—this important element of improvisation technique should be noted.

3. *Connectedness/Working Center/Zero Point/Readiness/The Moment Before/Stepping into the Unknown*. When these individual exercises in front of the group begin, the demonstrating actors must now begin to apply many training elements before they actually begin to move. Standing in the work space, they have to "go" to their *Working Center*, *connect* their consciousness and their body to it, reach the *Zero Point readiness* of *The Moment Before*, and only then *Step into the Unknown* of the improvised movement/phrase. Each individual exercise should be used to demonstrate the concepts of *connectedness* and *readiness*.

StickTalk

Another way of demonstrating this Feeling of the Whole very effectively is by bringing back that "unclassifiable" exercise StickTalk (Exercise 29). Using the same format, but with different sidecoaching, brings this exercise into line with the work on Move to Form, or the Feeling of the Whole. There is, however, one important emphasis, not mentioned in the original description of the exercise that must be added to in order to enhance the new "angle": *The Instant Endgame*. In the theater games format of improvisations (originally created by Viola Spolin and used by *everyone*), each "game" lasts no more than a minute or two. This means that as soon as two actors begin an improvisation they must immediately start looking for some way to bring it to an end. In this sense the StickTalk exercise belongs to the Theater Games category of improvisations. At the same time, it is an excellent vehicle for the Feeling of the Whole: once a basic "offer" has been made, the "StickTalk dialogue" begins, but, as it does, the two actors must *immediately* start looking for the final gesture, for closure. Repeated use of this game at this point in the training brings the Feeling of the Whole home in a very clear way.

42. MOVE TO FORM AND ZERO POINT

Armed with the experience of the whole from the two preceding exercises—Move to Form and StickTalk—we now move into an exercise where both the Feeling of the Whole and the Zero Point are worked in sequence. This is the next step up in the challenge of physical expression in the performance space, and the first exercise to provide a direct experience of that pure moment of creativity, the Zero Point.

Activity

The actors now start working individually in the space. Starting from their Working Centers, they give themselves a physical offer—as in the Move to Form exercise—and initiate a movement/phrase, working it through, from beginning to middle to end. This ending of the phrase is a pause (i.e. not a freeze), a Zero Point, the action-packed still point between two impulses, and it is from that point that the actors must now "surprise" themselves into the beginning of another movement/phrase. These movement/phrases must "take space" so that the actors begin to use the entire work space.

This is individual work, with no eye contact or physical contact with anyone else. After this has been practiced freely for a while, the actors should be reminded of the elements of variety—direction, level, pace, rhythm, amplitude, and quality—and these should be included in the exercise as well. (In a similar exercise, my Danish colleague in Chekhov work, Per Brahe, gives actors these qualities of movement to work with: *staccato*, *legato*, *lyrical*, and *chaotic*.)

Notes

1. The "layering" of training experience should go on constantly: even though the emphasis here is on form, the actors should now apply their work with centers and maintain a total awareness of every part of their body as they are moving. One of the ways to help them to check on this ability is to suggest to them that as they are leading with one part of the body they should also be able to know what the angle of their immobile

right heel is on the floor, or any other supposedly "irrelevant" physical detail not directly involved in the major physical impetus (see emphasis 1, below).

2. Concentrating on the Zero Point between two movement/phrases helps the actors "surprise themselves" into the next movement. "Surprising oneself" sounds like an oxymoron, but it is a prime tool of improvisation technique, and as such is a vital tool for any form of creativity. In this case, the technique for "surprising oneself" involves using the least likely part of the body, or starting off in one direction and changing on the fly, or using a metaphoric Soft Focus of the entire organism: allowing concentration/consciousness to relax, and just letting the body choose its moment to move, then following it into a form.

3. Having all the actors moving on the floor at the same time creates a complex space that challenges the actor's sense of improvisation. This is deliberate and the actors should apply techniques they have already learned earlier in the training: Soft Focus, Readiness, Stepping into the Unknown, No Surprises, No Mistakes, and so on to solve any "traffic problems" they may encounter.

4. Moving in abstract shapes through this chaotic space, the actors must incorporate any unexpected obstacle into the complete form of their movement/phrase—as if it were part of their plan of movement in the first place. They must bring the unfolding form to a close around, above, or below any other actor they encounter on the way, without a break in the movement (see *Emphases* below).

5. Remember the instruction in the activity description: after the actors have practiced this exercise for a while, add the requirement that they change direction, level, pace, rhythm, and quality with each new movement/phrase, or mix up their styles of movement using the concepts staccato, legato, lyrical, and chaotic.

Emphases

1. *The Feeling of Form.* The uncontrollable space, with so many people moving in it simultaneously, challenges the actors' feeling for form and the whole. The greater the stakes, the greater the learning benefits.

2. *Creative limits/freedom in limitations.* Here is Nachmanovitch on this: "(F)orm used well can become the very vehicle of freedom, of discovering the creative surprises that liberate mind-at-play" (84). In this exercise, the need to give the movement/phrase a form, and work it to closure, and to change the quality of movement with each new movement/phrase—all these are not restricting factors. On the contrary, as Nachmanovitch eloquently points out, they are liberating factors! The

harder we have to work to find our freedom of expression the more exciting our discoveries will be.

3. *Zero Point*. This still moment between actions, charged—indeed, action-packed—but unmoving, is inherent in the very idea of creativity. It is the crucially important beginning of the creative cycle: from Zero Point to recognizing, seizing, managing, and exhausting the creative moment, to recognizing the next Zero Point. This is that joyous moment of pure potential when anything can happen and something is about to happen, even if we don't know what it is. It has already appeared in the training in the moment before the walk begins in the walking exercises, or the moment when the first Mini–Maxi Walk ends, or the moments between touches in Touch Awareness.

4. *Variety*. This moves the actors toward the understanding of an important principle of the training: the possibilities of physical expression are *inexhaustible*, and the actors should always be seeking out their habitual modes of expression in order to overcome and surpass them.

43. FORMS SERIES

This is a follow-on from the preceding exercise, but has its own intrinsic benefits.

After working through a number of complete forms and Zero Points, the actors are now asked to create a series of complete movement/phrase forms as a running sequence, with no visible Zero Point in between. The sidecoaching tells it all: "You should all have a very clear sense of where each movement/phrase ends and the other begins, but I don't have to see it."

Notes

1. Variety is the name of the game here, as always. There should be absolutely no break in the continuity of the movement.

2. A suggestion: after watching individual actors do these series, ask all the actors to enter the space, and do four or five of these series back-to-back. Once again, the crowded space, filled with moving actors, sets up an excellent challenge.

Emphases

1. *The creative cycle*. Following the rise and fall of each movement/ phrase within the series as they are moving, the actors go through a

clear modeling of what it means to be aware, and more or less in control, of the creative cycle.

2. *Improvisation technique/thinking on one's feet.* This is the balance between thinking and doing, or thinking *while* doing; that is, creating new forms in total freedom, yet at the same time paying close attention—in equal measures—to form, the Zero Point, and variety (as well as many other elements already touched on in the training up to this point).

44. MOVE TO FORM—REPEAT (BODY MEMORY)

After the first two elements of the WarmUp, physical awareness and form, the Creative WarmUp now moves into its third element, Body Memory, still using the same basic unit of the WarmUp: the complete movement/phrase, with its form and completeness, or closure. *Body Memory* is a term, originating in dance, that describes the body's ability to "remember" movement as an embedded resonance. A totally nonthinking process, it is intimately related, as we shall see, to the entire aspect of physical awareness. Apart from its intrinsic value in relation to form, this exercise also creates an even greater challenge for the actor's creative freedom because it is even more restricted, and introduces a deliberate element of repetition into the execution of the exercise.

Activity

The actors are told to create a complete movement/phrase, then to repeat it as precisely as possible. At the end of the repeat, the actors reach a Zero Point and must "surprise" themselves, as before, into a new movement/phrase.

Notes

1. It is important to introduce the concept of Body Memory as a *nonthinking process.* Tell the actors not to work hard at memorizing the movement/phrase as they are doing it because this will limit the inventiveness of the movement/phrase itself. The sidecoaching here is simple: "Don't try to remember the move with your mind. Let your body remember."

2. At first, the actors will tend to try this out with simple movement/phrases. You should encourage them to experiment with increasingly complex phrases.

3. Stress the repetition training aspect of this exercise: each repeat is not an imitation of the previous movement/phrase, but a brand-new version of the same thing. Urge the actors to try to discover how to make the repeated movement/phrase no less a "first time" than the original, and just as surprising.

4. Reassure the actors that there is no such thing as a perfect, 100 percent repeat. They must definitely try hard to get there, but they should not get frustrated if they feel they can't get it perfect every time.

5. Going into the repeat, the actors should not move back to the spot where they began the initial movement/phrase. The repeat begins from wherever they end the initial phrase. Stepping back almost invariably causes a loss of the tonus of body/resonance that is vital for the physical recall of the movement/phrase.

6. If in the repeat the actors encounter someone in their way, they should solve the problem on the go, making the repeat as precise as possible under those changed circumstances.

Developments—Explosion and attack

Don't be alarmed! As you will see below, these are only references to body/mind-sets that add variety and an element of DangerWorks to this exercise.

Once the actors have grasped the basics of this exercise, tell them to try to "explode" into each new movement/phrase at the end of the repeat. This does not mean that they have to execute only very strenuous, high-energy movement/phrases. The reference to "attack" is as it is used in music—the energy/impetus with which any given bar of music is begun, even if it is soft and lyrical. In this case, the "explosion" of the "attack" only means that the actors should move *resolutely* into the unknown form of their next movement/phrase. Among other things, this helps eliminate whatever time the actors may be tempted to give themselves to think, recap, plan, or prepare—all of which are inimical to the spirit of improvisation.

Emphases

1. *Body Memory*. This is a new concept in the Logic of Training, and an important addition to the general aspect of physical awareness that has been the principle subject up to now. As the requirement for repetition grows (see below), the actors have to be able to rely on their "body memory" in order to free themselves to respond to images excited up by their movement/phrases—either the original, or the first repeat, or

the twentieth. This will become a very important element in the training later on.

2. *Repetition.* This basic aspect of training is now brought into immediate focus: creating a new movement/phrase, and then repeating it *absolutely* and *precisely*, but with something added—that something that makes the repeat as much, if not more, a "first time" than the original.

3. *Creative limits.* See the previous discussion in Move to Form and Zero Point (Exercise 42).

NB

This is a good example of how the Logic of Training suggests exercises as "models of behavior" that have a direct bearing on practical elements of the actor's art. The model of behavior here is that fundamental paradox of acting: a repetition that is, at the same time, a pristine, first-time act of creation. If the actors can learn how to do this in a movement/phrase, if they can discover what psychophysical array they have to call up within themselves to achieve this creative re-creation, they will have learned something of primary importance about their profession.

---

4. *Variety.* This is as detailed above but with a twist: introducing a hidden or inner variety into the repeat of a movement/phrase. One of the "secrets" that the actors will learn, or should be guided to discover, is this possibility of "inner variety" that makes the movement fresh, new, and like the first time, yet does not change its physical manifestation in any way.

5. *DangerWorks.* The "explosion" into the next move gives this exercise its DangerWorks quality. The more energetic the explosion the greater the risk of encountering one of the other actors in the space unexpectedly—and still completing the repeat.

NB

This is a good point in the work to remind the actors of an important aspect of their apprenticeship: the need for them to believe in the absolutely *limitless* possibilities of their physical expression. However harsh this may seem, it is a sound professional recommendation: Suggest to them that if they think—even for a minute—that they have nothing new to say or do with their bodies in one of these exercises, they should leave the workshop, turn their back on theater forever, and find something safer and less demanding to do with their lives!

The Creative WarmUp—A brief recap

Up to now we have had the following sequence in the Creative WarmUp Sequence, based on the fundamental concept of the center as a source of energy:

- *Moving from a Center*: abstract, free-form movement aimed at enhancing the actor's creative freedom and physical awareness in movement.
- *Move to Form*: enhancing the actor's sense of form, the whole, and Zero Point.
- *Move to Form—Repeat*: adding a basic element of *repetition training* in order to expand physical awareness into another dimension: *Body Memory*.

Now we move into the fourth element of the Creative WarmUp: the *sense of timing and duration*.

45. MOVE TO FORM—REPEAT WITHOUT MOVING (TIMING/DURATION)

Form in space and time is the essential unit of performance. While the preceding exercises concentrated on the element of form in *space*, this exercise deals directly with a modeling of the other part of this equation: *time* (or, in its translation into performance, *timing/duration*), without a sensitivity to which form cannot achieve closure.

The need for training in a sense of timing/duration is never questioned in the case of musicians and dancers. But, like connectedness and repetition, it is hardly ever addressed as a distinct training issue in most acting training programs. Timing/duration is therefore addressed directly in the Logic of Training, as an individual element, and as an essential part of the Feeling of the Whole.

> *Activity*
>
> As soon as these elements are trained they are put together in a sequence, the Creative WarmUp Sequence. This means that these separate exercises are, in fact, follow-on exercises; therefore, the *Setup* is always the same: all of the actors in the space simultaneously, training "alone in a group."
>
> Based on the preceding exercise (Move to Form—Repeat), this exercise involves repeating each abstract movement/phrase *without actually moving*. The idea is to create a complete movement/phrase

and then repeat it—in its entirety—but only as a *radiation into space* of the phrase's resonance in the body without the visible movement. After completing this nonmoving repeat, the actors "explode" once again into a new movement/phrase. The sidecoaching for this one is one of those simple but evocative paradoxes: "Do the entire movement again—just don't *do* it!"

Notes

1. More often than not, the first reaction to this is heads cocked to one side and a quizzical look on all the faces. "What do you mean, 'do without doing'?" First of all, then, suggest to your actors that tackling a paradox is a great exercise in creativity, and that instead of struggling mentally with the logic—or illogic—of the conundrum they should just *do it*, and find the answer in the doing. Then remind them of the last part of Staccato/Legato (Exercise 8) when they "move without moving" through the six directions, or the first moment of the Mini–Maxi Pacing (Exercise 13) when they were asked to feel "the desire to walk," to "see" themselves walking before they actually move—in other words, how they radiated their bodies' movements into the space before they actually started to move.

2. In the repeat the actors should not try to watch, as it were, a little image of themselves doing the movement/phrase in their "mind's eye." They only thing they should concentrate on is extending the physical resonance of the original movement/phrase out into the space.

3. Since they are actually doing the movement as a resonance in time—even if it isn't manifested in space—Body Memory plays the same role it did in the preceding exercise. However, since they are not actually extending the movement into space, all they have to go by is the memory of the duration—that is, the timing—of the movement/phrase, and that is the object of the exercise.

NB

There is a technique that I often suggest to my actors to help them do the complete gesture without moving, and that is "listening to the music of the gesture." What this means is that, as they are doing the gesture, they should get a sense of the musical form of the movement, for example "dah-dah, dah,dah-dah-da-*da*, dah, *dah*" and use that in the repeat to get the entire trajectory of the unmoving movement/phrase. While this may seem like "cheating" it is in fact a very effective tool for enhancing the sense of timing and duration— particularly the latter.

---

4. Here too, perhaps more so than in the preceding version, the actors should "explode" into the new movement after the repeat. They should be urged to use their Body Memory and sense of timing/duration in the repeat to follow the precise contours of the movement/phrase to its end, and, at that instant, to shoot out into the next movement/phrase. Strangely enough, consciousness of the coming "explosion" at the end of the nonmoving repeat renders the repeat that much more powerful and precise! This is because the actors must hold back their desire to go into the next movement, restrain their energies until they have played out the entire resonance of the original movement/phrase down to its most minute detail. Holding back in such a way creates a highly charged Zero Point—a potential that is held in check until the move-ment/phrase is completed. This gives the repeat of movement/phrase great clarity and precision.

5. Unlike the exercises for the Feeling of the Whole, where only a consen-sual evaluation is possible, here an experienced teacher/director can actually see if the actors fill out the time frame of a given movement/ phrase. Watching the original phrase—and creating his own musical phrasing for it—then watching the inner repeat, the teacher/director can indicate to the actors if they are (a) cutting short the repeat (i.e. not letting it resonate fully in the unmoving body); (b) giving it more time than the original, stretching out the resonance to a flabbiness; or (c) doing it just right.

NB

Actors doing this exercise for the first time generally tend to make the repeat shorter than the original. This should be noted. If this is a true "moving without moving"—the essence of radiation—then the phys-ical sensibility should have the *exact same duration* whether the actor is moving or not. The ability to do this, just like many other things in this training, is not a God-given talent. It has to be trained and takes time to develop.

Emphases

1. *Timing/duration*. This is an essential craft element, which, because it is isolated in the nonmoving repeat of the movement/phrase, can be

modeled in a practical, almost palpable, way. Repeated use of this exercise develops in the actors a sensitivity to timing as a fundamentally important part of virtually anything they do on stage, in rehearsal, or in a workshop.

2. *Body Memory, repetition, creative limits, DangerWork*.

3. *Radiation*. This is a fundamental goal of the training that has already appeared in numerous exercises before this one. In this case, it is modeled through the powerful radiation sent out by the very act of "doing without doing." This element will appear with increasing frequency as the Logic of Training progresses into the areas of the actor's work involving a conscious sending out of presence over a distance.

46. *PLASTIQUES*

This is the last element—to date!—of the Creative WarmUp Sequence, and it draws together most of the elements of both WarmUp Sequences. Once they are incorporated into training sessions, the *Plastiques* also serve as a good point of departure for whatever else is going to happen on that particular day after the WarmUp. It is also, as we shall see, one of the most potent points of contact with the Chekhov Technique.

The term *Plastique* (pronounced as in the French: *plass-TEEK*) is my modest homage to Jerzy Grotowski. The great Polish master coined the term "plastic exercises" to describe some of the most important elements of his physical training. In *Towards a Poor Theater* he defined these exercises as "the study of opposite vectors . . . vectors of opposite movements . . . and contrasting images." For him, and for his actors at the Laboratory Theater, experimenting with "opposite vectors" rendered each exercise "subordinate to research and to the study of one's own means of expression, of their resistances and their common centers in the organism" (139–40). It was this concept of experimentation with physical qualities, and the use of movement/phrases as research for the study of the actor's means of expression that led me to borrow the term *plastique* from the Master, with the greatest possible respect, and create these exercises.

Whereas up to now all these movement-based exercises have concentrated on repetition of whole movement/phrases that have been generated improvisationally from an inner impulse, the following exercise requires a more demanding form of physical awareness, followed by a more elaborate use of the creative moment.

Activity

Starting from their Working Centers and developing a flow of abstract movements, the actors are told to pay close attention to the fact that the continuum of physical expression is, in fact, a series of forms that flow into and out of each other as in Forms Series (Exercise 43)

This heightened awareness of the many mini-forms that go into a flow of abstract movement leads the actors to an awareness of particular forms within the flow that intrigue them, or give them unique pleasure. Finding a particularly "pleasing" or "intriguing" form in the continuum, the actor is asked to "pluck it out" of the sequence and repeat it in order to explore it further.

Selected in this way, this form becomes a *Plastique*: a complete movement/phrase, which is repeated as many times as possible. There is a difference here: the initial form plucked out of the flow is a "first draft" or "sketch"; the actors can experiment with variations—changing the timing, amplitude, or rhythm of the *Plastique*—until they find what is for them its optimal form, the one that gives them the greatest satisfaction. This *Plastique* is now repeated for as long as it holds the actor's interest—in other words, for as long as he can find something new to say with each precise repetition.

In each repeat there are the usual elements: Zero Point leads into explosion and attack, which leading into the basic training paradox: a series of "first-time" repeats.

When the actor's interest wanes, the *Plastique* becomes mechanical and the actor's center moves up from the Working Center into the head. When this happens, the actor must go back to the Working Center, pick up the thread of abstract movements, and continue moving until he "plucks out" another *Plastique* from the sequence.

Notes

1. There are a number of stages in the rise and fall of a *Plastique*:
   - Starting from a series of physical "offers" in the abstract flow of movement.
   - Identifying an intriguing/satisfying movement/phrase from within the flow.
   - "Plucking" it out and repeating it as a "draft."
   - Refining, modifying, experimenting with it until it feels right.

- Repeating it for as long as it remains interesting and fulfilling.
- Trying to find out how to make each repeat a "first time," and make the *Plastique* last as long as possible.
- Recognizing the end of the impulse when the center moves into the head and the movement becomes self-conscious, mechanical, and boring.

2. When the exercise is performed in front of the group, it is also an excellent opportunity for demonstrating what the actors have learned through other exercises in readiness. When an actor gets up into the space, watch for her state of readiness—of connection to the Working Center—before she begins to move. If you feel that the actor starts to move too soon, that she is not really centered or connected, stop her before she goes on, and tell her to start again. Or, if you feel that the actor is having trouble reaching that state of readiness, is working too hard to get there, once again stop the exercise and ask her to begin again.

NB

This state of readiness has a "look." With practice, the actors and the teacher/director can come to recognize it when it appears. Usually there is a steadying of the actor's breathing, the actor raises his head to look out with a Soft-Focus gaze that is oriented both outward and inward (ready to perform for others, while at the same time "listening" to the body), and a strong radiation of a Feeling of Ease. These are elements of the actor's stage presence, which, over a period of time, can be recognized, and used as clearly defined criteria for evaluating the relative effectiveness of any given exercise.

---

3. This is the first point in the training when, occasionally, close-up "active sidecoaching" might be necessary. This means stepping into the work space, close to the working actors, and sidecoaching them *as they are working*, directing them into a *Plastique*, or suggesting that they keep at a *Plastique* that they are about to abandon but is in fact still potent. This possibility of active sidecoaching should be explained beforehand, so that the actors will be able to listen on the go and apply what they hear without losing their concentration.

NB

Active sidecoaching should always be done from *behind* the working actor, so there is no visual intrusion into the work. This way the sidecoaching can be absorbed without a break in concentration.

---

4. There is a delicate balance that has to be found here between freedom and control. While moving in the flow, the actors should allow themselves to move without consciously thinking of a *Plastique*. Actively looking for a *Plastique* will hamper the freedom of the movements and result in an endless series of virtually "preplanned" *Plastiques*. The side-coaching makes it clear: "Don't *look* for a *Plastique*. Let *it* find *you*." The idea is just to enjoy the creative flow of movement, maintaining a physical Soft Focus and a high level of physical awareness, so that the actor will be able to recognize a *Plastique* when it presents itself. Once again, as in the Feeling of the Whole exercises, there are two clocks running simultaneously—one allowing the unconstrained pleasure of the free flow of movement, and the other a "*Plastique*-consciousness" idling in No Motion, waiting for a pleasing movement/phrase to appear out of the flow.

5. Referring to body/imagination connections, Michael Chekhov notes that an actor "cannot avoid gesturing or moving without responding to his own internal images." Moving into a *Plastique* will naturally arouse "*internal images*" to which the actor can respond. However, regardless of the nature of the images that appear, the overall form of the movement must remain abstract. Any slip into storytelling means that the actor has chosen a "plot line" that he will play out even unconsciously; as a result he will no longer be free to respond to random associative options. This can often be recognized when a moving actor corrects a supposed "mistake" because it doesn't fit the story line (see emphasis 5, below).

NB

There is an important element to watch for here, which determines the moment each piece of work either comes to an end or is stopped: the level of *connectedness* (see emphasis 4, below). The teacher/director should allow a *Plastique* improvisation to go on for as long as the actor is "connected"—deeply involved in his work and radiating a powerful stream of images to the observers. On occasion a truly connected actor can repeat a single *Plastique* for a fascinating fifteen or twenty minutes or more. In most cases, the exercise will come to a natural end as the actor simply "runs out of gas," or becomes—gradually or suddenly—self-conscious. The latter will be evident when you "see" his center move from the Working Center up into the head. In other cases, if the teacher/director feels that the actor is working too hard, is not deeply enough connected to his center, or is disappearing down his own black hole instead of radiating energies out, then an appropriate moment must be found to end the exercise.

Emphases

1. *Physical awareness*. This exercise—combining psychophysical energies into a single, complex whole that then emanates strongly out to the observers—is the culmination of the Physical and Creative WarmUp Sequences. It is based, first and foremost, on a very high level of physical awareness—the most important element in the actor's basic technique. Now no longer just a concept, here it has to be applied. As I move through the space in a flow of movements, without consciously creating a form, I must be so acutely aware of everything I am doing with *every part of my body* and how it affects my senses, that I will be able to pick out a movement/phrase from the continuum—a form that intrigues me, one that I would like to do again; and all this without even fractionally sacrificing any part of my creative/improvisational freedom. This keen awareness of my body in space—the simultaneous awareness of every part of my body at all times—is essential, I believe, to virtually any kind of character work in the theater.

NB

The practical applications of this kind of awareness are many and varied, and should be pointed out. One of the most important is the ability of the *Plastique*-trained actor to make immediate use of physical choices that occur unexpectedly in the course of a rehearsal or a performance, and then to remember them (using the "repeat without moving" technique) in order to perfect them on the following night.

---

2. *The creative cycle*. This exercise in effect models the entire creative cycle for the actor: recognizing the moment (the form within the continuum), seizing it ("plucking" it out and creating the first "draft" or sketch of the movement/phrase), managing it to exhaust its possibilities, sensing the waning of the creative fires, and seeking an impetus to rekindle the fire into the next creative moment. The repetitive nature of the *Plastique*, and the attempt to exhaust its potential, will help the actors model over and over again the end phase of a creative impulse: the "dying fall" of one creative moment that leads into the Zero Point, and the gathering of energies that then lead into the next creative moment. The actors will also become aware of how they can continue working *through* a Zero Point, making new physical offers as the previous creative moment is drawing to an end in their search for the next *Plastique*—without stopping the flow of physical expression.

3. *Exhausting the moment/first-time sensibility*. Perhaps more than any other exercise in the Logic of Training, the *Plastiques* exercise brings

these elements of the actor's craft and their relation to the concept of centers and connectedness, into very clear focus. Just finding a movement/phrase that an actor likes is not enough—he has to perfect it and repeat it for as long as he can make it interesting. The way to do that is to begin each movement/phrase as if he were discovering it for the first time. Doing this repeatedly, and asking himself: "What am I doing?" "What do I have to do to make it seem as if it's the first time?" will teach him something about his creativity, and help him understand how to make the fundamentally repeated act of theater endlessly interesting for the audience.

4. *Connecting*. The performance aspect of this exercise—doing it individually in front of the entire group—brings in a strong element of *connectedness training*. Starting from the point of departure (The Moment Before, when the actor has to connect to his Working Center in order to start the movement/phrase that initiates the search for a *Plastique*), through the complete execution of the exercise, which has to "reach" the observers, engage their imagination, and hold their attention, the entire sequence is an exercise in connecting. The only way an actor can engage and hold our attention is through the "first-time" sensibility of each repeated *Plastique*, and the profound connectedness of his entire organism—body and imagination—in the development of the repeated *Plastique* into its final form.

NB

A few years before I completed the first edition of this book, I gave a workshop to a mixed group of professional actors and students in Croatia. During one of the warm-up sessions, when we reached the *Plastiques*, the organizer of the workshop, a wonderfully talented actress by the name of Suzana Nikolic, found an extremely simple *Plastique*: sitting with her legs tucked under her, staring down at the floor in front of her with her brow slightly furrowed and her right hand supporting her torso palm-down on the floor, she repeatedly hooked her left thumb under her short blond hair, and pushed it back behind her left ear. As the other participants ended their work Suzana was eventually left alone in the middle of the space. From this point on, we all watched in utter fascination as she continued the *Plastique* for another twenty minutes with such concentration that we could not take our eyes off her. When at last she looked up, it was clear to all of us that she could have gone on for *another* twenty minutes, but that she felt awkward about taking up so much of our time. It was an extraordinary demonstration of the sheer power of concentration and radiation, not to mention the "first-time" sensibility that kept us rapt in attention.

---

5. *Improvisation technique.* "Expecting the unexpected" can keep a *Plastique* going for up to twenty minutes or more; if, after the *Plastique* has reached its optimal form, the actor begins each new repetition with the feeling that she has no idea where this movement impulse is going to end then she will be able to create the *Plastique* over and over again, making it new every time. Once again, remember that there are No Mistakes! No matter what happens, even in a repeat, there is nothing to correct—*ever*—in an improvisation! If something does change in the *Plastique* by accident, that same accidental move must be incorporated immediately into the next repeat of the *Plastique*, as though it had always been there.

The Creative WarmUp—Recap

Once you begin trying to understand the elements of creativity and developing methods for training it, you find yourself in a limitless world. Earlier I drew up a preliminary, and perhaps surprisingly long, list of "elements in training," all of which relate to the actor's performative expressivity. Well, the search is far from over, and here is a brief recap of the elements added to the training thus far as they have appeared in the Creative WarmUp:

The elements in Training II

Centers of Energy

"The Four Brothers": the Feeling of Beauty, the Feeling of Ease, the Feeling of Form, the Feeling of the Whole

Zero Point

Variety

The creative cycle: recognizing the creative moment, seizing, managing, exhausting, rekindling

The Power of Limits

Physical awareness

Body Memory

Timing/duration

And we have also added to the list of elements of improvisation technique things like No Mistakes/Retroactive Responsibility, Thinking on One's Feet, and Stepping into the Unknown. There is more to come.

The WarmUp Sequences—A review

With the introduction of the *Plastiques* exercise, all the basic elements of the WarmUp Sequences are in place. From time to time, variations, changes, and even new exercises are introduced, but whatever is brought in relates to the same logic, and aims at achieving the same effect on the creative organism of the actor.

The emphasis I have placed throughout on structure applies to individual workshop sessions as well—perhaps even more so. Whatever time frame you choose for working these exercises, each workshop session must end with a closure of some kind: a recognizable achievement, a discernible step forward, based on past exercises and processes. Don't labor any of these exercises beyond the actors' patience and abilities in any one workshop session—after all, these two WarmUp Sequences, with all their suggested exercises and in their proposed structure, will become a regular part of the workshop process, so there will be plenty of time to refine and deepen them. The frequency with which you introduce new exercises or additional steps to previous exercises is totally up to you, but the rule of thumb is *keep it moving*. No matter how important the WarmUp Sequences are, there are many more, equally important elements of the training coming up, and spending too much time on one element of the technique will bog you down and cause the actors to lose interest.

The entire trajectory of the two WarmUp Sequences, then, looks like this:

The Physical WarmUp

Personal Time
(transformation from "daily" to "extradaily" self)

Crossing the Threshold

NameBalls
(all the variations)

Staccato/Legato

Sticks
(all the variations)

Walking
(all the variations)

Partner Exercises
(open choice)

The Creative WarmUp

Centering

Free-form moving with a center
(creative freedom, abstract movement and basic physical awareness)

Move to Form
(the Feeling of Form and the Feeling of the Whole)

Move to Form—Repeat
(Body Memory)

Move to Form—Repeat without Moving
(timing/duration)

Plastiques

Once the group has reached a basic level of competence in all the separate elements of the Creative WarmUp, the exercises should be done in sequence in every workshop session.

As I mentioned earlier, looking for a new way to walk, throw a stick, or mirror a partner at every session over a year involves something akin to what marathon runners call "going through the wall": if you just keep at it long enough, eventually you will break through the psychological and physiological barrier, and the rest of the run turns into a virtually effortless breeze! And, like the marathon runner, there is hardly anything under the sun quite as wonderful as hitting that "zone" in the Training, reaching that moment of mind-less—or rather un-mind-ful—creativity when you simply can't go wrong, when ideas, each one better than the next, flow into your body endlessly, there for the picking.

Actors can be helped through this wall simply by urging them repeatedly to believe in their creativity, to understand that there is absolutely *no limit* to the forms of physical expression that the human body is capable of. What is more, they should be continually reminded that the learning process of a creative artist is a lifelong project that involves a great deal of hard—and not always exciting—work, leading only to occasional and temporary moments of great enlightenment. As such, it requires a great deal of patience and perseverance. This ability to turn first-time sensibility—the absolute prerequisite for the improvisation/creativity tandem—into second nature, into an instinctive, nonthinking part of their technique, provides actors with a tool of immense importance, regardless of the kind of theater they are interested in pursuing.

As the training progresses and proficiency grows in each component of the WarmUp Sequences, the actual time spent on doing the entire sequence is reduced. Eventually, the actors in the group can be simply given time to "work" the entire sequence of the Creative WarmUp on their own.

Taking this logic to its extreme, I often tell my actors or students that truly well-trained actors, those who have thoroughly incorporated these sequences into their psychophysical memory, can condense their WarmUp—for performance, rehearsal, or workshop—to the bare minimum (almost a form of psychophysical autosuggestion). In order to recreate the inner feeling of *Readiness*, which they know so well, all they need is the snap of a finger, the turn of a head, or perhaps a circular motion with one arm, and they will be "there." The only thing that actors at this level need is some solitude and silence, the inner connection to their readiness, and that one compact gesture (one is tempted to call it, *après* Michael Chekhov, the "psychological gesture" of their preexpressivity) in order to awaken all the necessary resonances of the actor prepared to engage in his or her craft.

BODY AND VOICE

At this point in the training, when the two WarmUp Sequences—the Physical and the Creative—are in place, the Logic of Training proceeds along the trajectory cited in Chapter 1 in the section "From body to voice to imagination" (pages 4–7).

These exercises can be introduced either parallel to the work on the Creative WarmUp, or in a staggered sequence—after the work on this WarmUp has begun. There is certainly no need to wait until after *all* the elements of the Creative WarmUp have been introduced and trained; the two are not mutually exclusive, and their different materials should be interwoven wisely in order to direct the actors into the most fruitful areas of research into their own creative selves.

Rudolf Steiner

When one thinks about the great innovators of modern theater practice, the name Rudolf Steiner does not come readily to mind. And yet, among the hundreds of books the extraordinarily prolific founder of Anthroposophy published in his lifetime (on everything from architecture to zoology), there is a volume entitled *Speech and Drama*, in which he elaborates in great detail his understanding of the production and function of speech in the theater. Being so close to Michael Chekhov in my own work, I was more than a little intrigued by Chekhov's great admiration for Steiner, and upon reading *Speech and Drama* I found many points of similarity between Steiner's concept of body/voice connections and my own understanding of connectedness in the area of voice work in Training. Here are a few selections from the book that give some indication of the direction we will be heading in this section:

> Speech as "formed gesture"—that is the highest of all. . . . Speech that is not formed gesture is like something that has no ground to stand upon.
>
> (80)

Please note that a *psychological expression must always, without exception, be associated with a feeling for sound.* It should be a strict rule for the student never in his practicing to make any bodily movement or action without its being accompanied by a particular sound-feeling.

(243; emphasis in the original)

Whenever some emotion has to be expressed, the student should on every single occasion practice it with some bodily movement or action, which again must invariably have its connection with formed speech.

(245)

All these extracts illuminate Steiner's version of what I have been calling *connectedness*: the desired "oneness" of the vocal apparatus with the physical, the psychological, and the imaginative mechanisms of the performer. Or, in the terminology I will be using in this section, the "necessariness" of a particular voice emanating from a particular body in motion, and its radiation of emotional quality into the performance space.

Steiner is also at pains to elaborate the profound connections he believes to exist between particular vowel and consonant sounds and particular areas of the body, and psychological states of being. For example:

When I intone *B*, there lies behind it an endeavor to imitate something that covers or protects. . . . *R* denotes that I am endeavoring to form a sound-picture in imitation of a process of commotion and excitement, or trembling. The consonants imitate; they shape themselves in imitation of forms or processes, of things or events in the world outside.

(135)

The basic connections between the moving body and the body's *sounding*; the concept of gesture as both the source and the form of sound; and the profound process of the "imitation" of our internal storehouse of memories, associations, images, and fantasies in particular vowel or consonant sounds—all of these have guided my work on the body/voice connections of the actor.

Body and voice: The premises

There are three important premises underlying this part of the training:

1. The emphasis in the voice work proposed here is on body/voice connections and their expressive potential, and not on the mechanics of voice production. In my own work with acting students I incorporate the training my students

get from professional voice and speech teachers in the areas of breath control, resonators, and projection into the workshop sequences. Whatever is learned in these technical classes devoted to voice is brought into the training to examine the ways in which voice and body connect in the physical expression of the moving actor in the performance space—in other words, the "organicity" of body and voice in the actor's performative expressivity. Without detracting anything at all from the absolute need for the serious actor to have a solid grounding in voice production, some of the exercises noted here can be effectively used even with beginning actors who have no voice training at all.

2. As Steiner suggests in his somewhat arcane manner, during a performance there can be no distinction between the voice and the body that produces it. In training terminology, this means that body/voice connections are interchangeable—the body can produce voice, and the voice can shape a body. Both possibilities need to be trained.

3. Entering into the area of body/voice connections requires a great deal of time, mainly because there are virtually no exercises that can be done on a group basis. It is entirely based on individual work and specifically detailed feedback. A teacher/director who intends to include this work in her workshop or teaching schedule must take into account the time-intensive nature of this work.

Body and voice exercises

In the first edition of the book I included at this point two ensemble voice exercises which over the years I have used less and less, therefore they have been moved to the book's website where anyone interested in them can have a look.

47. VOICE TO MOVEMENT

This is the first in a series of exercises that tie together the kind of physically expressive work from the warm-ups, and the idea of body/voice connections. Based on the concept that the moving body creates voice, and that voice can shape the moving body—this is the first attempt to explore how this connection works in the kind of abstract movement that is the core of the *WarmUp Sequences*.

(NB: at this early point in the voice training, this is a somewhat difficult, multiple-concentration exercise that must be worked up slowly and methodically. It requires a great deal of experimentation—and time.)

Setup

There should first be a demonstration with single actors, then the entire group working individually in the entire space.

Activity

An actor stands still in front of the group and, after a sign from the teacher/director, produces a sound/phrase—a complex sound impulse that may be formed from a random sequence of notes. It should be pointed out to the actors that here too, as in their work on forms in the Creative WarmUp, they should create the sound/phrase by "Stepping into the Unknown"—opening their mouths, allowing a sound to begin to emerge, and only *then* giving it a form, a beginning, middle, and an end. The actor is now asked to repeat this sound/phrase and—as in the *Plastiques*—work with it until he is satisfied that that is the sound that he wants to produce. The actor now "allows" the sound to reverberate into his body until it produces movement somewhere. These first stirrings are then expanded to the entire body, until a repetitive movement like a *Plastique* emerges. When it does, the actor should try to make the deep connection between body and voice last as long as possible. (NB: the sound/phrase should remain constant throughout the exercise. The only thing that should be adjusted is the body, so that it "fits"—"connects to"—the physical pose. Changing the sound/phrase to suit the slowly developing physical movement of the body defeats the purpose, because what we are looking for is the "creation" of a body to fit the sound that is already there.)

Emphasis

Body/voice connections. In daily life, our bodies and our voices are naturally "connected" and we don't spend even a single second making any kind of conscious effort to fuse voice and body into one. But performance is not daily life, and actors spend most of their professional lives inhabiting bodies other than their own, and so these supposedly "natural" connections cannot be taken for granted. How they work in the performance space has to be trained. And this is the object of the exercise: trying to understand, through a structured model of behavior, just how different, yet alike, these two modes of expression—body and voice—are, what needs to be done to make them interact creatively with each other in performance so that they function as different aspects of the same thing.

48. MASK—BODY—MOVEMENT—VOICE

Now we move in the opposite direction—from the body into the voice—with the help of an exercise suggested by Yoshi Oida.

Setup

Begin with individual demonstrations; follow up with everyone "alone in a group."

Activity

An actor is told to create a facial mask and make sure he feels it very clearly from inside. The rest of the body is relaxed at this point (see Figure 24). He should then allow the mask to "percolate" into the body, creating an entire physical form that supports the mask (Figures 24–27). Now, moving into his body—with the help of the physical awareness techniques from the WarmUp Sequences—the actor is told to allow that mask/body to begin moving. Once the mask/body begins to move, he should be sidecoached to allow the moving body to produce its voice, and then let that body's voice emanate from the body for as long as it is moving.

Notes

1. The facial masks should be different each time, and you should suggest to the actors that, after their extensive work on physical awareness in the WarmUp Sequences, even the slightest adjustment of the facial mask should lead them into an entirely new vocal world.
2. The actors should be told to take time between each one of these stages. They should make sure that they feel good about the mask itself, then about the physical expression of the mask in the body, and then about the movement and the voice. In each one of these steps they should experiment with different adjustments until they feel the connection.

Emphasis

Body/voice connection. This time from the moving body into voice. Each one of these expressive tools—body and voice—is unique, so that achieving a connectedness cannot be taken for granted. The fact that we produce voice from a mask/body does not mean that that specific voice is also automatically connected. Fine-tuning is almost always necessary. The adjustments needed to make body and voice connect on a profound

*Figure 24 Mask—body—
movement—voice: The "mask".*

*Figure 25 Mask—body—
movement—voice: The "mask"
moving into the body.*

*Figure 26 Mask—body—
movement—voice: The "mask"
moving into the body.*

*Figure 27 Mask—body—
movement—voice: The "mask"
in the body, producing a voice.*

level are the training element: modeling what needs to be done in order to connect these two different expressive mechanisms on an organic, resonant level.

49. *PLASTIQUES* TO VOICE

Growing naturally out of the previous exercise, this is the most important of the body/voice exercises, because of the complex—yet direct—way that it relates to the connections between the voice and the moving body, and the way it illuminates the idea that body and voice can be adjusted on the go, as it were, until they "fit." What is more, it also introduces the idea of the "necessary voice" reinforcing the concept of the moving body as the source of sound.

NB

Once this exercise is introduced and practiced to a satisfactory level of competence, the use of the voice in the *Plastiques* should be interwoven into the Creative WarmUp Sequence, and become the standard form of the exercise.

Setup

This is an exercise that requires individual demonstration—just like the original *Plastiques* exercise (Exercise 46) without sound. Depending on the size of the group, this can often take some time. However, there are no short cuts—time must be taken because it is only on the basis of individual demonstration and critiques that the concept can be made clear. Once the group has been trained in the basics of this exercise, groups can be formed for simultaneous work in the space.

So—the *Setup* is: one performer working in the space, all others watching.

Activity

An actor is asked to go to her center and begin to create a flow of abstract gestures until she finds a *Plastique*. All the steps elaborated earlier apply: find the movement/phrase in the flow, "pluck it out," modify and improve it if necessary, and repeat it in its final form with the utmost precision. As the *Plastique* appears to be reaching its optimal form—while the actor is still on an upward trajectory of finding everything that's interesting about it—the teacher/director should say, "Voice!" At this point, the actor has to do only one thing: "open the tap"—allow sound to emerge from the body simply by letting air pass over the vocal cords with enough vibrations to create a sound, and then continue the *Plastique* with its sound.

Notes

1. Initially, the most difficult obstacle in this exercise is "opening the tap"— just letting audible sound come out. In the early attempts there will be many instances of actors either stopping to move momentarily in order to find the voice, or stopping altogether, claiming that they can't find a voice—or that they can't do both at the same time. It is very important to stress here the basic Rudolf Steiner contention that the moving body is *always* producing a voice, even before one hears it. Or, to put it differently, *the condition of voice is movement*. So, in fact, the actor doesn't have to try to *do* anything—his body is already doing it. All he has to do is facilitate the actual production of the sound across the vocal cords into the oral cavity and out of the lips. You may have to try this a number of times with certain actors until they manage to produce a sound without thinking about it.

2. The training value of this exercise depends on defining whether or not the voice produced by a specific *Plastique* is "connected" or not. Defining the "connected voice" takes us again into the realm of subjective evaluation, but one that is based on parameters we are already familiar with such as connectedness, resonance, and The Feeling of the Whole. A truly connected *Plastique*/voice will partake of this Feeling of the Whole and give both the performer and the observers a profound sense of satisfaction—a sense of body and voice being one, or of that particular voice being the absolutely necessary extension of that moving body. Extensive training in the exercises leading up to this one and observation of others working in this way will eventually produce in the actors a good sense of what constitutes a "connected" moment, both in themselves as they are working, and in others they are observing.

3. A perfect fit—voice to body connection—will occasionally happen on a first try, but it is rare. What is more common is that a voice is sent out that is close but not yet "it." The actor must then continue the *Plastique*— without changing it (see list item 4, below)—and experiment with the sound until she feels it "fits." Once that happens, the entire voice/body complex must go on—as in the original *Plastique* exercise—for as long as she can make it interesting for herself.

4. Throughout the search for the voice, the *Plastique* must remain precisely the same. Since we are examining the birth of sound out of movement, in this case looking for the connection of a sound/phrase to a particular movement/phrase, the exercise becomes useless if the actor changes the form of the *Plastique* to suit the voice. The exercise that follows this one—*Plastique* Putty (Exercise 50)—addresses this possibility directly.

Emphases

1. *Connecting.* This element of the training is taken to a more complex level here, as the voice is added to the physical work. What we are looking for at this stage is a practical experience of the differences between body and voice, and the possibilities for adjusting either one to make the total expression a unified one.

2. *The Necessary Voice.* This is a term that will become the staple of any future evaluations in the voice work exercises. It derives from the concept that a moving body necessarily produces a particular voice, and in evaluations of voice work, the most frequent question is, "Was *that* voice the necessary extension of *that* body?"

3. *Body/voice connections.* This means repeating this exercise in the training in order to help the actors understand what it means to let the body produce its voice, and to adjust the voice to suit a particular movement/phrase. After a period of time, and based on this kind of training, actors will know, in rehearsal or performance, when their bodies and voices are connected and when they are not, and they will make automatic adjustments whenever necessary without even thinking about it. This technique, then, which is difficult to learn at first, eventually becomes—as all good techniques should—second nature.

4. *Complex concentration.* This is a difficult exercise because the actor's concentration must be divided equally between (a) finding the "right" form of the movement/phrase; (b) maintaining the physical precision of the *Plastique*; (c) enabling a Soft Focus of the consciousness to allow a voice to come out effortlessly; and (d) making conscious modifications of the voice until the "connection" is found. As all of this is happening, the actor must maintain a profound connection to the form and resonances of the *Plastique*. The ability to achieve all of these simultaneously is an indication of an advanced level of training.

NB

Active sidecoaching becomes even more important in this exercise. The teacher/director should be ready to enter the work space, and coach an actor—from behind—to seize a potential *Plastique*, or continue working one, or modulate the voice to find the connection, and so on.

---

50. *PLASTIQUE* PUTTY

A follow-on exercise from the previous two, combining in one exercise the move from body to voice and from voice to body. Exercising the Voice *Plastiques* requires a great deal of time, and the following exercise should not be introduced until the concept of Voice *Plastiques* is well absorbed.

Setup

The actors stand in a large loose circle. Each actor should sit down after completing his part of the exercise inside the circle. This will make it easier for those working in the middle to choose their partners, as stipulated in the exercise below.

Activity

Step 1: One actor goes into the center—and there should be plenty of room for people to work there—and begins the *Plastiques* to Voice exercise. Once he has created a complete sound and movement *Plastique*, he makes eye contact with one of the actors in the circle and "gives" his sound and movement/phrase to the other performer in a "mirror." When the first actor feels that the second actor has acquired the Voice *Plastique*, he moves out to the periphery, leaving the center space free for the second actor to work with the acquired Voice *Plastique*.

Step 2: The second actor now works to make the adopted Voice *Plastique* her own—without changing it in any way. When the actor reaches this point—and some sidecoaching may be necessary to help the actor get there—the teacher/director now gives the following instructions:

1. "Stop the voice, continue the movement." (The actor does so, continuing the adopted *Plastique* without audible sound.)

2. "Now find your own voice for that same movement." (The actor does so, "listening" to her own body and making the connections to her voice for that movement.)

3. "Stop the movement and continue the voice." (The actor stops the adopted *Plastique* and remains now with her new voice, but no movement.)

4. "Now, find your movement for that voice." (The actor does so until a completely new *Plastique* appears, which she works until it is "right.")

5. "Give it to someone." (At this point, she takes the *Plastique* to someone standing on the periphery and "gives" it to him in a "mirror," and the whole cycle begins again.)

Variations

The order of the sidecoaching can be reversed: the second actor "acquires" the given Voice *Plastique*, and is then told to stop the movement, and continue with the adopted sound/phrase only; then to devise a new movement for that voice; then to stop the voice and remain only with the new movement; and finally, to find a new voice for the new movement.

Both ways of doing this exercise are useful and should be alternated in the workshop.

Notes

1. Clearly, if the training exercises are going to be "interwoven," this one can only be used after the group is proficient in the mirror exercises.
2. Stress to the actors that when they give their Voice *Plastique* to someone on the periphery, they should not leave the mirror until the new partner has fully acquired the *Plastique*.
3. There should be no relaxation in the transitional moments, between the old sound/phrase and the new movement, and between the new movement/phrase and the new sound/phrase that arises from it. The actor in the center is moving and/or sounding all the time in a continuous flow throughout the exercise.
4. Once again the question of the "quality" of connectedness arises, and once again there is no easy answer. The only suggestion I have is that a deeply "connected" piece of work will simply shine. It will be markedly

"seductive" and exciting, firing the imagination of the rest of the group even if they don't understand its sources. An unconnected one will, by the same token, be uninteresting, lacking in resonance.

Emphases

1. *Body/voice/body connections.* These are the object of the exercise. However, in this variation of the *Plastique* to voice exercise there are added training benefits, since no matter which way you choose to run the exercise the actors have to deal with the body/voice connections on two different levels, or in two different directions—voice to body and body to voice.
2. *Transformation.* This is the first time in the training that anything resembling a "role" appears. The actors entering the circle must "take on" something they did not create and make it their own. What the actors have to do in order to do this should be the object of the Actor's Catechism in this exercise, and the process should be discussed when the exercise is over.

There is another sequence of exercises (Exercises 51–55 below) that does not relate directly to the body/voice connections we have been considering here, but is a very effective tool for emphasizing directionality, vocal energy, and vocal precision. Where these exercises should be brought in is open to the teacher/director's discretion, although clearly they should come in with some connection to the specifics of the exercises detailed above.

51. VOICE PRECISION I

There are a number of variations to this exercise, all of which are physically demanding and should be used only after the Physical WarmUp. (NB: the notes and *Emphases* for *all* the variations appear at the end of the Voice Precision sequence, so read the entire description before proceeding with the first exercise.)

Setup

The actors should stand around the work space, facing the walls from about a meter or so away.

Activity

The actors are asked to choose a very specific "target" on the wall—a spot, a hole, a nail, an electrical outlet—and send out a vocal impulse as precisely as possible to that point, and with enough energy to go to the "target" and come back. The "vocal impulse" can be anything at all except words.

As soon as they sense that the sound they sent out has "hit the target" and "returned" all the way back to its source—the diaphragm—they are to take two steps backward, then do it again. They keep doing this until they reach the opposite end of the room, or that point in the space, which, they feel, is as far as they can distance themselves from the "target" and still produce enough vocal energy for the sound to "go" and "come back."

52. VOICE PRECISION II

The actors now spread out in the entire work space, and, from a stationary spot send out sounds, choosing a different target for each vocal impulse. As in the previous version, when the sound/phrase comes back and "hits" the bottom of the diaphragm, they should send out a new sound, but only after turning and choosing an new target. The choice of targets, of course should be varied in terms of relative distances.

53. VOICE PRECISION III—VOICE AND RUN

Everything remains the same, except for one thing: as soon as a returning sound "hits" the bottom of the diaphragm, the actor turns and runs quickly to another place in the room, stops and sends out a new sound/phrase to a new target.

54. VOICE PRECISION IV—VOICE AND RUN WITH ONE TARGET

The same as above, with this difference: the actors use the *same* target throughout the exercise. No matter where they run to in the work space, they must send their sounds out only to that original target.

55. VOICE PRECISION V—VOICE AND RUN, ONE TARGET, AND DIFFICULT PHYSICAL RELATIONS

Multiple targets once again, but the actors must now send out their sounds from a difficult or contorted physical position: on their backs with their legs over their heads, out of a handstand against the wall or a headstand on the floor, legs apart looking backward through their legs, and so on.

NB

Eventually, when the actors feel freer in this exercise, they can use *each other* for the physical difficulties (e.g. leaning palm-to-palm with their legs planted as far as possible away from each other; one actor wrapping her legs around the other's waist and leaning down back-wards to the floor, while the standing actor counterbalances, etc.).

Notes for all the variations

1. Remind the actors about using only vocal sounds, not words and not mechanical/percussive sounds such as hissing or clicking.
2. Remind the actors that they have to send out enough vocal energy for the sound/phrase to "make it" to the target and back. You should demonstrate this by asking an actor to send out a weak sound with little vocal energy, and let the actors "see" how it "falls to the floor," either on the way out or on the way back—for lack of energy.
3. Tell the actors that they must "follow" the sound in their imagination—as though it had a shape in space—as it makes its way out and back. For example, a simple "Bah!" sound is easy to follow, but if the actor sends out a longer, more complex rising and falling version of the same sound, with different emphases and tempi for each segment, then he must wait until the entire "train" of sounds has "reentered" his diaphragm, before choosing the next target.

NB

Remind the actors that this is not an exercise in the imagination, so they shouldn't get carried away by visions of a serpentine sound/phrase that looks like a polka-dotted Anaconda with ten parallel sets of Cupid's wings, yellowing fangs, carrying a straw handbag with sour cream dripping out of a hole in the bottom! A simple image of sound-waves is quite enough.

---

4. The actors should be warned beforehand that since everyone is working at the same time, there is a great deal of noise in the space—sounds and bodies "flying" through the air to many different targets. This demands a great deal of concentration.
5. Actors should be encouraged to work with as great a variety of distances as they can.

Notes to steps 3 and 4 (sounding and running)

1. When their sound "comes back," the actors should "explode" into their run—just turn and blast away through the space. Anything may happen on the way, anyone might be in his or her way—and they have to "expect the unexpected." Remind the actors about Soft Focus and Readiness.
2. Now that there is an imperative to rush ("exploding" to a new location in the space when the sound comes back), remind the actors that they have to wait until the *entire* sound/phrase returns to its source before "exploding" away.

Emphases

1. *Vocal energy and control.* As the name of the exercise implies, the main object of this exercise is to teach the actors that the voice, like the body, is energy that can be controlled for effect. Repeated use of this exercise develops in the actors the ability to project their voice to a very precise location with exactly the right quantity of vocal energy.
2. *Physical awareness/body-voice connections.* In this case, learning through modeling exactly which body–voice connections help them send out a sound/phrase to a target, reach it, and come back.
3. *Concentration.* Maintaining a clear focus on the target and the trajectory of your sound with so many other actors and sounds crossing the space.
4. *Soft Focus/spatial awareness.* Exploding into the space at the end of each sound/phrase without knocking in to anyone.

NB

The Voice Mirror exercise (Exercise 38) can be brought back into this part of the work, giving it a different sidecoaching emphasis: the actors should see a "reflection" of their body/sound by watching their partners move and sound in exactly the same way as they are moving and sounding.

Body to voice connections—Parting thoughts

The voice work in the Logic of Training is based on a relatively small number of exercises that deal primarily with discovering the necessary connections between the voice and the moving body. This is a long and arduous task, one that requires a great deal of time, but with perseverance, it is tremendously rewarding. Following the logic of the "physical-to-physical/vocal" trajectory mentioned in Chapter 1, and based on the extensive training thus far of the actors' physical expressiveness, voice becomes an integral extension of the body, not an "add-on"; voice and body complement each other to the point where they are interchangeable. As we shall see, a truly "connected" actor can move just by "sounding," or "sound" just by moving. Finally, this training helps the actors understand once again a basic concept in the Logic of Training: that the freedom of the voice is enhanced by the precision with which it is used.

From here we are just a step away from the final segment of the training trajectory—the Body–Voice–Imagination—and a few steps away from the move into words. But let's take one at a time, and move first into the extraordinary world of the creative imagination.

SOAP BUBBLE PUSHING—TRAINING THE IMAGINATION

Introduction

Paradoxically, the less one gives the imagination, the happier it is, because it is a muscle that enjoys playing games.

—Peter Brook

Imagination grows by exercise and, contrary to common belief, is more powerful in the mature than in the young.

—W. Somerset Maugham

Both of these quotes refer to an important starting point for this section: the fact that the imagination can be trained.

Talking of "less," Peter Brook is of course referring to his extended love affair with what he sees as the prerequisite for creativity—"emptiness"; Somerset Maugham stakes an unusual claim for the greater power of the mature imagination, and the fact that it can be developed "by exercise." This, as opposed to the mere "availability" of childhood imagination (see my note on Pablo Picasso and his children in Chapter 1). But what interests me in all of these is the concept of the imagination as a *trainable* tool. Once this is acknowledged, the world of actor *"formation"* opens up to the almost infinite possibilities of training the imagination—the actor's most powerful tool; the "laminate" that binds the many layers of the actor's art into a communicable whole and renders them perceivable as a potent communication to the spectator.

Demonstration exercises

Imagination Training must, I believe, begin from a practical understanding of the way in which the creative imagination works, leading eventually to an understanding of the possibilities we have as actors to harness our imagination for creative purposes. If we can be persuaded that this mysterious brain function is also susceptible to a measure of control, we might be able to surrender more easily to the more complex body/imagination and body/voice/imagination exercises that form the backbone of the training. So here goes!

NB

The next four exercises take us briefly out of the physical work into mostly verbal work (using words, but not as "text"). There are two important things that should be borne in mind: (1) even in this stage of the work every workshop session should begin with the Physical and Creative WarmUps, and (2) these exercises are mostly "demonstrational"—although they can also be repeated as a training. Once the actors have reached a fair level of proficiency, these exercises can be integrated into the physical and vocal work of the earlier sections.

---

56. SOUND PICTURES

This is a classic example of an exercise that is easy to do but takes pages to explain. So, first of all, have patience! Read the description of the entire exercise (steps 1 and 2), then try step 1 and you'll see how easy it really is. Once you get it and want to use it with your actors, the best thing to do is to explain the ground rules, then try out a few examples and take it from there.

Setup

The actors should spread out at random in the space and sit upright on the floor. Emphasize to the actors this is *work* and the body needs to be alert, so there should be no sitting on chairs, leaning against walls, or lying down.

Activity/Step 1

Suggest to the actors that it is virtually axiomatic that every stimulus—physical, aural, or olfactory—excites up a visual association into our mind's eye. This "excitation of images" is part of our most primitive defense mechanisms. For our own protection and reassurance we need to know what it is we are touching in the dark recesses of the closet, what is making that strange sound outside our door, or what that slightly scorched smell means. So when stimuli like these reach our brain, we immediately look for their sources by scanning our imagination for all the possibilities: an extraterrestrial in the closet; or the familiar feel of that old sheepskin coat; a burglar rifling through the desk—or the kids coming home at 2 a.m. munching potato chips from a cellophane bag; a fire in the basement—or the neighbors grilling shish kebab in the wee hours. In each of these cases, we scan hundreds of pictures per second until either all the facts fit and we are reassured that there is no imminent danger or else *nothing* fits and we reach for the phone to call the police as our adrenalin level goes through the roof.

This "scanning" involves a rapid reviewing of all the details of the pictures that pop into our heads until we come up with one *effective* detail—the most important detail in the picture. Using one of the examples above—the potato chip sound—the effective detail we might "see" in our imagination is a grubby teenage hand in the bag of potato chips. Since that fits in with all the other sensory information we may have at that moment, the image of the teenage hand in the chips satisfies us as to the source of the noise. Zeroing in on the effective detail, then, relieves the tension, allows us to "turn off" the high-powered scanning, and lets us ago back to our normal, relaxed state of attentiveness—until another sound/stimulus sends us on our way again. This is the basic premise behind this exercise, and must be explained before embarking on the work.

Now, tell the actors that when the explanation is over they will be asked to close their eyes and listen, concentrating on whatever sounds they hear, in the room, in the building, or from outside. They should try to isolate each specific sound-stimulus, and separate it from its background or ambient noise. From there, the exercise proceeds as follows:

- As soon as they hear a sound they are to try to immediately "see the picture"—the visual association—that comes into their mind's eye.
- As soon as the image is excited up, they should try to scan it as thoroughly as possible looking for the effective detail. You might suggest to them that this scanning can be done with the help of cinema techniques: zooming out, zooming in, or panning from one side of the picture to the other in order to find the effective detail.
- As soon as they find that effective detail, they should then "clear the slate," or "delete" the screen in their heads, and wait, with a blank screen, for the next stimulus to excite the next image.

Notes up to here

1. Tell the actors that as long as they are working on any one stimulus they should ignore any others that may be heard in the room. This is easy to do simply through autosuggestion—just as people who live near bus or train routes "blank out" the sounds of the busses or trains that they are used to hearing.

2. Tell the actors that each sound stimulus should produce its own unique image, that they should avoid creating a consecutive story out of the successive sound stimuli. This involves a true "deleting" of the screen of their imagination each time so that they can let the next sound excite its own image.

3. If your work space is in a particularly quiet area, the teacher/director should produce the sounds with whatever is handy—a plastic bag, a radiator grille, coins, or a bottle of water—leaving suitable intervals between each one for the actors to "work" their images.

4. After letting the actors do this for a few minutes, tell them to open their eyes, and ask them to relate briefly what they experienced, noting the original sound stimulus, and what image it excited up in their imagination. There are a number of possibilities:

- Some actors will tell you that they didn't see anything.
- Others will give you a detailed description of the one-to-one images that were excited into their mind's eye by the sounds; if you rattled a water bottle, they will tell you that they "saw" a water bottle.
- Still others might tell you that even though they recognized the sound—the water bottle—what popped into their heads was a totally unexpected and surprising image of, say, underwater corals.

For those who saw nothing, suggest to them that they are simply being over-protective and not allowing their imagination to wander freely for fear of what they might see. Encourage them to try again with a Feeling of Ease, and not to worry about it too much if they still don't "get it"— eventually it will come. For those who gave you a detailed description of the "real thing," ask them if they can describe the actual process that occurred in their imagination, i.e. how they got to the effective detail in each case.

5. More often than not, actors will talk about "moving around" within the visual association that popped into their heads, examining various details in the picture, and then locking in on the most important detail. Indeed, many of them will try to describe what they "saw" as "zooming in," or "zooming out," or "panning," with their "mind's-eye camera." As for those who talk about being surprised by the images that came up, this too is very important for the rest of the exercise, and should be pointed out immediately as a good example of where the exercise is heading.

Emphases

1. *ImageWork or pushing the soap bubble.* This is the first instance of this phenomenon in a manner that is directly perceivable by the actors. In this metaphoric rendering of the mechanism of the imagination, the image that is excited up into the mind's eye by the external sound-stimulus is the soap bubble. In order for this image to yield its wealth of details it has to be "pushed"—scanned by the camera in the mind. This is an extremely delicate operation: pushing the bubble too hard will burst it and cause it to disappear; pushing too gently will get us no information at all; pushing resolutely but carefully will help us keep the bubble/image in our mind's eye *and* allow us to scan it for the effective detail. This element of "pushing" the imagination—henceforth *ImageWork*—is a seminal concept and the basis for subsequent exercises on the imagination.

2. *The stimulus/image syndrome.* As explained earlier, sensory stimuli provoke visual associations on condition that we render ourselves available—*disponible*—to them.

3. *Readiness.* The kind of readiness required for this exercise is different from the physically-induced readiness of the WarmUps. Using the experience gained from the physical exercises, readiness leading to an availability to the imagination has to be consciously induced as a nonmoving activity, a clearing of the slate and expectant waiting for the next image to bounce off our imagination and excite a picture.

4. *The fullness of the imagination.* It is very important to point out to the actors that the instant these images are created, they appear in our mind's eye crammed with details waiting to be "looked" at. For example, the sound of a laugh coming in from the outside might bring to mind a laughing face, but it will always be a very specific person in a very specific locale—not just a generic laughing person. All we need to do is to make ourselves available—in other words to go into a Soft Focus of our consciousness—and our imagination will supply us with all these details and many more we are not initially aware of.

5. *Working the imagination.* The simple act of "deleting the screen" after the actor finds the effective detail involves active intervention in the functioning of the imagination. This very early, primitive form of "working of the imagination" gives us a foothold for what follows.

Activity/Step 2

Having established the direct effect of sounds on our imagination and discovered that we can also—naturally and without any visible effort—"work" or control our imagination to a certain extent, we move on to a more complex level.

Suggest to the actors that they can, by an act of will, bypass their defense mechanisms and excite up a raw, "unmanaged" image that does not correspond directly with the object that made the sound or with logical reality of any kind. Hearing a bus rev up after changing gears at the corner, we might find ourselves—surprisingly and unexpectedly—"looking" at the image of a large chain saw, which, when we "zoom out," we find lying on a frozen lake in the Canadian Arctic. Zooming out a little bit more we might "see" a cut-up caribou staining the snow with its blood, and a high-powered rifle lying next to it on the ice with smoke coming out of the barrel. The effective detail might be, in this case, the bright pink spots of blood, the smoke from the rifle barrel, or the chain of the saw.

One way of clarifying the process involved in this exercise requires some more cinema terminology. In 35-millimeter cinema technology, our brain responds consciously to only one out of every sixteen or seventeen frames of film shown on the screen. The rest we take in, but only subliminally. Using this as a metaphor, you might suggest to the actors that if they simply give a visual identification to the source of the sound (hearing a bus = seeing a bus), then they are protecting themselves by seeing the "normative" sixteenth frame. But,

---

if they make themselves "available" by allowing their imagination to work in Soft Focus, they can actually catch an unprotected earlier "frame"—the eleventh or the eighth—that may be essentially different from the source of the sound (hearing a bus = seeing a chain saw/ caribou/smoking rifle on the ice in Canada).

Now go through the exercise again, giving the actors more time to listen to sounds, either from the surroundings or those you make, and after a few minutes check the results. This time you may still get some people who didn't see anything, or simply tried hard to identify the sources of the sounds, but in 99 percent of the cases you will get some wonderful and unexpected fantasies arising out of the sounds. When that happens, lead the actors to discover all the details of the picture by asking questions about what they saw. (NB: the questions should be as neutral as possible, so as to avoid imposing details on their images.) For example, if the actor who has come up with the Canadian image tells you that all he saw initially was a small part of the chain saw and a hand resting on it, you might ask, "Was there anything on the hand?" The answer might be, "A glove," in which case you could go further and ask, "What color was the glove?" Or else the answer might be, "A ring," and you might ask, "Is there anything on the other hand?"—thus causing the actor to involuntarily "pan" to the right in his imagination to check out the other hand.

Since this is merely an introductory exercise, it should be used for demonstration purposes for a short period of time, then given to the actors as "homework," calisthenics for the imagination that they can do anywhere.

Emphasis

Pushing the soap bubble or ImageWork. If by an act of will we can consciously direct our "camera in the head" to zoom in or out or pan to the left or right in order to find the effective detail we are looking for, or if we are able to "delete" a picture from our imagination at will, then we become aware that the imagination is subject to some control. That is an important first step in learning how to train the creative imagination.

57. DISTANT ANALOGIES

Another form of calisthenics for the imagination, this develops the actors' ability to intervene in, direct, and, to some extent, control their imagination.

The name derives from the concept of "distant analogies" proposed by Filippo Tommaso Marinetti and his Futurist friends as a way of kick-starting the creative imagination. The more "distant" the analogy, they claimed, the more powerful the "kick" to the imagination.

Setup

The actors pair off in the space, standing fairly close together and facing each other. If the number of the group is uneven, one trio can be created. There is a great temptation to do this exercise with eyes closed, but this is an exercise that helps actors learn something about the *conscious* manipulation of their imagination for acting purposes, and for that they need to be up on their feet, eyes open and *working*.

NB

Because of the supposedly relaxed, verbal nature of this exercise and the need to concentrate on the visual associations of the imagination, there is even more of a temptation to do this sitting down. Don't give in to the temptation! This is an exercise for *actors*, and the physical tension and alertness provided by standing up with their eyes open is an integral part of the process. Once actors really get going in this exercise, the tension involved in "working" the imagination makes them look more and more as though they are on the starting line for the finals of an 800-meter race—and *that's* what we're looking for!

Activity

The actors now use words to excite each other's imagination, and it goes like this: *Actor A* brings to mind a picture at random, selects an object from that picture and names what he sees for *Actor B*. This object—for example "horse," "fountain pen," "bottle," "eyebrow," and so on—should be given to the partner as a simple noun with no descriptive adjectives. Let's use "horse" for now. *Actor B* now has to let that word excite up her own mental picture of a horse, and then she must "scan" that picture in her imagination—zooming in or out, panning right or left—looking for a detail from that picture to give back to *Actor A*. BUT—the image given by *Actor B* to *Actor A* must be something that is *as distant as possible* from the original stimulus. The idea, of course, is to surprise *Actor A* by coming up with a totally unexpected image.

Example

A "asks" his imagination for a picture to begin the exercise and up comes with a beribboned circus horse. As he is concentrating on the image, a bareback rider materializes, doing graceful somersaults on the horse's back as it pounds around the sawdust. Of the many potential details from this image, *A* chooses the horse itself, and says only "horse"—not "circus horse," or "pale colored horse"—so as not to limit *B*'s imagination in any way.

Having said that, *A* now "deletes" the circus, horse, bareback rider, and all, and waits with an "empty screen" for *B*'s return image.

For *B*, the word *horse* excites up the image of a horse's head, tilted up at an angle, mane blowing in the wind, teeth bared, in a large grassy meadow surrounded by a white wooden fence. *B* now scans this picture for a "distant" detail with which to surprise *A*. *B* will first consider, say, the horse's mane, then discard it because it's too close to the original stimulus— "horse"—and thus too obvious. She may then zoom out to "meadow," which is less directly related but still relatively uninteresting and not at all surprising, And then, finally, she zooms in on the horse's head again, and chooses a detail from the original image, which is not obvious and could be quite stimulating—"teeth."

Hearing *B* say "teeth," *A* lets his imagination loose and sees, say, a small, cramped dentist's office with an aquarium fixed into the wall in front of the dentist's chair. Scanning this picture rapidly, *A* will instantly discard the "drill" or the image of an open "mouth" as being too close to "teeth," too obvious and too uninteresting, and, zooming in on the aquarium, will say "seaweed."

B goes into her own underwater scene, but soon discards it because it gives her related images that are too close to the original, and she "asks" her imagination to make an associative leap to something else. Her imagination immediately complies, and, concentrating on the seaweed, *B* now sees limp, dark green weeds on a small, white octagonal dish. Zooming out, she instantly "sees" where she is: in a Japanese restaurant, complete with red, dragon-motif wallpaper, shiny lacquered dishes, and a bustling sushi grill. Scanning the busy restaurant for a "distant" detail, *B* zooms in on the chefs, and very quickly says "butcher knife." In this way, we have moved, in associative leaps—aided by a conscious "working" of the imagination—from "horse" to "teeth," to "seaweed," to "butcher knife." Worked well, this should take less than a minute, and the two actors go on like that for as long as the exercise continues.

Notes

There are a number of rules to be followed relating to the nature of the exchange:

1. The actors must not use verbal associations—only image associations. Watch out for those who, when they hear "sun" answer "moon," or when they hear "fire" answer "water." These are intellectual exchanges that do not require imaging of any kind. Whatever the actors offer each other must come from a detailed image they "see" in their imagination, in order to provide their partners with something they can see as well.

2. For the same reason, the offers must not be too generalized, as, for example, getting "tower" and answering "Prague," or getting "pacifier" and answering "blue". Such generalizations will force the actor receiving them to spend a great deal of time reducing them to any kind of workable detail. Concepts should also be avoided (for example, if—for whatever image—the answer is "awkward" or "apathy") as these are too general, and will either require too much time to create a respondent image, or not excite an image at all.

3. The opposite is no less important: don't constrict your partner's imagination by giving too many details. If, example, for "mouse" the answer is "a slightly yellowing stalk of wheat, half eaten by the ravens, its upper part broken and hanging by a thread in a recently harvested wheat field after the rains," your partner will either get bored halfway through, or get angry at you for not leaving any room for his imagination! "A stalk of wheat" will do just fine.

NB

A good sign of progress in this exercise is when you begin hearing groans from actors who have been given images that are too close, too obvious, or too uninviting.

---

4. Time is of the essence. Urge, coax, or berate any actor who takes more than fifteen seconds to come up with a reply. Taking too much time will (a) instantly kick in all of our ever-vigilant defense mechanisms and steer us safely out of any problems (and the last thing we want to do when we are exercising our imagination is be safe!), and (b) defeat the purpose of learning how to "work" the imagination, how to make demands on it, and force it/allow it to provide the answers.

5. It is a good idea for the teacher/director to walk around the room listening in briefly to these exchanges and pointing out any associations that are too close or too obvious, too vague or too conceptual. From

time to time, as I listen in, I also ask actors to reconstruct an associative chain, e.g. hearing "red ant" in response to "soap dish," I might ask how this response came about, just as a way of encouraging the actors when they get the idea and do the exercise well.

Emphases

1. *Readiness/availability.* This was a major element in the preceding chapters, where it was related to a physical orientation of some kind. Having set that up as a standard for the beginning of any kind of physical work, here we are setting it up also a prerequisite for enabling our imagination, for opening the door into the realm of images that will occupy us in a major way in the following sessions. The way the exercise is described makes it quite clear to the actors that it is going to take them from one surprising image to another; there is nothing they can do to prepare themselves to field these surprises creatively except to generate in themselves a readiness coupled with a mental Soft Focus/Feeling of Ease.
2. *Working the imagination.* To do this exercise well, a delicate balance is required between figuratively sitting back and allowing the imagination to free associate without any constraints, and actively intervening in its workings—zooming in or out, panning, discarding, or "demanding" associative leaps. The issue of time is intimately involved in this. As we noted above, too much time between image stimulus and response allows for too much conscious intervention, so try to stick to the fifteen-second limit for each answer. The idea is to reach the point where this form of associative dialogue runs rapidly, smoothly, and effortlessly from image to image with just enough conscious intervention to enable the imagination to provide the required images.

58. TRIPLETS

This is the same exercise but with a twist: competition is added to increase the element of time pressure and emphasize the concept of "pushing" the imagination or *ImageWork*.

Setup

Groups of threes stand in close circles in the work space.

Activity

Actor A throws out an image and the other two scramble in their imaginations for the response just like in the previous exercise, except that they know that *only one of them* can provide an answer. As soon as A has given the opening image—say, "needle"—she must "delete the screen" and wait for the other two to pick up the challenge. *Actor C* makes it first with "lettuce leaf" (having gone at the speed of thought from "needle" to a syringe, to a junkie holding the syringe in an alleyway, to a "lettuce leaf" hanging from the dumpster the junkie is leaning on). *Actor B*, who was busy going from "needle" to "socks," to "sneakers" to "basketball," now has to give up on the image of the sweaty gym, and immediately begin working on *B*'s offer of "lettuce leaf." Occasionally, a single actor will have to "delete the screen" repeatedly as she keeps losing the race to the image. (NB: the groups taking part in this version can be enlarged to a maximum of five, but beyond that the exercise gets cumbersome and ineffective.)

59. RANDOM TALK I

Still within the framework of demonstration exercises for the workings of the imagination, this is an important exercise that provides an excellent model for training our imagination and illuminates very clearly a number of important elements of improvisation technique. Here again we have a simple exercise that is very easy to demonstrate and enormous fun to do, but that requires extensive explanation. *Pazienza*! Read the whole description and then try it out.

Setup

Two actors are seated, facing the observers, with their chairs angled in toward each other. It's hard to explain logically why this exercise can be done on chairs, while for the other imagination training exercises I insist on the actors sitting upright on the floor or standing up. Perhaps it's the ambience of a café conversation that I look for here. In any case, two things should be noted: first of all, when actors really get into this exercise, the sheer imaginational effort involved soon pushes them to the edge of their chairs anyway, and second, over the years, this has simply proven to be, in my experience, the best way of doing this exercise.

Activity

On the face of it, this is a language-based "situational improv," and, as such, a radical departure from everything done in the Training thus far. If the structure of the training is maintained, this usually does not cause a problem, and the apparent departure is understood within the overall framework of the demonstrational part of imagination training.

The fictional premise behind this exercise is that the two actors were together at some event the night before, and are meeting the morning after to gossip about it. There is only one catch: there are no givens in this exercise, so they have no way of knowing where they were or what they did the night before—until they start talking about it. The exercise is *not* a quiz, so the object of their conversation is not to discover the "secret"—a surprise party or the opening of an avant-garde installation—but rather to allow the imagined event to invent itself as they follow the vagaries of their individual—and joint—imaginations.

Before the examples, here are a few more rules:

- As part of the premise, the two participants were absolutely insep-arable during the "event" and saw all of the same things, so there should be no questions, only remarks relating to jointly experi-enced moments. For example, instead of asking, "What was she actually wearing?" the actor should say something like, "If only she hadn't been wearing that thing again!"
- For the same reason—in order to allow their partners maximum room for imaginative freedom—the two participants must try to avoid specifics for as long as possible. The idea is to find generic substitutes for names, colors, styles, clothes, or any physical details relating either to the "characters" or physical surroundings of the event. People should be referred to as "them," or "what's-his-name"; places as "there," "over there," or "inside"; and objects or animals as "that thing" or "those whatchamacallums."
- The tricky part is that in order to move the improvisation forward, they *have* to add details to give each other something to work with. But again, since they both "saw" everything together, they should be able to add details and avoid specifics at the same time. For example, instead of saying, "I wonder why Gary and Linda were scratching the wall at the far corner," one of them

could say, "Wasn't it weird when those two did that crazy stuff in the corner?" We now have "those two" instead of "Gary and Linda"; "doing" something "crazy," but not necessarily "scratching the wall"; "in the corner," but not necessarily the "far" one. This leaves the partner with ample room to imagine his own couple (two men, two women, two monkeys) doing whatever it is he sees them doing in his imagination. Played by two adept people, this game can become gaily cutthroat as each one tries to force the other to commit to a specific detail, and then the game becomes about how *not to commit* and still move the unraveling story along for as long as possible.

Example

A: (*Using a virtually standard opening for this game, she says the first thing that comes to her mind within the general parameters of the premise*:) I thought it was terrible!

B: (*Not having much to work on, he furiously prods his imagination for an image*)
Yeah . . .
(*locks on to "terrible," and "demands" an image, getting, say, a small messy students' flat with dirty socks hanging from the ceiling, and says:*)
. . . all those . . .
(*—about to say "socks" but avoids specifics*)
. . . things hanging down from the ceiling.

A: (*She "demands" an image of a place with "things hanging down from the ceiling" and gets, say, a large hangar-type building with enormous bright floodlights hanging from the ceiling; moving around the image in her imagination, she also has a flash image of great doors clanging shut all around the hangar and people scurrying toward the middle of the space, and says:*)
Wasn't that hysterical how everyone ran into the middle when they shut the doors?

B: (*The students' flat that he saw earlier had only one door, so now he has to adjust the picture in his imagination: keeping the socks hanging from the ceiling, but adding more doors, with the result that the space grows. A few people—"they"—run from one door to another banging them shut. A flash image free associates with this, and in his imagination, after shutting the doors "they" begin hosing down everyone in the flat with water, and he responds:*)

Yeah! If only they hadn't turned on . . .

(*—is about to say "those hoses" but escapes specificity to:*)

. . . the water!

A: (*She is trying to adjust to the water now, and scans the hangar with the closed doors and people scurrying toward the center of the space, adds the water flowing freely from a bank of taps along one wall and flooding the space, and zooms in on one couple standing motionless in the middle of the space:*)

But those two were really nuts! They just stood there as if nothing was going on!

B: (*The words "as if nothing was going on" skips him away from the students' flat, which dissolves now into an image of two people facing each other, wearing nothing, and he replies:*)

They weren't wearing anything anyway, so what did they care?

A: (*She now has to deal with unexpected nudity—A porno film? An arty affair? A Happening? Pressed for time, she responds with a dull offer that falls a bit flat.*)

Yeah, they always do that.

(*A better answer might have been:* "except for those weird things around their wrists," *which would have opened up any number of avenues for development.*)

B: (*Having a very weak offer to work with, he jogs his imagination with a self-offer: he asks his imagination to make the nude couple dance; his imagination complies, and—surprisingly—also provides them both with red patent leather shoes studded with rhinestones, so he replies:*)

But this was the first time they did it with those shiny shoes on!

Without the annotation, this exchange would sound like this:

A: I thought it was terrible!

B: Yeah—all those things hanging down from the ceiling.

A: Wasn't that hysterical how everyone ran into the middle when they shut the doors?

B: Yeah! If only they hadn't turned on the water!

A: But those two were really nuts! They just stood there as if nothing was going on!

B: They weren't wearing anything anyway, so what did they care?

A: Yeah, they always do that.

B: But this was the first time they did it with those shiny shoes on!

This could be a totally logical conversation between two friends overheard on a bus or in a waiting room. Who could guess that this is in fact a *carefully crafted* bit of nonsense that requires a great deal of technique and imagination training in order to make it sound so completely natural?

The conversation has to be "pushed forward" all the time, so details must be added—with as little specificity as possible—in order to give both partners something to work on, or else the mutual sparking of the imagination dies. For example, answering the question we suggested above, "Wasn't it weird when those two did that crazy stuff in the corner?" with, "Yeah, it was really funny!" would be totally useless because it provides absolutely no stimulus to the imagination. But if, in answer to the question about what those two weirdos were doing in the corner, I would let my imagination loose, "see" the Grecian urn behind them fall off its pedestal and onto their heads, and say, "Yeah, especially after that whatsis fell all over them!" I would be giving my partner a wonderful "whatsis" to work on, one that is not only a "whatsis" but a "whatsis" that can fall not only *on* someone but also *all over* someone!

Unlike the Sound Pictures or Distant Analogies exercises (Exercises 56 and 57) where each image had to be different and unconnected to the previous one except by association, in Random Talk the story line *must* be continuous and images should be carried over all the time. What is more, if at any point any specific detail is mentioned—for instance, "She was wearing that unbelievable yellow skirt again"—it immediately becomes a given and a permanent part of the event that cannot be denied or blocked. If, for example, *A* replies aggressively, "What skirt? She was wearing slacks!" this is a "block" that stymies *B*, who now has to reorganize in order to pick up the flow of images again. As any good improviser knows, one should always say "Yes!" to any offer, no matter what.

NB

The beach game of paddleball—played with two large wooden paddles and a small hard rubber ball—provides a wonderful metaphor for *any* good improvisation, but particularly for this game. Paddleball is a game that is played without any form of scoring—there are no points given or taken away, and so, as in any good improvisation, there are no winners or losers. The only object of the game is to keep the ball in the air as long as possible. This does not necessarily mean that the partners have to make it easy for each other. On the contrary, the two players can best display their skill only if they have to field exceedingly difficult shots that have been hit as hard as possible, with as much spin, curve, or "body English" as possible. The really important thing is that however difficult you make the shot for your partner, you must always *make sure that the ball is returnable*. And no matter how difficult the return is, it should look effortless. There is no better metaphor for a good improvisation!

Notes

1. This exercise—like many others involving the creative imagination—is a great deal of fun. But, once again, beware of the sheer seductiveness of the imagination, and don't forget that this is a training exercise. It has to be worked over and over again, until the actors fly with it, and turn it into a technique they can apply to their craft.
2. This is an excellent exercise for demonstrating "good" and "bad" offers in an improvisation—any improvisation, not just a verbal one. Good and bad offers in this game are absolutely clear, as in the example above, and the teacher/director should use the opportunity to point them out. Another ball metaphor can be used to describe the difference between a good offer and a bad one. Suggest to the actors that an improvisational dialogue is like a well-inflated balloon. Good offers keep the skin of the balloon taut and smooth and make it easy to bat back and forth; bad offers let air out, making the skin sag and wrinkle and demand more of an effort because the balloon first has to be inflated again and only then batted back to the partner.
3. Turning the game into a contest—a winnerless contest like paddleball, in which the patter is kept up at breakneck speed, and no image, however bizarre, kooky, or outrageous, is discarded—keeps the two participants in a constant state of readiness.
4. The basic improvisation technique of keeping all your options open as long as possible by not committing to specifics, is wonderfully exercised here, and can be described by the paddleball metaphor. As long as the two players stay far away from the concrete, in other words do not commit to specifics, their room for maneuvering is almost infinite. Playing their improvisational "paddleball" well—executing spectacular shots without giving in to specifics—will give the two improvisers a great deal of leeway for invention.

Emphases

1. *ImageWork.* This exercise provides actors with what I believe is a crystal clear model of how their associative imagination functions, and how, with training, it can be "worked" on demand. This is about as close as one can get—consciously, and "learnably"—to the actual workings of the creative imagination.

2. *Improvisation technique*. The form of this exercise also provides us with a great tool for illuminating some of the most important elements of improvisation technique:
   • Always saying "Yes!"—even to the most outlandish of offers.
   • What makes an offer "good" or "bad"—interesting or dull.
   • The idea of "accepting" or "blocking" improvisational offers.
   • Keeping one's partner—and oneself—off balance, with "one Foot in the Air," for maximum creativity.

60. RANDOM TALK II—ABSTRACT VARIATION

This is an advanced version of the above, and a very pure exercise in *ImageWork*. It is also a difficult exercise and should only be done after the two previous exercises have been thoroughly trained, and a fair level of competence has been achieved.

Setup

As above, two actors are seated at angles to each other.

Activity

This is the same as before, but with a difference: there is no premise of a commonly shared experience that is being gossiped about. The idea is to try to hold a conversation that is *completely abstract*, based only on associative images. In effect, this is an expansion of the Distant Analogies exercise into conversational form. The dialogue here has to be even more "distanced" because the two participants are not sharing a common experience, nor do they have to relate directly to any givens that might come up in the conversation.

Regardless of the completely disconnected nature of the dialogue, the actors must maintain etiquette of conversation, responding politely and *immediately* to their partner's offer *as if it were a perfectly logical answer*. These elements of conversational etiquette might be any one of the following: "Yes, but . . . ," or "Of course, however . . . ," or, "That's very true, nevertheless . . . ". All are to be used instantly, while the actors are seeking their oblique, image-fueled response. This is extremely important because: (a) it is completely legitimate to take a few seconds to start running the imagination search engine, and (b) it also forces the actors to commit to talking even before they

---

have actually finished working their imagination for a response (as in Tristan Tzara's Dada dictum, "Thought is made in the mouth"). By starting to speak before they are "ready" the actors have lifted their metaphoric feet into the air, and now they have to work their imagination harder, pushing it, saying to it, as it were, "Faster! Faster!"—and in the process learning even more about the way in which they can train themselves to "work" their imagination so that it provides them with the fuel they need for their creativity.

Example

A: (*Looks out the window of the studio, sees some scaffolding, and says, off the top of her head—but carefully leaving options open for B:*)
What a ridiculous piece of equipment that was!

B: (*Instantly:*)
Yeah, wasn't it?
(*As he fast forwards his imagination to one of those absurd "machines" created by French Surrealist sculptor Jean Tinguely, he zooms in on a cog wheel, and adds:*)
All those . . .
(*He is about to say "wheels" but junks it because it is too close to the idea of "equipment," and appeals to his imagination for help, so he zooms back from the cog wheel, sees it transform into a large rickshaw wheel, zooms out some more, finds himself in a market in Bangkok, gazing at some dog meat for sale, and says:*)
. . . disgusting lumps of . . .
(*—about to say "meat" but avoids specifics and ends up with:*)
. . . red junk.
(*And all this took ten seconds!*)

A: (*Instantly:*)
Disgusting? No, not really, it's just that . . .
(*She races the pictures by in her head: red junk > > > strawberry Jell-O > > > bits of fruit suspended in the Jell-O > > > zooming out to the glass dish with the Jell-O, sitting on the table in Grandma's kitchen > > > scans the kitchen frantically and finds the blue Wedgewood plate hanging over the table > > > zooms in again, this time to the Chinese dragon motif on the plate > > > free associates with the dragon, and comes out with:*)
. . . that it's so difficult to see anything when there's so much fire and smoke.
(*In twelve seconds, tops!*)

B: (*Instantly:*)
Naturally. However . . .
(*The wheels race: "fire and smoke" > > > fire engine careening around a corner > > > dalmatian on the seat > > > Disney's* 101 Dalmatians *> > > patch over one eye > > > free association—through the patch to pirate > > > Captain Hook > > > zooms in on the hook hand > > > zooms in on the hook > > > the image gels and he zooms back: the hook runs through someone's shoulder and, zooming out: there's Rod Steiger, in a camel-hair coat, hanging from a meat hook through the shoulder in* On the Waterfront. *Breathless from the image chase, he says:*)
. . . he probably hated the thought of . . .
(*was about to say "all that blood" but it's too close to the lumps of meat she saw before in "Bangkok"—so she distances it and says:*)
ruining his coat like that.
(*A record!—covering all that distance in seven seconds flat!*)

Here's that conversation again, as an eavesdropper might hear it:

A: What a ridiculous piece of equipment that was!
B: Yeah, wasn't it? All those . . . disgusting lumps of . . . red junk.
A: Disgusting? No, not really, it's just that . . . that it's so difficult to see anything when there's so much fire and smoke.
B: Naturally. However . . . he probably hated the thought of . . . ruining his coat like that.

To outsiders this, of course, makes no sense whatsoever, but for the participants it has the inner logic of the engaged imagination of two good improvisers who have learned how to "push the soap bubble" with impunity and style! Played well, this a giddying exercise that raises beads of sweat on the participants' foreheads, and leaves them gasping for breath as they race from image to image, zooming in, zooming out, free associating, intervening to choose the most distant image possible in order to "feed" the partner as quickly as possible with creative surprises—and all this while keeping up the tempo and ambience of a polite conversation over tea and crumpets.

As I said in the introduction to this section, the imagination is an endless world, and I could go on listing scores of exercises that fit into this category of preliminary "calisthenics for the Imagination." But demonstration exercises like these do not engage the body, and engage the voice only functionally—to provide verbal evidence of the workings of the imagination. Assuming, as I do throughout the book, that each exercise suggested here will be used repeatedly and extensively, we need to move on, and tie in these "technical" exercises for the imagination with the work on the body that preceded this section. This means making a large step toward understanding the seminal concept of connecting: training the intimate creative symbiosis that exists between the body and the imagination of the creative actor.

BODY AND IMAGINATION

The actor imagines with his body. He cannot avoid gesturing or moving without responding to his own internal images.

—Michael Chekhov

I can think of no more succinct way to state the training purposes of this section: shaping the imaging function of the body into a consciously applied technique. With connecting body, voice, and the imagination as the ultimate goal, once again we travel along the trajectory suggested in the opening and begin with the non-vocal body.

Raise your arm. Now why are you raising it?
—You asked me to.

Yes but why might you have raised it?
—To hold on to a strap in the Tube.

Then that's why you raised it.

(82)

This is how Keith Johnstone describes a moment in an improvisation class on spontaneity in his wonderful book *Impro: Improvisation and the Theatre*. In the terms set out in the previous section on Imagination Training, what happened to Johnstone's student is very simple: by raising his arm and being urged to push his imagination, the student excited up an image of himself in the Tube (the subway), raising his arm to steady himself, and thus was given the "right" answer. What is more, I have no doubt that the picture excited by the gesture was full of endless detail, because—as I suggested above—our imagination is inexhaustible, infinite, and irrepressible! This next section of the Logic of Training builds on the premise stated at the beginning of the section on the imagination: that in a state of performance and "availability," any stimulus—any stimulus at all—provokes the actor's imagination and brings associative images to mind. The readiness to receive images created by movement is the next step in the training.

Imaginary objects

An easy way into this aspect of the training takes us into the area of imaginary objects, not only for their "sense memory" value, as is the case in the Stanislavsky System or in Method training, but as a lead-in toward understanding the ways in which the body and the imagination interact, sparking each other in an endless cycle of creativity.

NB

Before you begin working with this family of exercises it is very important to point out the differences between this use of imaginary objects and mime. Mime involves creating *illusions of reality* through conventions, and as such often creates a stylized version of objects—as, for example, the sign of thumbs hooked together with fingers and palms flapping that signifies a bird or a butterfly. In these imaginary objects exercises, what we are looking for is not the sign, but the *object itself*, as if it were physically present in the space. Using the same example, in this technique of imaginary objects all we can do with a bird or a butterfly is "hold" them gently on our palms, or let them fly away from there.

---

61. THE BASIC IMAGINARY OBJECTS EXERCISES— "REAL" OJBECTS AND PLAYING BALL

These are the most basic of Imaginary Objects exercises, devised for the most part by Viola Spolin, and I bring them in here only because they are "prerequisites" that introduce the concept. They are the fundamental platform without which none of the following exercises will make sense.

Activity 1—Real objects

This starts with homework: ask the actors to practice at home picking up a glass, opening a book, leafing through a magazine, unscrewing a light bulb, taking a match out of a box, and so on. They should then put the object away, and do the action again, this time without the object, as precisely as possible. This repertoire of remembered actions with objects is then brought into the workshop session, and performed before the group.

Note

The creative imagination is not only irrepressible. It is also very tricky—so much so that at times it has to be carefully controlled otherwise it can get totally out of hand! This exercise in using imaginary objects is one of those instances. What I am referring to is something one might be tempted to call the "Sorcerer's Apprentice Syndrome": actors start out with a single object and within seconds scores of objects are filling up the empty air. Ask an actor to work with an imaginary bar of soap, and in no time at all we have a full-blown "soap opera": using the bar of soap gives birth to a tricky tap that insists on letting out only boiling hot water, a plug that doesn't fit the drain, and a towel that comes off with the towel rack! This, of course, is all very natural and a wonderful testimony to the fascinating riches of the imagination. However, for the purposes of this exercise and the ones that follow from it, caution the actors to stick to the one object they are working on.

Emphases

1. *Working the body/imagination tandem.* Acquiring a rudimentary under-standing of the connections between the body and the imagination by making every effort to maintain the *reality* of an imagined object.
2. *Controlling the imagination.* However strange this may seem, particu-larly after everything that has been written here about creative freedom, this a highly important concept on two counts. First of all, it is only when we try to block the endless stream of images that appear when we let the imagination loose that we can begin to understand the powerful dynamic of the creative imagination. Second, throughout this training I have been emphasizing the need for *control* as the necessary prerequi-site for the acquisition of a technique. Letting the imagination run wild is a lot of fun, but if we don't know how to control it for creative purposes, that's all it will ever be—just fun, not a professional tool. Reassure the actors that their imagination will be given free rein in due course, but in order to enjoy that part of it even more, they should practice restraint on this one.

Activity 2—Playing ball

There are endless variations on this, but basically they involve throw-ing an imaginary ball from one actor to another and trying to make sure that the entire group has the *same* ball. This can be done in couples or in a circle with the full group, and the variations include, among many others, changing the ball's size and weight.

This is, of course, a very basic exercise and the amount of time you will want to spend on it depends totally on the nature and qualifications of the group you are working with. As an introduction to this section of the training, Playing Ball is another platform: setting up the basic "language" of using an imaginary object in many different physical ways.

62. OBJECTS OUT OF THIN AIR

With these two platforms in place, we now begin to use them as we move into the body/imagination connections that are now the main subject of the training.

Setup

This should be exercised individually by each person in the group, in front of their colleagues.

Activity

This exercise is basically the same as the Basic Imaginary Objects exercises, except that instead of working with an object you have practiced with at home you now simply put your hand out into thin air, straighten your fingers or curl them in, and discover what you have there. A softly-cupped palm might "produce" a "gold chain," which you might then begin pouring from one hand to the other, or holding by the ends with two hands and twirling around itself. Or else you might put two hands out a certain distance and angle one from the other, let your imagination put something there between those two hands—say, a concertina—and then work with it for a minute or two.

Note

As in the Sound Pictures exercise (Exercise 56), there may be actors who put their hands out, curl their fingers, watch their hands with bated breath, then break away and say, "I can't find anything!" Just reassure them that there is *always* something there, all they have to do is use the *via negativa*: they have to avoid blocking its appearance in their imagination. Remind them of earlier techniques that they have worked with extensively up to now, particularly Soft Focus; tell them just to put their hand out, and not to think about anything, so that whatever is there in their imagination will be allowed to appear. Have patience—working this close to the imagination is no less a DangerWorks exercise than throwing sticks!

Emphasis

Body/imagination connections. On the most preliminary level—by moving the hand in some way, curling or straightening the fingers—we are inviting the imagination into our physical expression. This is the basic unit of the connection between moving and "imaging."

63. TRANSFORMATION OF OBJECTS—THE BASIC EXERCISE

From the creation of individual imaginary objects, we move now into the creative "magic" of the imagination's flow! Careful!—if you really let yourself sink into this exercise it is a giddying experience that is sometimes hard to stop!

NB

There is virtually an endless number of exercises using imaginary objects, as even the most cursory glance at any manual of improvisation or theater games will reveal. Over the years, particularly when training actors for improvisation groups, I have indeed used numerous variations of this basic exercise for training and in performance. However, the process of refinement that produced this book also produced the concept of seminal exercises—using the *same* basic exercise for numerous training purposes, depending on the angle, the sidecoaching, and the inflection. The following basic exercise is just such an exercise.

Setup

Individual actors perform in front of the group or in front of smaller subgroups.

Activity

An actor is asked to put his hand out, "find" an object in the air, and begin using it as an imaginary object. Then, as he is using it, he has to allow it to transform into another object, use that new object, and, in a similar way, allow that to transform, and so on. The actor continues transforming objects, one out of the other, for as long as he can, or as long as you have time for it in the training. (NB: watch out for what I have called "soap operas"—a proliferation of related, but *different*, objects. Remind the actors about control, and tell them to stick to one object at a time, with no connection between the various objects that appear save the associative connection of the body/imagination tandem.)

Sidecoaching

First of all, the basic body/imagination premise has to be reiterated here— namely, that in a state of performance, all physical stimuli excite up images and visual associations. Therefore, if we let the imagination loose, using one imaginary object can lead us to discover another imaginary object made of the same material—thin air. To demonstrate this put your hand out into the air, palm up, and "allow" an object to form there. Now work with the object, and by working it making it present, real (twirling the gold chain, carefully leafing through the pages of the diary, trying out the hat, or tying the bandana around your neck). Now put your mind into Soft Focus, and, by relaxing your attention, "allow" the object to transform itself—*through the action*—into another object. Don't force it! Don't think about what it reminds you of! Just let it be and it will transform before your very eyes! Stephen Nachmanovitch refers to this process as "surrendering"; Jerzy Grotowski calls it *via negativa*. In both cases we are trying not to prevent the imagination from going through its paces.

Example

Using the same "gold chain," an actor might do the obvious and tie it around her neck or twirl it by the ends, but that might come to a dead end as the gold chain simply refuses to transform into anything else. The way to jog your imagination is by using the same technique of the "distant analogies": doing something unexpected with the object to "kick start" your physical imagination. You might, for example, try to balance the gold chain upright in your palm, holding one end of it in the right hand and letting the other end dangle on your left palm. As you apply Soft Focus to that, the gold chain goes stiff, the clasp at one end no longer tickles your palm but pricks it instead, and the other end that you are "holding" between your thumb and forefinger grows thick and bulky and—*voilà!*— the golden chain has suddenly transformed into a jewel-encrusted dagger! Or, having tried the "hat" on your head in a number of positions, or twirled it around a finger stuck into its crown, once again you find yourself with a hat that won't change. Try raising both hands to the brim, lifting it up over your head, then tilting your head up and back as far as possible to look at it. As you do so, the soft felt turns hard, the high crown flattens out and you suddenly find yourself looking at your own "reflection" in a small, square mirror that for some reason you are holding over your head. To make the dagger or the mirror—as the case may be—transform into something else, you might need to do some more "jogging" of the imagination in the same way.

Notes

1. Emphasize to the actors that the only way they can give us the reality of the object is by "using" it—in other words, letting the body stoke the imagination. Watch out for actors who *demonstrate* objects instead of *using* them. The most common of these evasions is the "Door Syndrome" in which an actor comes in front of the group, traces the outline of a door with his finger in the air, then opens it and walks through. The "demonstration" is clearly a defense mechanism designed to protect the actor from any misunderstanding on our part: he wants to make sure in advance that we all know that he is in fact creating a door for us. This should be pointed out, if it occurs, as something to be avoided.

2. The "substance" of the object should remain "palpable" or intact at all times. This ensures that the objects will indeed transform one out of the other. If, for example, an actor starts off with a "banana" and then "eats" it, or creates a "wine glass" and smashes it to the ground, he will have to start all over again with a totally new object. That's not a transformation of objects, the seamless flow of imaginative connections through the body, which is what this exercise is all about—it's just work with two separate objects. What we are examining here is the connection between the body and the imagination—in this case the flow of movement of the hands and body with this object, which creates the next object. Letting go of the object and thinking up the next one means evading the training purposes of the exercise.

3. The actors should also keep "working" the objects continuously, so that their physical movements stimulate the transformations, and the objects

transform only in their hands—as they are being used—and nowhere else. One of the more common evasions of this exercise is to throw one thing into the air (say, a "jewelry box") and then catch something else on the way down (a "laundry basket," for example). This gets a laugh, but again defeats the purpose. In those few seconds that the "jewelry box" is in the air, the actor is racking his brains for another object, instead of using his body to discover it.

4. Remind the actors about Soft Focus and Readiness, and stress that to do this exercise they must concentrate only on working the object, not on the transformation. Not thinking about it will bring it about—thinking about it will keep it at bay.

NB

This is good place to elaborate a bit on Viola Spolin's concept of "No Motion," to which I referred earlier. The reference is to something that the actor keeps in a kind of inactive but expectant repository in the back of her head, for whenever it needs to be turned into active energy. The application of No Motion to this exercise is as follows: since you have described the exercise as one in which the actors have to transform one imaginary object into another, tell them to store this instruction in No Motion—someplace in the back of their heads—and leave it there as an inactive potential that will be triggered when the conditions are right. In other words, as they are working on one object they know they have to transform it, but this knowledge is inactive, held as a potential in No Motion. Since this knowledge is there, just waiting to be triggered, they don't have to think actively about the transformation—they can just let it happen, knowing that the information in No Motion will kick in automatically when the time is right.

---

5. Watch the actors' faces and body language, and watch out for those who are head centered (i.e. thinking hard about how to change a "banana" into an "umbrella"). Sidecoach them to use a lower center and to stop thinking about the transformation. They should simply enjoy working the one object, and let the other one appear like magic from the first one—as it inevitably will if it is "invited" through a kind of active indifference.

6. Thinking too hard about what to do with the object will more often than not cause the object to "refuse" to transform. The way to bypass this is to do what I suggested in the example above: sidecoach the actor to do something unusual with the object—"smoke" the "golden chain," "read" the "bandana," or make a "loudspeaker" out of the "magazine."

Concentrating on this unexpected activity will take the actors out of their heads and into their hands that are working the object, and in that state of mind, No Motion will kick in and the object will transform magically by itself.

Emphases

1. *Body/imagination connection.* Given the right conditions—being in the body (low centered) and not in the head (high centered)—the body and the imagination become one, following Chekhov's claim that "the actor imagines with his body."

2. *Imaginational flow.* The object of this exercise is to make the actors aware of the infinite endlessness—a deliberate tautology!—of their imagination. The actors should be encouraged to seek that level of creative concentration that enables them to discover a never-ending chain of objects that appear willy-nilly in their hands, and keep transforming with each slight shift of balance, angle, effort, or grasp. The actor shifts imperceptibly from consciousness to No Motion "unconsciousness," from control to surrender. In this way the actor tunes into the flow of her imagination, and lets it lead her for as long as possible—in other words, for as long as the body/imagination connection can be maintained.

3. *Readiness/Soft Focus or "surrendering"*: Nachmanovitch, who, as usual, is succinct on these, writes in his *Free Play*, "To *try* to control yourself, to *try* to create, to *try* to break free of the knots you yourself have tied is to set yourself up at a distance from that which you already are. . . . This paradox of control versus letting things happen naturally cannot be rationalized, it can only be resolved in actual practice" (141–42, emphasis in the original). What he suggests is to "(r)elax, surrender to the bafflement . . . and the solution will come. Persevere gently. . . . Stay close to the zero mark" (141). Nachmanovitch's "surrendering" goes hand in hand with the previous note about "flow," and cannot be emphasized enough. It is the very stuff of the training at this point.

NB

In all the sheer fun of working the imagination, don't forget the automatic self-learning mechanism—the Actor's Catechism. So here it is again: "What am I doing when I allow an object to transform?" "How am I doing this?" "What psychophysical state of being makes it possible for me to do this?" Or, if the exercise doesn't seem to be working, "What's missing?" "What do I have to change internally—in my mind and/or body—in order to make this thing work?"

Body/Voice, Imagination, and Body/Imagination—A pause for perspective

Having come so far in these past two sections of the training—Body/Voice, and Body/Imagination—let's pull back briefly and put these developments into the perspective of the training process. First of all, let's take a look at the elements that have been added:

<u>*Vocal energy*</u>

Voice precision

Body/voice connections

The Necessary Voice

Speech as formed gesture

Sensory stimulus-to-image

The fullness of the imagination

ImageWork: controlling/working the imagination

No Motion

Associative imagination/imagination's flow

Surrendering

Through constant repetition, these new elements of the training accumulate in the creative/expressive organism of the actor by a process of "layering"—the actor adding knowledge about his creative/performative instrument in "layers," one on top of the other, as they are accumulated along the trajectory of the training—until a point is reached, somewhere down the line, when the discrete techniques are "forgotten," or transformed into a marvelously complex, totally coherent, unconscious part of the creative processes.

NB

An evocative metaphor for this process of layering is the traditional way of making Japanese swords, the *kata*. Master sword makers hammer out the molten piece of metal they have chosen for the sword, and then fold it over and hammer it again, then reheat it and fold it again. They repeat this process seven or eight times before they declare the sword complete. Thus the finished sword contains *inside it* all the layers that were folded over, but they are not visible in the *kata* itself. The sword has seemingly "forgotten" all the layers that it is made up of, but they're all there as an integral part of its tensile strength.

In order for this intricate, delicately organic process of layering and "forgetting" to take place, structure is of the essence. The training must have a logic that renders the creative psyche available at each point in the process to accept and incorporate—to literally *place in the body*—the next step on the ladder. A procedure that lacks structure—or one that has no structure that the actors in training can discern—makes this process of acquiring knowledge about the creative instrument exceedingly difficult, forgettable, needlessly mystifying, or altogether impossible—or all of the above.

In my own work, at this point in the training, a typical three- or four-hour session is divided into two parts: half of the session is devoted to the repetition of the WarmUp Sequences and half to the learning of new techniques and processes. Whatever happens, I don't recommend working the WarmUp Sequence for more than two hours at a time, so if a given workshop session is longer than four hours, the division of time changes.

The body/imagination part of the training is far from over—in fact, it has only begun. Having trained the actors in allowing their imagination to work *externally*, through objects, the emphasis now shifts to the *internal* connections between the body and the imagination, with the help of a different, and crucially important, "family" of exercises: the statue exercises.

Statue exercises

This is another familiar cluster of improvisational exercises that appear in many different variations in almost every book ever written on improvisation and/or theater games. Starting perhaps from Michael Chekhov's group-oriented "Composition Exercises" and some of his exercises relating to the *Psychological Gesture*, to aspects of Vsevolod Meyerhold's études in Biomechanics, to the many variations on the theme of statues in the "bible" of improvisation, Viola Spolin's *Improvisation for the Theater*, these exercises involve the creation—at least initially—of a *tableau vivant*, some sort of static pose that is either an end in itself or the beginning of an improvisation when the "statue" comes to life.

After years of refining the process, I have included only those exercises that I have found to be the ones most directly applicable to the learning process suggested here: those that provide a clear, *practical* understanding, through modeling, of the powerful way in which the body and the imagination interact *internally* when the actor is in a state of performance. What is important here is the move from imaginary objects that are handled, and exist outside the body, inward now to the body as a stimulus for the imagination. In a way, we are closing a circle, because after the "break" taken for the demonstrational exercises of imagination training, the Training now reconnects with the all-important element of physical awareness that was such a central part in its earlier stages. The statue exercises focus on one of the most important elements of the training as a whole: awareness of the fact that for a trained performer, even the tiniest change in physical posture has an enormous impact on the creative imagination—which in turn has an enormous impact on what the performer radiates to the audience.

And one last note before moving into the exercises: the statue exercises bring the training close to a totally new area—*transformation*, as each new statue develops into a completely visualized "other." An actor/statue can often be seen to relax visibly into the new body/character, indicating that a process of transformation is going on inside. What is more, the actor will sometimes be reluctant to let go of her "character" when the exercise moves on to the next stage. All of this has to be handled with care, once again because of the seductive ease of slipping into the endless flow of the engaged imagination and allowing actual character work to take over the *training* for character work. A brief anecdote will, I believe, help put this into perspective. In the advanced stages of a training program, a student remarking on an exercise said something about, "When we're acting . . . ," to which I immediately replied, "But you're not acting now." The student: "Why not?" Me: "Because you're not doing the most important part of acting yet— you're not *transforming*." The student: "So what *are* we doing?" Me: "Training your creative instrument so that it will be *able* to transform—when we move into work on character and scene."

Essentially what this means is that if you want the training to be effective, the objectives of these exercises have to be kept absolutely clear. This is one of the reasons why you will see in the following section recommendations to stay away from psychology, feelings, and emotions. If the siren song of the imagination begins to lure you and your actors into "characters," my recommendation is that you follow Odysseus's example: tie yourselves to the mast, put wax in your ears, and sail past the temptation.

64. THE BASIC STATUE EXERCISE

Not only is this a "basic" statue exercise, it is, for my money, the *only* statue exercise that is truly useful for a general training of the actor's instrument. The other variations are mostly useful for ensemble training, and for developing improvisational material through theater games, both of which are outside the scope of this book.

> *Setup*
>
> One actor is standing, with her eyes closed, and one "sculptor" is standing behind the actor and "sculpting" her into a "statue." This can

be done first as a demonstration, and, if you have the time, individually with each member of the group. It can later be done in the entire space in smaller groups.

Activity

The performer closes her eyes and concentrates—that is, brings her center down into the Working Center. The sculptor should wait patiently until the performer relaxes, and displays the kind of visible Working Center-concentration that the group has learned to recognize as a readiness for creative work.

The sculptor can now begin moving parts of the performer's body, placing them in any position he sees fit (see Figures 28 and 29). When the "sculpture" is ready, the sculptor says "Okay" and goes to sit down. The statue is then asked to remain with eyes closed, and to describe who she is, where she is, what she is wearing, and so on in great detail—all in the first-person singular (see example below). With no givens except the input from her physical position, the statue must "go to the body," relax the imagination into a Soft Focus mode, and "see" all the details.

Figure 28 The basic statue exercise.

Figure 29 The basic statue exercise.

Sidecoaching the statue

The sidecoaching for this exercise—which is in fact more of a "questioning"—should be done carefully so that nothing you say will impose anything into the picture from outside.

Let's assume that the actor has been "sculpted" so that she stands with her feet far apart, both knees bent, one slightly more so than the other. Her left arm is bent at the elbow, drawn back behind the body; her right arm is held straight down her side, with the back of the right hand pressing, palm turned out, on the right thigh; her head is on an angle to one side, facing down. A typical exchange with this actor might go like this:

Who are you? (*The standard opening question for this exercise.*)
—I'm not sure, (*All she "sees" is dirty, cracked concrete*) . . . but I'm outside somewhere . . . on a sidewalk.

Are you a man or a woman?
—A man (*There is a surprised smile as she suddenly realizes that she knows she is a man.*)

What are you wearing?
—Well, all I can see is one long, ragged sleeve covering my right hand right down to the knuckles. (*The pattern and texture suddenly come into focus and she adds:*) It's made of burlap.

Zoom out . . . what do you see?
—I'm covered in a dark brown . . . almost black burlap cloak of some kind.

Is it day or night?
—Evening . . . (*The picture suddenly expands, and "he" looks down a long street to the right and sees*) . . . sunset . . . there's still some light.

Are you alone?
—No. (*She shakes her head as "he" suddenly becomes aware of many pairs of shoes moving through "his" field of vision.*) There are a lot of people passing by but I can't see their faces because I can only see the ground immediately in front of me.

Are you wearing anything on your feet?
—Sandals . . . (*She sees ragged edges.*) . . . torn (*Zooms in and realizes that they are made of*) . . . leather! . . . with no buckles, just sort of knotted thongs.

How old are you?
—Young, but prematurely old (*She has the sensation of having an emaciated face.*).

Meaning . . . ?
—(*She zooms out an sees herself almost bent over double.*) I'm not an old man, but my body is bent and feeble.

Are you wearing anything under the burlap cloak?
—(*The unexpected question surprises an instant answer out of her imagination:*) No! Just a kind of twisted cloth around my groin, like an Indian holy man. (*Her hand involuntarily scratches her chest, and she adds:*) And the cloak itches!

This questioning can go on a little further, but in most cases, the longer you question the statue, the more likely it is that she will begin adding details that were *not* there at the first moment of revelation.

NB

Take some time to clarify the method that should be used to question the statues:

- *Stay away from psychology*! Statues should not be asked how they are feeling. All we are interested in are the *visual* details.
- The sculptors should not plant any details in the statues' minds. Instead of asking, "Why are you wearing blue shoes?" the question should be, "Are you wearing anything on your feet?" Or, instead of asking, "How many rings do you have on your fingers?" the question should be, "Are you wearing any jewelry?"

Notes

1. There are a number of simple rules to follow in this exercise:

   - The "sculpting" should be continuous, without any pauses between moves.
   - The sculptor should not place the statue in any kind of storytelling pose (praying, embracing, fighting, etc.). On the contrary, the sculptor should treat the statue's body as a random collection of articulated limbs that can be moved in many different directions with no necessary correlation between them. This keeps the sculptor from creating a predetermined story that the statue simply has to play out, and gives the statue only an abstract physical combination that she has to make sense of.
   - The sculptor can move any part of the statue's body repeatedly until he is satisfied with the results of his sculpting.

- Facial expressions can also be sculpted, but only at the end of the sculpting, so that the statue does not have to maintain a difficult facial mask for too long.
- The statue should be told not to change the position of any part of her body after it has been sculpted. If, for example, the sculptor closes the statue's fist loosely, not allowing her fingertips to touch the palm of her hand, the statue must not "correct" it or "finish" it by clenching the fist tightly.
- There should be no talking between the sculptor and the statue. The sculptor can move any part of the statue's body simply by putting pressure on it, or physically moving it, and, of course, the statue should respond easily, without any opposition.

2. Suggest to the statue that every physical stimulus—a part of her body being moved by the sculptor—brings an image to mind, and that as soon as such an image appears she should "work" it until her position is changed again by the sculptor. At that point—as soon as she is touched—she must "clear the slate" of any image she has been "working," to free herself to work with the next image provoked by another change in her body position. This is an important introduction to the advanced version of the exercise, but it also gives the actors a first indication of the way physical movement impacts on the imagination.

3. If at the end of the sculpting the statue hesitates, or says that she doesn't "see" anything, sidecoach her to "demand" some help from the imagination—as the actors have already learned to do in earlier imagination training exercises. Alternatively, you can suggest that she scan her imagination for the tiniest detail (the angle of a hand, a fold in a skirt) then zoom out or zoom in, as the case may be, and give a detailed description of the person she has become.

Emphases

1. *Physical awareness—Body/imagination connection.* As mentioned in the introduction to this "family," this is the first exercise that emphasizes the *inner* connections between the *body* and the *imagination*; as such, it is an important step toward the most advanced techniques of the Logic of Training.

2. *ImageWork.* Having practiced this repeatedly in the imagination exercises, the actors should now be adept at "making demands" on the imagination, and this exercise gives them a different model of behavior to practice.

NB

One more word about staying away from psychology in the questioning of the statues. This exercise deals *only* with the development of the actor's ability to understand and control her imagination. Feelings, emotions, sensations, and the like are a long way down the line, and relate more directly to work on character and scenes, all of which will be dealt with extensively in the concluding chapter of the book on the Chekhov Technique. Feelings and emotions will appear naturally in many exercises as a *result* of a particular movement pattern or vocal pattern, and they will be discussed as part of the strength or weakness of any particular exercise, but they are not the *object* of the exercise. So if the actor/statue starts telling you how she feels or what her parents did to her as a child, ask her to "stick to the facts" and forget about the psychological complexities of the "character."

65. ADVANCED STATUE EXERCISE

This is a direct follow-on exercise, and the *Setup* is the same as before.

Activity

This version picks up on an earlier suggestion to the statues, that every stimulus, even the most minute, excites an image, so that every time the sculptor moves a part of the statue's body, an entirely new statue/character appears.

In the chapter on "Sensitivity" and the "Psychological Gesture" in his *On the Technique of Acting*, Michael Chekhov describes a very similar exercise, when he talks about creating a Psychological Gesture then making a minute alteration to the overall position and paying attention to the internal changes that occur. "The more you become sensitive to such alterations in your Gesture," he writes, "the more imperceptible changes you must make. The position of your head and shoulders, arms, hands, elbows, the turn of your neck and back the position of your fingers, all will call up your creative spirit corresponding to Qualities and Feelings. Go on exercising this way until you feel that even the slightest idea of a possible change makes you react inwardly" (79).

Following Chekhov's concept of "sensitivity," in this exercise the instruction is that every time there is even the briefest pause in the sculpting—every time the sculptor lifts his hands from the statue—the statue must *immediately* start describing aloud, *with no prompting*, the persona she has become. From the sculptor's point of view, this means that after each physical change he must allow the statue a brief moment to describe her persona (see the note below on the rhythm and frequency of these changes).

Once the statue has started the description, she should be ready to stop instantly, midword or midsentence, the moment the sculptor touches her again. The instant of contact is the signal for the statue to immediately "clear the slate," to prepare herself for the next image that will come once the next physical adjustment is completed. Again we are in an exercise that involves a "calisthenics of the imagination," but on a much more complex and profound level.

NB

Note that in Chekhov's exercise the emphasis is on the emotional changes that occur with each physical alteration, rather than the excitation of a "persona." My recommendation to avoid slipping into character work renders this training, in a way, a "pre-Chekhov" training—concentrating only on preparing the actor's instrument for the many different forms of transformation that they will contend with in their professional life in the theater.

Note

The rhythm and nature of the sculpting change as the exercise progresses.

1. The intervals between one sculpting adjustment and another should diminish gradually, so that the sculptor leaves the statue less and less time in between adjustments to start working her imagination and describing each new persona.
2. The physical adjustments made by the sculptor should also diminish gradually, so that by the end of the exercise a typical bit of "sculpting" might involve no more than changing the angle of the top section of the right forefinger.

Emphasis

Body/imagination—Minute sensitivity. This involves leading actors through a model of behavior during which they can experience the essential symbiosis that exists between the body and the imagination in a state of performance, where even the subtlest physical adjustments have an instant effect of the imagination. All the exercises of the WarmUp Sequences relating to physical awareness come into play here, as the Minute Sensitivity to the body that is trained daily in the warm-ups is now channeled into the imagination as well—and Connecting, the goal of the training, is now beginning to take palpable shape.

From this "basic training" in the body/imagination symbiosis, we can now move into the most complex and rewarding section of the Logic of Training—*Imaging*.

Vanishing cream—Thoughts to go before the final chapters on training

For a few months before I originally submitted the manuscript of this book to my publishers, a well-known cosmetics firm had been airing TV ads for a new facial cream. The ad showed the portrait of a woman painted in the Old Masters style, with her hair drawn back in a bun. Although the classic eighteenth-century features of the woman were clear and striking, her face was crisscrossed by the unflattering craquelure of old paint. The hype for the facial cream talked about putting on this particular cosmetic to overcome the ravages of time and aridity, and as the words droned on, the cracks on the woman's face mysteriously disappeared and the skin in the portrait transformed into a glowing suppleness.

In a way, the concept for this ad is a wonderful metaphor for what takes place at the end of the training cycle. Having worked along the various trajectories to an ever-growing number of individually-named—and thus separately-learnable—techniques, we are now going to carefully apply a cream to erase the cracks that have separated all these distinct parts of the training thus far. This, then, is about what has to occur beyond the acquisition of discrete techniques in order to render the art of acting seamless. It's about learning how to forget the techniques we have acquired and allowing them to fire up the incredible vanishing/presenting act that occurs every time the "I" of the actor transforms into the "other" of the stage persona.

At this point in the training we are on the threshold of the next major step, which might qualify as a trajectory in its own right and will be the subject matter of the concluding sections of the book: *from training to character*. The training described up to this point has one main purpose: to prepare the actor's creative instrument for any form of character and text work that he might choose to do in his professional career. However, before moving into that final chapter, there is one more step to be taken: into the intricate, complex, exhilarating, sometimes frightening, and sometimes awe-inspiring process of advanced *ImageWork*, where everything I have tried to construct in the Logic of Training thus far, comes together, and Connecting becomes no longer a goal—but a tool.

IMAGEWORK

In the early training for centers, and particularly in relation to the Working Center, I said that images *could* be used, but since it was far too early in the training at that point to introduce work on the imagination, I recommended just mentioning the possibility, without recommending any images. The idea of an "image" that I am referring to is a single, more or less coherent mental picture—a "hot sun," a "piece of ice," or a "transparent veil"—that we "place" in the Working Center, so that it causes us to move through the evocative power of the imagination. The ability to "work" a specific image like that and the ability to manage it over a period of time, exhaust its possibilities and use it repeatedly without losing its potency—these are the subject matter of this section.

This is the final part of the Logic of Training, and while much of what appears here can be expanded in many different directions, structurally speaking, this, I believe, is as far as "instrument training" like this can take the actor without reference to character, scene, or text. Ideally, an actor who has proceeded intensively through this training over a year or so should be able to bring to any work on text and character a finely tuned instrument, sensitive to the slightest nuance of the actor's three basic tools—body, voice, and imagination—and their profound interconnection. The actor should also be able to bring these skills fully to bear on his or her contact in real time with an audience through radiation and creative cooperation, together with a thorough incorporation of the "primary colors" of the actor's craft: improvisation/creativity, connectedness, and repetition.

Before we embark on this fascinating last leg of our journey, a few notes are in order:

Stepping into *ImageWork*, we are moving into an area of the greatest complexity, the greatest difficulty, the greatest riches, and the greatest potential for misconceptions. I say this advisedly, referring to times when actors go through the motions but are not really *connected*. This is not always noticeable, and even the most experienced teachers/directors can be moved by an exercise that has actually been done quite technically with no deep resonance. The greater the experience of the teacher/director, the less likely this is to happen, but it should be noted and attention must be paid. At the same time, as we have mentioned earlier, actors in advanced stages of training may feel they are going through an exercise technically or superficially and still *genuinely* move their observers because of the now innate strength of their radiation.

The sheer psychophysical energy required of the actors in doing many of these exercises is enormous, and as a result they should not be labored beyond a certain limit. If working with the imagination goes on too long, there will come a breaking point, when the actors feel "milked dry" and have no more resources for delving once again into the world of their imagination. This is the reason why all of these exercises should have fairly limited timeframes.

Structure

In this final section, the entire vocabulary of the techniques we have been working with comes into play, through the continuing use and development of the Warm Up Sequences and the addition of new techniques. By the time we head into this part of the work, the actors generally work through the Warm Up Sequences on their own, with their own points of concentration, and with no sidecoaching. Occasionally I will intervene when an actor seems in need of direction, does something particularly interesting or connected that needs reinforcement, or ends the warm-up long before he has really warmed up for the work at hand.

This sequence, like all the others, has an inner trajectory of its own, which moves not only from the abstract to the concrete, but also from the exterior to the interior, from the palpable to the impalpable, and—closing a much larger cycle set out at the very beginning of the book—from the moving actor to the unmoving actor. At the same time, we are also moving from the world of more or less measurable results, to the immensely variable, immeasurable (and often downright misleading!) world of images. We are, in a word, closing the gap between training and performance.

The exercises

66. QUALITIES AND CENTERS

Setup

All the actors work individually in the space.

Activity

The exercise begins with the actors concentrating on their Working Centers and walking through the space on their own, making no contact with anyone else. Before they begin moving, they should be told that as they are walking they will be given a series of adjectives each one of which will define the *quality* of their centers (e.g. "smooth," "flat," etc.). As soon as they hear the adjective, they should allow their centers to assume that quality ("smoothness" or "flatness"), and begin moving with that quality as a center. Since their centers are the only energy source for all their movements, they are to move through the space now in response to that specific kind of energy. The actors should experiment with that quality in all parts of their body and try out different combinations of movement, until a different quality is introduced by the teacher/director.

Notes

1. A partial list of qualities may include actual physical categories, such as smooth, flat, sharp, jagged, round, shiny, rough, thin, brittle, flexible, or hard, or more difficult ones such as transparent, opaque, fragile, luminous, or even simple colors: red, black, green, blue.

NB

Using "generic" qualities like these ensures that the training remains in the abstract for a little while longer before moving into specific, concrete images. It gives the actors the freedom to choose *any* image—or many different images—for "flatness," "sharpness," or "brittleness," and provides them with as much room for improvisational/creative space as possible.

If, in response to such qualities as "transparent" or "blue" you get perplexed looks from the actors, sidecoach them not to give it a second's thought, but just to *move* with whatever their body does in response to those images. There used to be a sign on the door of Blair Cutting's old Chekhov Studio in New York that said, "Check your brains at the door!" This is one instance when this idea comes in handy!

---

2. The actors should be encouraged to use elements from the WarmUp Sequences in this work, for example, using the center/quality to create forms or *Plastiques*.

NB

It is extremely important to emphasize to the actors that when they are working through this exercise, they should remember that they are a *what* not a *who*, a *quality* and not a *psychology*. Don't let the actors slip into the relative ease—and the trap—of getting involved in psychology or playing a character. They should remain at all times in the abstract realm of qualities—which gives them much greater freedom and many more possibilities than the conventions—or possible stereotypes—of a psychological construct.

---

3. The actors should be encouraged to experiment with the radiation of the given quality out of their body to the far reaches of the room, just as they do in the Creative WarmUp. (See the variations, that follow in Exercises 67 and 68.)
4. The Actors' Catechism should always be at work:

   - What does it mean to radiate "smooth" or "flat" energy?
   - What kind of effort is involved in each one?
   - How difficult—or easy—is it to retain that image throughout the work?
   - What do I have to do—what kind of psychophysical organization of my body and psyche do I have to activate—in order to respond to these different qualities?

5. Like many other exercises outlined here, this is an exercise that should be used as many times as necessary until the actors reach a fair level of competence, and basic understanding of the idea of working with a center/quality.

Emphases

1. *The imagination working the body.* For the first time in the training, the actors are now being asked to turn their imagination into an active tool that they use to direct their physical expression.
2. *Working with an image in the center.* Even though no specific images are mentioned here, the actors will be using images anyway, because they will automatically translate, say, the quality of "sharp" into the image of a knife or a razor; the quality of "brittle" into a dry leaf or a thin piece of glass, and so on. (NB: because of its importance to all subsequent training, this emergence of images should be discussed after the exercise.)

67. CENTERS—COMPLEX QUALITIES

This is a follow-on exercise that is usually done as a direct continuation of the previous one. Because of its importance to the rest of the work, and the possibility of working it on its own as well, it appears here separately.

Setup

If it is brought in as part of the previous exercise, then all the actors are on the floor, working the last quality. If it is worked separately, then it starts with all the actors spread out in the space in a state of *Readiness*.

Activity

The activity here is exactly the same as in the previous exercise with this difference: the center becomes a complex of qualities—still without naming a specific image. For example, you might say that the center is "soft, round, and warm," or "small, hard, black, and cold," or "large, yellow, light, and fluffy," and so forth.

Note

The actors should be sidecoached to regard each of these clusters of qualities as one thing, a single, coherent "something" with many qualities. They should be urged to "work" these centers, with all their qualities, in any way they can, alternating their concentration from one component quality to another, or—what is more likely—translating these multiple qualities into an "image" that they work from. Once again, they should not be given an image, just the composite of qualities.

Emphases

The *Emphases* are the same as in the previous exercise except that the actors will now be even closer to the concept of images, simply because an image is, by definition, a collection of physical properties and qualities. Thus, "large, yellow, light, and fluffy" will inevitably be translated into a yellow powder puff, or "small, hard, black, and cold" will undoubtedly appear in their imagination as a frozen squash ball or something similar. The only thing separating the work now from actual work on images is the fact that the teacher/director is remaining in the abstract in order to give them the greatest leeway: all he is giving them at this point is a quality cluster and allowing them the freedom to create their own images out of the cluster.

68. CENTERS—RADIATING THE QUALITIES

Once the actors have understood the way the basic exercise functions, the teacher/director can bring in another element from earlier parts of the training—*radiation*—tying it in now to its ultimate source, the creative imagination.

Activity

As the actors are still moving in response to the center and qualities— single or multiple, as the case may be—sidecoach them as follows:

- "Begin working your way to a standing position, and as you do, reduce your physical expression so that in the end your are standing up and nothing is moving except the highly active image in your center."
- "Now, choose a target—a very specific point in the space (as in Voice Precision I, Exercise 51)—and 'send out' the image to that point in the space. Don't forget to ask yourselves the question: 'What do I have to do in order to radiate?' 'What am I actually *doing* when I radiate?'."

NB

Remind the actors once again about the technique of the Actor's Catechism: they may not get an answer to these questions, or they may get an *intuitive* answer that they cannot articulate in words; the important thing is to ask the question and initiate the search for the answer.

- "Now, when I snap my fingers, you should 'turn it off'—keep the image but stop radiating it—then choose another target in the room, and 'turn it on,' and ask yourselves the appropriate questions: 'What is the difference between being on and being off?' 'What do I do to turn it on or off?' and so on. Vary this by radiating different images at the same target, choosing from among those given during the exercise."

69. ROPE DANCE

The original idea for this exercise came from a wonderful book by Lea Bartal and Nira Ne'eman, *Movement, Awareness and Creativity*, and has undergone a number of metamorphoses before taking its place in this training. Over time, this deceptively simple exercise has turned into a crucial exercise that usually marks a watershed in the training, as the actors begin to understand, through practical models of behavior, the concept of *connectedness*—the enormous power of their imagination manifested through physical expression. The length of the notes and *Emphases* is one palpable indication of the exercise's "seminality."

Setup

Making yet another small step toward the concrete, we move now from the personally created, internal images based on "generic" qualities of the previous exercise to work on a palpable physical image. The image in this case comes from a length of rope—about 1.2 meters long and half a centimeter thick (so that it has some weight)—preferably white and as neutral as possible, made of very smooth, easily flowing material that does not kink. This exercise is performed individually by each actor in front of the group.

NB

The reason for using a white, flexible rope for this exercise is that it is neutral, shapeless, and abstract. There is no way the actors can determine or influence the shape of the image it will create, so they have absolutely no foreknowledge of what they will be working with. All they need to do is engage their readiness and begin from an absolute Zero Point: the moment when—as we shall see—the rope settles into its image on the floor.

Activity

An actor is asked to hold the rope loosely coiled in his hand, stand close to the front edge of the work space (nearest the observers), and "center." When the actor reaches a state of readiness (when his center has moved visibly down from the head to the abdomen and there is a relaxed preparedness in his entire being), he should throw the rope in the air—without watching it, just maintaining Zero Point readiness—and let it land on the floor (see Figure 30). Throwing the rope near the front edge of the work space generally ensures that the work space remains free for the working actor to move in, and that the actor will not touch the rope during the exercise (see note 6 below).

A smooth, flexible rope will land on the floor in a random, abstract pattern. Suggest to the actor that this pattern is an image that he must now "take in" into his Working Center—and move in response to that image for as long as the image nourishes his movement. I have found that the most evocative way of describing this activity is to tell the actors to look at the Rope/Image as it lies on the floor—and *dance it* (Figures 31–33). After doing a number of demonstrations, it is very important to point out to the actors to begin moving *instantly* as soon as they hear the sound of the rope landing on the floor—a quick look, and the "dance" begins (see note 2 below)

The exercise can end in a number of ways: (1) when the connection between the Rope/Image and the actor's Working Center fades—in other words, when the actor's center moves back into the head and into self-consciousness; (2) when the actor "runs out of gas" and simply cannot go on.

The actors should be told that there are a number of possibilities of using the rope as a controlling image in their Working Center:

- They can remain in eye contact with the rope all the time, and engage in an ongoing "dialogue."
- They can look at the rope, "take in" the image it gives them—a small part of the overall pattern (a loop, a tight knot, a frayed end, etc.) or the whole thing—and work that until they exhaust it, then come back for another "charge" from the rope, take that away and work it until it ceases to nourish their movement, and so on.
- They can take one look at the rope image and work it without looking at it again until the image is exhausted.

NB

Initially, this may seem like a regression to a more "primitive" form of *ImageWork*, but the Rope Dance is, in fact, the first in a sequence of exercises, leading to the most profound way of using images (see Object/Image Dance, Exercise 71). To get the whole picture, you might want to read through the entire sequence of Exercises 71 through 76 before going on.

Figure 30 Throwing the rope: Centred, not looking at the rope until it lands.

Figure 31 Working the rope/image.

Figure 32 Working the rope/image.

Figure 33 The rope dance.

Notes

1. Once again, when introducing the exercise, remember the idea of "dancing" the image on the floor. This will help the actors understand the idea of taking the image into their center and translating it into movement.

2. Absolutely no time for thinking is allowed! The actors should be told to start moving a split second after the rope hits the ground. All they need is enough time to get a visual image of the rope on the floor—a *coup d'oeil* (a "hit of the eye"), as they say in French—and they should be off and running.

3. There is a useful rule-of-thumb that can be employed here to short-circuit the thinking process. If you—the teacher/director—manage to sense a delay and say "Too late!" somewhere between the moment the rope hits the ground and the time the actor begins to move, then the actor is, indeed, too late—she has allowed herself too much time to think before moving. Stop the exercise, point out the delay, and tell the actor to start again.

4. Encourage the actors to use the rope in the same way that they used the qualities in the previous exercise: as an image that "moves" them because it is "in" their Working Centers. This is a creative dialogue that moves back and forth between the image on the floor and its physical manifestation in space through the actor's body. Clearly we are not talking about any kind of "copying" of the Rope/Image, but a creative adaptation of the physical image of the rope into the "dance." Without waxing too mysterious about it, it's almost as though the actor is "possessed" by the rope from the inside; she is not moving of her own volition but *being moved* by the image of the rope she has "taken" into her center.

NB

Some years ago, while doing this exercise in one of my classes, a young woman "hit the zone": she connected in the deepest possible way to the Rope/Image as her body and her imagination joined in an extraordinary symbiosis. In this wonderful psychophysical state of performance, she created a stunning, deeply moving, kaleidoscopic Rope/Dance, moving from one physical image to the next, each one more surprising than the one before. We watched her in awed silence for nearly twenty-five minutes until she simply ran out of strength— not inventiveness—and collapsed on the floor. What was no less fascinating was the "report" the young woman brought back from her sojourn in this "other" world of pure creativity: she could not remember a single thing about the entire exercise! All she could remember was a heady sense of infallibility and pure joy—which is nothing but the exhilarating "high" of the Creative Moment in full bloom.

---

4. Tell the actors that if, in the course of their dance, they find a movement/ phrase that they like, they should repeat it in a *Plastique* and work it for as long as it intrigues them. If this takes them away from the rope for a minute or two, that's fine (see note 6); the Rope/Image is just a catalyst for movement, and whatever they find they should explore as fully as possible.

NB

In this and all the subsequent *ImageWork* exercises, I often use active sidecoaching, mainly to encourage the actors to go on rather than succumb to the temptation to stop. Remind the actors beforehand that you might come into the work space so that they don't freeze up when you do.

---

5. It is important to explain to the actors that, despite the fact that the Rope/ Image is a total abstract, it is, nevertheless, a coherent image—an entirety—and they have to relate to it as such. This means, among other things, that the "dancing" actor should not touch the Rope/Image or disturb its integrity in any way during the dance improvisation. What is more, at the end of the exercise, the rope should be left on the floor exactly as it is, so the image can be visually referred to in the critique session (see emphasis 1, below).
6. There are a few important points that should be stressed relating to the nature of the exchange that is about to take place between the observers in the group, and the dancer/actor:
   • As always: *no audible responses from the observers*!
   • If the dancer is lucky, and she "hits the zone" as in the example above, and begins to improvise the dance with a deep Feeling of Ease and sense of infallibility, she can lose herself in the Rope/Image, but she must always remember that there are observers out there watching her and that she must radiate to these observers whatever it is that she is experiencing. "Losing oneself" in an image is wonderful if you can do it, but never at the expense of communicating with your audience! An actor who disappears down her navel in an orgy of physical introspection defeats the purpose of the exercise and, ulti- mately, is simply boring to watch.

NB

It is not a bad idea to set the standard for this exercise by talking about one of its ideal forms: an actor taking a single *coup d'oeil* from the Rope/Image and letting it take her away for twenty minutes to half an hour of endless physical inventiveness. Use this opportunity to tell the actors that one of the objects of the exercise is to make the Rope Dance—or the creative moment—last *as long as possible* before the center returns to the head, or the creative connection—the "muscle" —between the image and the body is lost.

Emphases

1. *Responding to an external image.* On the face of it, responding to a fixed image like the randomly shaped rope on the floor seems much more demanding, and hence more difficult, than responding to the open-ended abstraction of a quality of "smoothness." In fact, the opposite is the case. Once the actors understand that they have the freedom to "work" the whole rope or any small part of it, it becomes a virtually inexhaustible source of stimuli for movement. In the critique sessions at the end of each individual work, the actors should be asked what exactly they were working on, and they should be encouraged to show the group exactly which loop, which knot, or which coil inspired their movement/phrases. As we shall see very soon, an actor who can "work" a Rope/Image well (for ten to twenty minutes of totally concentrated body–image dialogue) can work *any* image.

2. *Connecting/centering.* Throughout the training there have been many opportunities to point out moments when actors are "centered"— *connected*—or not. However, this exercise—like the individually-performed *Plastiques* exercise—offers a unique opportunity to actually watch this at work with absolute clarity and almost mathematical precision.

   First, the moment before the rope is thrown should be a Zero Point, a moment of relaxed readiness with a low center. By this time in the training, the process of centering—of lowering the center before working creatively—should be visible as the actor's face and body transform from protective self-consciousness to vulnerable readiness. By now, the group should have no trouble distinguishing between a moment of connectedness and a moment of unconnectedness. This exercise, which can be stopped by the teacher/director—even with the rope in midair—to point out the level of connectedness, is an excellent vehicle for doing just that. Second, during the exercise itself, trained observers—like a group that has been doing this training for a few months—can see or sense the cycles of connectedness, particularly at moments of transition, when one stimulus from the Rope/Image ends and the actor looks to the rope for a new stimulus. It is at these moments that the center tends to "wander" up to the head and the focused energy that was at work up to that moment begins to dissipate. At these fragile moments, if the actor allows herself even a second to think about what she is doing, the chances are she won't do it and will prefer to end the exercise. If instead she gathers herself together and decides to try and get another "shot" from the rope, and begins working without thinking—that is, she looks at some point in the Rope/Image and just allows her body to respond to the shape without giving it a second's thought—at those moments you can actually "see" the center sinking down again into the abdomen as instinct takes over from intellect and the body sings.

3. *Exhausting the possibilities/expanding the creative moment.* Having come this far in the work, with all the previous training in the *Plastiques*, to mention just one of the techniques, the actors should know that in every exercise they do they have to work through repeated creativity cycles: seizing the creative moment and then managing it for as long as possible, until its potential for psychophysical "nourishment" is exhausted, and only then going on to initiate an openness for the next creative moment. In the case of the Rope Dance, the actors should be encouraged not to give up, to work against their tendency to allow their center to move to the head and stop the exercise. They should challenge themselves: How long can I keep this going while staying truly connected? What more can I take from the rope to give me another "shot?"

NB

This exercise is usually the first in the Logic of Training that can lead the actors to touch upon and radiate into the space what might be called "emotional material." If an actor is capable of surrendering herself to the many abstract images that emerge as she is working, the images will function like Rorschach blots, moving the actor into areas of emotional involvement with the associative nature of these fleeting image forms. This kind of deep searching is an important step in the training, and, like many other illuminations that may occur on the way, often appears unbidden in a particularly well-connected exercise. When it does the actors should be encouraged to explore it fearlessly. However, it should also be carefully monitored so that it does not descend into any form of realism (e.g. some kind of "narrative," with the rope as the antagonist). This is unlike Method training, in which the actual *facts* of the "emotional material" are what count; what I tell my actors is very simple: "I don't care what the source of this material is; all I care about is your ability to transform it into *art*, into something that seduces me into *my own* imagination, associations, and memories."

70. THE ROPE DANCE CYCLE

This is, in a way, a variation of the Rope Dance, and it is not, strictly speaking, a separate exercise. Nevertheless, it is brought in here as an independent exercise because it can be developed in many different ways into many different variations, and has its own slightly different *Emphases*.

Setup

Divide the group into smaller groups of three to five actors each, depending on the size of the studio space you have at your disposal. Give each group a rope, and send them to different corners of the room, leaving enough space for them to work simultaneously without intruding on each other's space. They should sit down, and one actor at a time in each group gets up to work in front of that group.

Activity

The first actor gets up, throws the rope and does the Rope Dance, as in the previous exercise. When he is finished, he leaves the rope on the floor *exactly as it is*, and a second actor gets up from that group to work the same image in a Rope Dance. When all the actors in the group have worked that Rope/Image, the cycle begins again: the first actor who originally threw the rope gets up and works the same image again, as do all the others in turn. The number of full cycles of work in each group depends on what the teacher/director's goals and time frame are at this point in the training.

Emphases

1. *Repeating ImageWork.* This means approaching an image that, to some extent, has already been explored or "solved." (Occasionally actors will talk about the Rope/Image as an "enigma" and the dance

as a way of working through to its "solution.") The actor has to prepare himself—that is, face the Rope/Image—differently; he has to "connect" differently, and find a starting point for the exercise, this time not from the virgin image created when the rope hit the floor, but applying Centering, Readiness, Zero Point, Stepping into the Unknown, to a Rope/ Image that has already been expressed in movement.

2. *Repetition.* Doing the cycle means that each actor works the same Rope/Image at least twice (depending on how many times the group works off the same rope/image), and watches it being worked many more times by the others. Nevertheless, the actors must find new stimuli, new ways of seeing the rope, new angles of vision, or new ways of working the same visual elements of the rope, but differently.

A note to this and the subsequent exercises

As I pointed out in the introduction to this section, when we move into the area of *ImageWork*, we are also moving into an area of the impalpable, where the distinctions between profoundly connected work with an image, and work that is only technically competent, are sometimes very hard to call. The observers' visceral response is really only one way of measuring the degree of "success" of a Rope Dance—or of any work on an image. If you as spectator feel yourself "seduced" by the work, drawn into the imaginative world of the dancer with nothing more to go on than a feeling, a sensation of having had your imagination fired by watching the working actor being fired by his imagination—then, generally speaking, this is a deeply connected work.

Occasionally, too, there are great differences in what the actor feels about a Rope Dance and what the observers report back to him—for better or for worse. An actor may feel absolutely wonderful about his exercise, only to be greeted by less than enthusiastic responses from the observers. The opposite may also occur— the actor may feel thoroughly dissatisfied with work he may have felt was technical and unconnected, while the observers might be unanimous in their praise, talking about how profoundly they were moved by his dance. This is an important moment, and some time should be taken to talk about it, because it has a great deal to do with (a) understanding the axiom of observation and critiques, namely that "the audience is always right," and (b) the growing body of self-knowledge that an actor acquires in the training. These moments of disparity between self-criticism and observers' evaluation are moments of enlightenment when an actor can discover his true power as a performer. An actor with a solid background in the training thus far may feel that in a given exercise he is only partially connected, or even not connected at all, and yet something profoundly resonant will still radiate unconsciously from what is, by now, a highly trained organism. This could be a first indication that some of the techniques learned on the way to this point have already been "forgotten," incorporated, or integrated, to the point where they have become second nature and appear unconsciously or involuntarily in the actor's performative expressivity. This is a power that has to be explored when it appears, so that it can be harnessed and turned into a technique that is available on demand.

From the actors' perspective, they should be able to tell you after the exercise if they felt they were working too hard at it or if they managed to get "inside" the image and work effortlessly through it with an endless stream of stimuli. In those rare cases when everything comes together and an actor does "hit the zone," there is nothing to report! The actor simply doesn't remember anything except an exhilarating sense of infallibility, a feeling of not being able to do anything wrong, a wonderful, simultaneous sense of containment and freedom.

With so many important training concepts emerging from a "simple" Rope Dance, these exercises can become a very important platform for many different aspects of the training. This is one of the reasons why the group should not be in any hurry to move on to anything else. The rope work should be repeated frequently until its basic concepts are thoroughly incorporated. This is particularly important in view of the fact that the Rope Dance and all its variations are "basic training" for the more complicated and difficult challenge coming up: working with concrete images.

71. OBJECT/IMAGE DANCE I

The move from the abstract to the concrete continues inexorably. Now we move from the virtually unlimited possibilities of the white rope, to trying to find the same kind of freedom in the specificity and limitations of a real object.

Setup

Individuals work in front of the group, then the entire group works "alone-in-a-group."

Activity

There is a certain procedure that I generally employ when introducing this exercise: I suggest to the actors that having spent some time on working with Rope/Images, there is no reason why they can't use the same technique to "dance" *anything* at all. At which point I usually take off one of my dance shoes—a fairly dilapidated brown leather number with large stitches—lay it down on the floor in front of the group, and ask someone to come up and "dance" the shoe (see Figure 34). If the work on the ropes has gone well, it takes only a second for someone to get up, glance at the shoe, and start moving with a center that is "brown, rough, low-slung, containing, and open." Once this first attempt is finished, and without a critique of any kind, I take anything else that may be handy—a water bottle, a book, a scarf, a pair of sunglasses—and put it down in front of the group, asking someone to do the same thing with this new object.

Notes

1. The Object/Image used in this exercise should be simple in form and not complicated or highly detailed. For example, working with a water bottle means relating to the fact that it is tall, transparent, "containing," and blue—but no more than that. Working with an espresso machine—just to take an extreme example—involves an object that is so intricate

Figure 34 Object/Image Dance I: Dancing the shoe.

and comprises so many different qualities that it is not easily susceptible to abstraction into a dance. To avoid this, I have occasionally limited my actors to using only objects that are similar to the three archetypal forms suggested by Rudolf Steiner and used by Michael Chekhov: stick, ball, and veil.

NB

As my colleague in the Chekhov work, Lenard Petit, says in relation to these archetypal forms, each archetype is a "family" and there can be many variations based on these three basic physical forms. An anchor chain, for example, is perhaps a distant relative, but still part of the "Veil" family, just as a toothpick can be included in the family of "Sticks." Thinking about Object/Images in this way helps (a) keep the images simple, and (b) open up a vast anthology of images.

---

2. The actors should not touch the object at any time during the exercise. It should just be there, like the rope, on the edge of the performance space, so that the actors can glance at it from time to time when their connection to the image wanes and they are looking for another "charge."

3. If during the course of the work on this image, other images are excited into the working imagination (after all, the body is moving and generating images all the time), they should be worked briefly just like the different parts of the rope. After working through them for a while, the actor should go back to the object to reorient with the "anchor image" and let it take him in a different direction.

4. Tell the actors that if at any point voice appears in their work, they should welcome it, make sure it is "connected" to the moving body, and be ready to end it if it is no longer necessary. (NB: at this point we are still talking about using only voice, not words.) Be careful, however: don't allow this possibility too early in the training of this exercise, or you will find voice taking over and being substituted for a great deal of physical commitment. One way to avoid any such takeover is to limit the actors to voice *only* when a *Plastique* appears in the work.

5. After watching someone take the plunge and work off the dance shoe, it usually takes even less time for the next person to get up and work the new image—and from here on, there are any number of possibilities:
   - Like the work with the rope, let each actor work individually on a different Object/Image in front of the group, and critique each piece of work looking for criteria of connectedness, "seductiveness" (in the sense of drawing the observers into their imagination through the

actor's involvement in his imagination), and seamlessness—shifting through a series of creative moments, emanating from the same Object/Image, without visible Zero Points in between.
- Split up into groups and work an Image/Object cycle, like the Rope-Dance Cycle: a single object "worked" by everyone.

Emphases

1. *Working a complex, physical image.* This ability opens up a vast resource for the actors—no less than *anything at all in the material world around them*—so that its development is crucial as the actors move into the more advanced exercises toward the end of the training.
2. *Responding to external stimuli.* Often when I am working on this exercise the actors get markedly skittish as they begin to respond physically to almost any thing they see—even when they are not in the studio! In a state of performance, virtually anything can set them off—and this is one of the main objects of the exercise!

NB

Note, too, that images will often continue to reverberate inside an actor even after the exercise is over. Recently, an actress I was working with finished a particularly powerful exercise with an object, and long after she sat down she kept shifting and turning and simply could not find a comfortable sitting position. Before I managed to ask her what was wrong, she blurted out plaintively, "How do I *stop* the image from moving me even after I've sat down?"

---

3. *The Necessary Voice.* Having introduced this concept in relation to the *Plastiques* to Voice (Exercise 47), this now becomes an integral part of the actor's technique as he is working in the space and an integral part of the vocabulary of evaluation. With experience, this "necessariness" is fairly clearly discernible, and you should be prepared to sidecoach an actor to stop the voice and just continue the physical work if the voice begins to lead the body or is not deeply connected to the image and emanating from the moving limbs.

NB

Having moved into *ImageWork* using real objects, a word is needed about animal images. Generally speaking I avoid doing this kind of work, even though I do realize its potential for character work and the fact that in many acting schools—such as Lecoq in Paris—working on the physicalization of animals is a major element in the early part of the training. One of the reasons for my reluctance to use animal images is that since they involve a kind of copying rather than creating, I feel they do not provoke the actor's creative imagination the way the more abstract objects do. A clear, blue water bottle can be worked as an image only through a flight of the imagination, a leap of faith "through the bafflement"—as Stephen Nachmanovitch suggests— into something that is *substantially different and exactly the same at one and the same time*. There are very few things in the work of an artist that are more fulfilling, more *fecund* than facing a paradox and finding the bizarre, outlandish, surprising, and yet perfectly under- standable solution. Hence—at least for training purposes—I believe inanimate objects should always be preferred over animals or humans of any kind.

Before we leave this exercise, here is a cautionary tale that tells us some- thing about the need for close monitoring of what I called earlier "emotional material," and about the sheer power of the imagination. More importantly, it also tells us something about the delicate line between control and lack of control that can often appear quite unexpectedly, and harmfully, in this strange and wonderful art we are dealing with.

Having reached this point in the training with one of my classes, using an early version of the Object Image exercise, I asked my actors to bring to class an object they would like to work with. One of the actors got up to work, placed a plain, quite delicate drinking glass on the floor, and began "working" this image. At some point, contrary to the rules of the exercise that stipulate no touching or using of the object during the exercise itself, she picked up the glass in her hand and, before any of us had a chance to react, she closed her fist, crushing the delicate glass in her palm, and of course began bleeding profusely from multiple cuts. And yet—and this was the most extraordinary part of this bizarre incident!—she continued working without even the slightest grimace of pain for the few seconds it took me to come to my senses and stop her. When I did, she looked at me uncomprehendingly and said, "Why did you stop me? I was just getting into it!" When I took her hand and showed her the bleeding palm, the apparent anesthesia of the *ImageWork* wore off instantly and she started screaming with pain.

In the thirty-odd years I have been teaching, this was—thank God!—a singular event; nothing in my experience has even come close to this kind of momentary loss of sanity. However, it was, in its own eerie way, one of the most extreme examples I have ever encountered of the incredible power of the imagination. And, in the same breath, it demonstrated to me how close we always are to an abuse of this power if we're not careful. Dealing as we are in this training with pure improvisation and, as a result, with the actor's deepest personal materials, care must be taken.

72. OBJECT/IMAGE DANCE II

We now complete the cycle. We started this section with qualities, worked internally as images ("soft," "sharp," "transparent," etc.), and then went on to working on gradually more concrete external stimuli such as ropes and objects as images. We now move the work back into pure imagination.

Setup

As has been the case in these advanced exercises, this one, too, is initially worked individually by each actor in front of the group. Later, this can also be worked as an "alone-in-a-group" exercise, with everyone working in the space without contact.

Activity

In this exercise, the actors must now demand an image from their imagination, and then work it physically for as long as they can hold on to it in their imagination. The actors should be coached once again to use the three Steiner "families" of images—stick, ball, and veil—to find simple images. Since these images are created in the imagination, they may be fantastic (e.g. "a cloth flower with sharp steel petals"), visually poetic ("a sharp, triangular piece of glass with a drop of blood at one corner"), or "realistic" ("a sunflower"). Whatever they are, they have to be "workable"—that is, they have to provide the actor with an enigma to explore, a fruitful stimulus for movement.

Ending this exercise involves a process similar to the one used in Centers—Radiating the Qualities (Exercise 68): the actors gradually reduce their physical work as they get themselves back into a standing position, holding on to the image and radiating it to different targets in the space—until the teacher/director ends the exercise with a soft handclap.

Notes

1. The actors should be urged not to spend too much time looking for an image. Sidecoach them: "Take the first thing that comes to mind and *move—now!* If it doesn't work, stop and choose another, *but don't think!*"
2. Here, too, the moving body will naturally excite subsidiary images—additional images excited by the movement. These should be worked—briefly—and then the focus should be returned to the original anchor image. One of the goals of this exercise is to retain a chosen image for as long as possible, so shifting from one image to another defeats the purpose.
3. Voice—but no words—can be brought in if it emanates from the moving body and is therefore "necessary."

Emphasis

Making the image last. Everything we have done in this process thus far—the enormous body of training knowledge that has been gained—has been layered-in to empower the actors in the area of acting technique set out in the beginning of the book: connecting body, voice, and the imagination into a powerful stage presence. The concept of this exercise, using an image to create a coherent performative expression and making it last as long as possible, is one of the reasons why I embarked on this entire complex of exercises, trajectories, tools, and skills in the first place.

As I understand the actor's craft, virtually everything an actor does in training, rehearsal, or performance is connected on the deepest level to the imaging function of the creative organism. Consequently, the entire complex of a training structure like this aims itself toward the understanding—and inculcation—of this single, all-encompassing technique. And here we are, at that juncture, bringing to bear everything we have learned in order to try and discover what it is we have to do to make an image that we have created in our imagination serve us powerfully over a period of time in live contact with an audience; what it is that renders this imaging function the most powerful tool we have as actors and makes it possible for us to reach out and fire the audience's imagination, touch its soul repeatedly to make communication in the theater occur, to create the *art* in theater.

73. BODYSONG

With this in mind, we move now into the next step: using images in contact with other actors and their images.

Bodysong is an exercise that I owe to one of Perter Brook's leading actors, Bruce Meyers, and it is one that has developed in my work into an excellent vehicle for moving into the transitional stage between training and rehearsal since it requires the retention of an image throughout a physical dialogue with a partner. It is also a necessary prelude to the exercise that follows it—the Image Dance.

Setup

One actor works an image, joined later by a second actor—as explained below.

Activity

One actor gets up on the floor, chooses an inner image, as in the previous exercise, and begins to move in response to that image. At least initially, there should be no use of the voice at any time during the exercise (see note 4, below).

Working on his own, the first actor responds to the image he has selected, and when he finds a *Plastique* he wants to explore, goes into the repetition. This *Plastique* is also an invitation for someone to come and join him in the work.

The person who accepts the invitation and comes onto the floor must come in "empty"—with no image of his own, drawn only by the "seduction" of the first actor's *ImageWork*.

When the second actor comes in, this becomes a jam session in movement: the first actor moves with his image and tries to respond solely from within that image to the second actor's offers, while the second actor responds in movement (as in Energy Exchange, Exercise 27) to the qualities emanating from the first actor's *ImageWork*. This Give-and-Take goes on until the "muscle" of the imagination tying them together disappears.

Notes

1. Remind the first actor to choose a simple "material" image.
2. If no one comes in on the first *Plastique*, the actor should go on working with the image until he finds another *Plastique*, and offers that as a new invitation.
3. Unlike some of the other Partner Exercises mentioned earlier, in the BodySong, physical contact is not only allowed, but unavoidable, and

the actors should be reassured that this is an integral part of the exercise. (NB: it should be pointed out that this is *not* Contact Impro, and the actors need not remain solely within the lift–pull–push weight-sharing parameters of Contact.)

4. There should be no voice!—at least not at first. If you allow voice to be added here, you make it almost impossible for the actors to remain in the abstract. The actors' natural survival techniques will lead them immediately into a kind of gibberish dialogue that will very soon deteriorate into bad text and even worse plot, to the obvious detriment of the quality of their physical expression. This is a movement–image exercise, not a verbal improv. Conceivably, this exercise can be worked up into voice, but only after a significant, nonvocal basic training.

Emphases

1. *Retaining an image with a partner.* Working with a partner involves a great deal of outward-oriented focus, as you try to see and respond to all the offers you get in response to what you are offering. This sometimes makes it difficult to retain the image strongly in your imagination as you find yourself concentrating more on your partner than on the image. This is the point of the exercise: learning how to do both.

NB

This kind of work very often raises questions among the actors about how to retain an image over a long period of time, particularly with a partner. Attempting to do so and "losing sight" of the image causes a great deal of frustration, since the actors feel inadequate—as if they can't do what you are asking them to do. The answer, as suggested to me by another colleague in the Chekhov work, Jörg Andrees, is yet another paradox: you don't always have to actually *see* the image in your mind's eye in order to move. Often it is quite enough to let the initial stimulus received from the image move you, then to keep it in "No Motion," and continue working with its resonance. From time to time—if and when you feel the initial resonance fading—the anchor-image is brought back into sharper focus, from "No Motion" in the back of the head to "Motion" in the body.

---

2. *Foot in the Air/Creative imbalance/Stepping into the Unknown.* The partner aspect of this exercise brings us back to some basics of improvisation technique. Occasionally, actors watching someone in a BodySong *Plastique* will be uncertain about entering the space, even

though the invitation from the first actor is crystal clear. They, too, should be urged not to think, but to follow the creative cycle: get up, put themselves in precarious balance by lifting one Foot in the Air and then Stepping into the Unknown—joining the actor working in the space.

74. IMAGE DANCE

This is an exercise that follows naturally from the BodySong exercise. It is also a rehearsal tool of great importance, which will be elabopated upon in detail in the chapter on the Chekhov Technique.

Setup

The entire group should spread out in the work space.

Activity

The actors are asked to choose an inner image and begin working on their own in the space, initially making no contact with each other. In this first phase of the exercise, they should not use voice. As a matter of course by now, if and when they find *Plastiques*, they are to go into the repetitions for as long as they interest them.

When the actors are deeply involved in their *ImageWork*, the teacher/director should direct them toward a partner so that they begin working in pairs, as in the BodySong exercise, except that this time *both* partners have anchor images. If you have an uneven number of actors in the group, tell them that an actor left without a partner should continue working on his/her own image until the partners are changed.

After letting the actors work through this dialogue of images for a while, tell them to separate and continue working on their own. As they do so, sidecoach them to use their time alone to regain the anchor image, to assess what they have learned about it, how they work with the image, and what the image does to—and for—them. After a short while, the teacher/director should create new pairs for this work. This switching of partners is done three times. The image, of course, remains the same throughout.

After working alone, working with a partner, then working alone again—three times—the exercise should be wound down in the same way as in Object/Image Dance II (Exercise 72)—the actors working alone again, reducing the physical movement until all that remains is the standing, unmoving body, radiating the image to different points in the room. A soft handclap ends the work.

At the end of this cycle, there should be a critique session, which is no less important than the actual exercise itself. Ask each one of the actors in turn to talk about the qualities they *received* from the partners they worked with—not about *their* own qualities or images. This critique session is based on the same principles used throughout the training for evaluating a colleague's work, and has a number of important rules that should be followed:

1. The most important part of this critique session is for each actor to *listen* to what his partners received from him without reacting in any way—no smiles or grins, no nodding of heads in agreement, just listening. There should also be no discussion at this point. Every actor in turn gives his impressions of the qualities he received from the three people he worked with.
2. During this part of the critique session, the actors should not reveal the images they were working on. The personal images will be made known at the end of the critique session. This is very important because it gives each actor the possibility of hearing from three different partners what he or she was radiating, before the partners know what image the actor was working with.
3. *The descriptions of each encounter should refer only to the qualities that were radiated and not to psychology.* Just as in all the *ImageWork* exercises thus far, actors working images are a *what*, not a *who*; therefore there is no point in discussing "character traits." They can say that what they got from a partner was "warm" and "flowing" and "flexible," or "sharp" and "hard" and "jerky," but not "friendly," "lovable," "aggressive," or "threatening." At this late point in the training we are still—as always—holding on to the abstract for dear life! Talking about psychological characteristics limits the dialogue of images, funnels it into predetermined plot patterns or character molds that limit their improvisational freedom and their creativity.
4. At the end of the critique session, each of the actors should mention the images they were working on—and surprises usually abound!

The importance of this session lies in the feedback that each actor gets from different partners, which gives them a good idea of what it was they radiated—or if they were radiating anything clearly at all—while working on that particular image. It is a highly illuminating session, and one that can either be very rewarding (hearing from their partners an exact definition of the qualities they hoped they were radiating) or, surprising (hearing from their partners that they got something entirely different, or that what they were sending out was unclear, even though they felt it was crystal clear).

Working this exercise repeatedly in training, the actors begin to sharpen their self-awareness in the area of radiation—that is, what it is they are *radiating* at any given moment on the stage. (NB: this is a vital step toward their understanding of the basic, all-important imaging function of the creative actor in every aspect of his professional work.)

NB

Voice—but still no words—can be used in the partner work as an option. It should not be brought in as a matter of course, nor should it be used in every encounter—unless it emerges *necessarily* from the physical expression. Once actors begin to distinguish between those moments when voice is necessary—emanating unavoidably from the body—and moments when it is unnecessary—when the body is *not* making audible sound—they will have learned an important lesson about the connections between the body and the voice, the body and the imagination, and the voice and the imagination.

Notes

1. It's generally a good idea for the teacher/director to make up the pairs on the floor as this exercise progresses. This way, duplications of partnerships can be avoided, and the teacher/director can also make interesting combinations on the spot, based on specific work being done by certain actors.
2. Stay on your guard in the critique session, and make sure the remarks relate to qualities only, and not to psychology.
3. The teacher/director should point out the fact that this exercise is just one step away from work on character—a step that the training does not take but it does prepare them, as we shall see, for detailed work on character in the Chehkhov Technique.

MOVING INTO TEXT—AT LAST!

The time is ripe, after months of preparing the instrument through all the trajectories of the Logic of Training, to deal with one final element of training—*language*, the final step in "instrument training," before the actor moves into text, character, and scene.

Actors undergoing all the trajectories of the Logic of Training have, hopefully, learned a great deal about the Creative Moment, Creative Freedom, Improvisation Technique, *ImageWork*, and Connectedness, and how all these feed into—or are fueled by—Repetition. Through this process they have hopefully also acquired "habits of creativity" that will allow them to now approach language freely and creatively, without allowing its built-in patterns of meaning to overtake and suppress their other creative processes.

Language is a multileveled sign system with an extensive range of metaphoric, emotional, psychological, and historical baggage firmly attached. Our own speech patterns and verbal associations are imprinted onto our mental circuits from childhood, and as a result turn into habits that are extremely difficult to break. The training I am proposing here demands the continuous application of creative freedom in *every* area of performative expression, and language is no exception. The idea is to find ways of breaking down our habits of language by breaking down words into their component parts—syllables and phonemes—so that we can use language not only as a lexical tool that addresses meaning, but also as a highly evocative *sound tool* that affects our imagination and sensibilities through its many different aural effects, and—as Rudolph Steiner suggests in *Speech and Drama*—through the profound connections between particular vowel or consonant sounds and our emotions. I have found that deconstructing language in this way provides actors with a wealth of hidden possibilities for their associative imagination, and helps them acquire another important professional habit: listening to words *for their sounds*, and thus turning language into a highly charged creative tool, liberated from the strictures of meaning or, conversely, imbuing the surface meanings of words with a world of aural associations. The following exercises suggest some ways of acquiring this important habit.

NB

This next exercise (Exercise 75) should be preceded by "basic training" in the technique, beginning with an explanation about the nature of the "phoneme"—the smallest unit of vocalization. For example, the word "dance" is made up of the following phonemes: *deh – ah – nn–ss*. After that, preliminary training for this exercise should include training using either single words or short lines of text rather than the complete poem. Read the description of the entire exercise and then you can make your own decision concerning the extent of the basic training you would like to do based on your acquaintance with the group you are working with.

---

75. MOVING POETRY

For the purposes of this exercise I have found that the best vehicle is the form of the Japanese *haiku*, although conceivably it could be done with any short, complete poem. The reason for this is that the exercise works best with a short poem that has a single powerful image.

The actors are asked to choose a *haiku* that intrigues them and then to analyze the chosen poem. This is homework for which no professional training in literature is required; it is simply a question of responding to verbal imagery and resonances, because what they are told to look for is a totally subjective understanding of the poem's central quality. Time should be given in the workshop sessions to talk about this analysis, and help each actor define these qualities. This is, of course, a highly subjective process, and *there can be no right or wrong*.

The actors are now asked to choose an image they think will give them this same quality in a movement exercise. Discovering these images involves "interrogating" the quality as in this example:

What central quality did you find in the poem?
—Melancholy.

When you think of "melancholy" what's the first thing that comes to your mind?
—A faded photograph.

Zoom in.
—The corner of the photograph is creased and brown.

Clear the slate. Think again: "Melancholy" . . .
—An empty house.

Zoom in.
—Dust balls on the floor.

The actor now has two potential images to work with: the creased, brown, dogeared corner of a photograph, or a lonely dust ball on an empty floor.

Activity

Since this is a complex and multistaged exercise, rather than embarking on a lengthy description prior to the exercise itself, the best way to describe it is to get an actor to go into the space and lead him or her through the exercise from beginning to end, as follows:

Step 1:   The actor getting up to work is asked to stand up and recite the poem, simply and clearly. He is then asked to begin "working" the chosen image in movement, without voice, as the group has been trained to do with internal images. If *Plastiques* appear, they should be worked through.

NB

a. It is extremely important to remind the actors at this point about elements of the Creative WarmUp such as Forms, Form/Repeat (Body Memory), themes and variations, and physical awareness, since they will have to bring all of these to bear on the subsequent steps of the exercise.
b. It's very much a matter of choice if the teacher/director wants the working actor to tell the group before he begins what his image is for the poem. There are advantages to hearing it first and having it as a reference during the exercise, and other advantages to letting the actor work and giving him a critique of his work, and only afterward hearing from him what image he was working on.

When you as teacher/director feel that the actor is truly *connected*, moving easily and inventively in the space, driven by his image, say "Voice!"—at which point the actor should "open the tap" of his vocal apparatus, and allow the moving body to produce its sound, but no words yet. This should be a *Necessary Voice*, deeply connected to that body in that movement pattern. The actor can, if necessary, spend some time adjusting the voice until it "fits"—but without stopping the "dance" at any point.

When body and voice are connected and the physical and vocal work is flowing in a creative dialogue with the image, the teacher/director says "Text!"—at which point the actor should begin saying the words of the poem. However—the text of the poem is to be used as follows:

- The actor must say the words of the text in the order in which they are written in the poem, but the words of the poem *do not have to be intelligible*. He concentrates on the phoneme structure of the poem, playing with the individual phonemes as long as he likes, modulating, lingering, repeating and so on, but bearing in mind all the time that he must move forward through the words of the poem.
- Those phonemes and syllables that emerge are all stimuli to the body and the imagination, and the actor should respond to these resonances, in movement, voice, and text, exploring whatever they excite into his imagination at any one time during the exercise.

Step 2:   When the actor has gone through all the words of the poem, and the image/dance of the poem comes to an end (these two are not necessarily concurrent: occasionally the "dance" will continue long after the words are finished), the actor is asked to stand in front of the seated group, and repeat the poem and the dance, but more or less in place, in a highly reduced form. By applying Body Memory and running through his mind's eye the flow of images evoked by his movements and vocalizations, he now produces a still distorted but nevertheless more intelligible version of the *haiku* image/dance. This is often an exaggerated, even grotesque, rendition of the poem, which is okay, as long as the words are now more intelligible.

Step 3:   The final stage of the exercise involves saying the poem once again, reducing the vocal and physical expression even further to a now "normal," everyday recitation but retaining the results of the first two stages of the exercise as a subterranean, but strongly radiating, resonance. The desired effect is a layered rendition of the poem, through a powerfully connected expressive organism.

Notes

1. This is an extremely difficult exercise, and should not be attempted before all the other steps leading up to this point in the training have been thoroughly exercised and incorporated into the actors' technique.
2. Sidecoaching is very important here, and it begins with the teacher/director's choice of the moment to move the performer from his purely

physical work into the physical/vocal work ("Voice!") and then to move him into verbal work ("Text!"). These commands have to be given only when you feel that the actor is truly connected to his imagination, and then only when his voice, body, and imagination are one. Active side-coaching is very useful here, and the teacher/director should be ready to go into the performance space, get behind the working actor and help him as he is engaged in the process. The sidecoaching might urge an actor to repeat a certain phoneme or syllable, expand a physical movement, or readjust the voice to connect it more deeply to the body, or else it might suggest to the actor that a certain moment is very powerful and resonant, and that he should pay attention to it in order to remember it.

Emphases

1. *Working an image.* This is as before, but with the added difficulty of doing so with all the "layers" of connecting body, voice, and the imagination, and using words. In the final phase of the exercise there is also the complex task of working all the images that came up during the moving part of the exercise—without moving.
2. *Breaking down language.* This is one of the most important aspects of this exercise: breaking down language habits and searching behind the pedestrian, "daily" understanding of words for their sound value as stimuli for the "extradaily" imagination.
3. *Remembering found material.* This skirts very close to rehearsal techniques, which are indeed just around the corner at this stage, so it is a legitimate emphasis at this point. Basically, this exercise involves the kind of repetition that is used in rehearsals: an actor works through a moment of the play or a moment in the life of the character he is about to portray, and when he finds something useful in the rehearsal process, either the director jumps up and shouts "Yes! Keep it!" or the actor does. In either case the actor now has to commit to physical and verbal memory a momentary flash of inspiration. In Moving Poetry, the actor working in the space is working through an almost endless stream of invented, created moments, all of which he will be asked to "reactivate" in the second presentation of the poem. So, the Catechism has to be employed once again: How do I do that? What do I have to do to remember the voice, the imagery, and the physical metaphors that occur in these totally improvised moments and fractured language while at the same time retaining the creative freedom of the exercise?

76. POEM CHOREOGRAPHY

This exercise is an optional addition to this sequence, but one that I have found to be extremely powerful and interesting—and a first step into the many elements of performance that lie just beyond this initial period of training: incorporating found material, working through improvisations to a fixed form, making choices, and the ever-present paradox of first-time repetition.

Setup and activity

There is no one way of setting this one up, and teacher/directors can take it in almost any direction.

Often, having taken a group through the Moving Poetry exercise, I will then take a week or so—depending on the size of the group—and work with them individually to try to develop a sequence of movements derived from the *ImageWork* on the poem. Using this reduced set of movement/phrases or *Plastiques*, the actors then connect them into a choreography that is the best possible expression of the poem in words and movement. This way of creating a finished piece of performance is very similar to Eugenio Barba's concept of "montage"—generating a great deal of material through improvisation, then "cutting and pasting" different parts of that material into a sequence that creates a powerful, effective performance. This new organization of the improvisational material is often intuitive, based on a sense—no more—of which physical image might work best with which particular word or set of words in the poem. (NB: a camcorder or a detailed written record of the original is indispensable here.)

Creating the montage requires the actors to make some hard choices, and select only the most effective physical images, movement/phrases, or *Plastiques* that emerged in their original work on the poem. A poem that they managed to open up into fifteen, twenty, or even forty-five minutes of extensive physical and vocal work, resulting in many different movement/phrases, *Plastiques*, and "phoneme-gestures" now has to be distilled into a two- or two-and-a-half-minute piece, with perhaps no more than five or six basic movement components—and, of course, the entire text of the poem.

In this part of the work I try not to be a director, but only a facilitator, leading the actors to their *own* choices and providing them with an outside eye and a critique. The result of this collaboration is a brief choreography of the poem, which the actors must now rehearse until the teacher/director feels it can be performed before an audience. (NB: in a two-year course with a group of actors, I will use this exercise as a showcase for the end of the first year of training.) When a "moving poem" like this is done well, it produces a highly unusual and often mesmerizing physical, vocal, and verbal expression of the poem.

The presentation of these pieces of choreography before an audience involves four stages that illuminate the process:

1. The poem is "recited," simply, without any special emphasis.
2. The rehearsed poem-choreography is performed.
3. The actor speaks the poem again standing up and facing the audience, but he is allowed to add to the vocal rendering of the words much of the "exaggerations" of the choreographed version.
4. In the fourth and last phase the actor is asked to make some even more severe choices and compress the entire physical, imaginative, and emotional content that he discovered in the poem into a still, virtually nonmoving "rendition" in a "normal" voice. The attempt, of course, is to try and imbue the "normal voice" rendition and virtually still body with those subterranean currents of radiation that will allow all the highly charged material from the earlier breakdown of the material to be there as a palpable part of the actor's presence even if they are not overtly visible.

77. THE UNMOVING ACTOR MOVING AN AUDIENCE

There is only one logical conclusion to this Logic of Training, and it takes its place as the last exercise in the process.

Using the platform of the Moving Poetry exercise, and having gone through the freedom of the *ImageWork* improvisation and repeated the poem twice using all the physical and imaginative resonances without moving, the actor is now asked to perform the entire poem, with all its levels of physicality, imagery, and verbal metaphors—*without moving a muscle or saying a word*. Only a few of the actors in any group will be able to do this immediately—or ever—but those that do will close the cycle we began at the beginning of the book: they will be touching upon that paradigmatic moment of the unmoving actor moving an audience when the many layers of theater—*presence*, *form*, *resistance*, *paradox*, *enigma*, and *contact*—all coexist simultaneously in a vibrantly *connected* instant of shared imagination in the performance space.

CLOSING THE TRAINING CYCLE

Recently I heard of a famous sculptor who was found one day weeping at the foot of his greatest creation. Taken aback by this outburst, a worried friend asked him, "Why are you crying over this statue? It's perfect!" To which the sculptor replied, "That's why I'm crying—there's nothing more I can do with it!"

The Logic of Training proposed in this book is *never* going to cause me to cry over its perfection, for the simple reason that its development can never truly end, and therefore perfection is simply not in the cards. The concepts that lie at the heart of this form of training are endlessly variable, and if I thought for one moment that they have an *end* of any kind, or felt that in my own work I am merely regurgitating what I have already digested over and over again rather than constantly learning and relearning the very techniques that I am teaching—I would retire to the Judean Desert and spend the rest of my life in a dark cave, contemplating the salty wastes of the Dead Sea in the distance.

Nevertheless, this cycle of the training can be momentarily brought, if not to an end then to a halt here in order to move into the next step: the practical application of these techniques to the basics of theatrical performance: transformation/ character, text, scene-work, rehearsal techniques, and performance. Given the body–voice–imagination basis of this training, *ImageWork Training* leads naturally into the form of theater training elaborated in Chapter 6, A Marriage of True Minds: *ImageWork Training* and the Chekhov Technique. The connection of this form of training to the Chekhov Technique is natural, but it is my belief that the models of behavior included in this training are a preparation of the actor's creative instrument, with all its tools and skills, so that he or she can bring a finely-tuned, profoundly *connected*, professional sensibility to any form of theatrical expression.

Training like this is a long journey, and it is, I believe, the most rewarding journey possible, because it comes so close to the very core of what constitutes the creative moment in the actor's art. In working with a group of actors through these exercises, we are dealing almost exclusively with the sources of the actor's creativity: *Improvisation/Creativity*, *Connectedness* and *Repetition*, as they are manifested in the actor's *body*, *voice*, and *imagination* in all their myriad connections, and radiated to the audience. I can think of nothing in this world that excites me more than watching a moment of pristine creation as it unfolds in the real time and space of the performed event—*never to reappear in exactly the same form ever again*! This is the beautiful irony of our boundless fascination with theater both as spectators and as performers—that no matter how many times a performance occurs, it will always be that profoundly satisfying paradox: a first-time repetition.

Having the repeated opportunity of taking this journey so close to the sources of theatrical creation is the guiding joy of my professional life. All I can hope for is that something of my own fascination with these processes has come through in all the sections of this Logic of Training, and that it will help you come as close as you can to this "signaling through the flames" that is the creative moment in theater.

AFTERWORD TO THE FIRST EDITION

Any theory is a rendering into form of what has been learned intuitively or experientially, and tested in practice in some kind of controlled environment. But once again the Pirandellian paradox raises its head: as soon as I complete this book, a process that has been evolving for thirty years will be delimited by the front and back covers of the printed volume. I will have taken everything I know and cut it off from its organic source, removed it from the flow of time, and in so doing—the brilliant Italian would tell us—rendered it "dead." What a relief! Then I will be free to go on delving into this mystery that has been the absorbing passion of my life, cast aside everything that I have written here, and start the journey all over again!

—*Tel Aviv, August 2001*

CHAPTER 5

A Marriage of True Minds

Imagework Training and the Chekhov Technique

When the late Mala Powers told me, after participating in my 1993 workshop at ATHE, that what I was *doing* was Chekhov, I was genuinely intrigued and responded by saying, "You have to explain this to me." She replied by inviting me to the workshop she was giving the following day on the Chekhov Technique and promised me that I would see the light. And indeed, that is exactly what happened: watching her demonstration the following day, I realized that for years, somewhere in the subconscious of my work, there had been a powerful underground current flowing inside me that connected me to Michael Chekhov like the "muscle" I describe in the Mirror Exercises above. From just an intriguing name I heard in my distant past as a student at Tel Aviv University, "Mischa" suddenly became my retroactive mentor, a Master and a colleague, and the techniques he developed—the natural continuation of *ImageWork Training* into character, text, rehearsal, and performance.

This then, is my tribute to this belated spiritual/professional connection: a detailed account of the profound affinities between *ImageWork Training* and the work of Michael Chekhov, based on the training I have developed that is aimed at preparing the actor's instrument to take the fullest advantage of the riches Chekhov bequeathed to us.

The Chekhov Technique—Parallels

Before going into the specifics of the ways in which the instrument-training of *ImageWork* prepares the ground for the Chekhov Technique, it is important to point out the elements common to both. Most of these are seminal, multileveled correspondences which, in practice, overlap. There are four areas where the parallels are very clear:

1. improvisation/creativity
2. body/imagination
3. *ImageWork*
4. the Psychological Gesture.

Improvisation/creativity

In Exercise 12 of *On the Technique of Acting*, Chekhov gives an example of how the actor can develop what he refers to as the "Creative Individuality" by repeating a simple gesture "like cleaning a room, finding a lost article, setting the table," and trying to find a new way to do it each time. He then goes on to explain the benefits of this exercise:

> By doing this exercise you will develop your originality and ingenuity, and with them you will gradually awaken the courage of your individual approach to all that you do on the stage. As a result, you will later on be able to improvise on the stage quite freely at all times. This means that you will always find new, individual ways to fulfill old business, remaining within the frame given by the director. *You will discover that the real beauty of our art, if based on the activity of the Creative Individuality, is constant improvisation.*
>
> (2000, 19, emphasis mine)

This clear link between the creative individuality and improvisation is directly connected to the improvisation/creativity tandem that lies at the basis of *ImageWork Training*, and is a focal point for the connections between the two techniques.

Body/imagination

As we have seen, *ImageWork Training* is based almost entirely on the *natural* connection between the body and the imagination of the actor in the performance space. This is a fertile meeting ground of the two techniques, and consequently it will figure prominently in the following sections on the uses of *ImageWork Training* throughout the work on the elements of the Chekhov Technique.

ImageWork

This area of acting training is perhaps the most "muscular" connection between *ImageWork* and the Chekhov Technique; no less than the actual embodiment of the underground current that connects the two. On the one hand, there is hardly a single element of the Technique that is not related to the imaging function of the actor's creative individuality. On the other hand, the ultimate goal of the whole cycle of *ImageWork Training* is to inculcate in actors the ability to access and use the creative imagination as an on-tap technique in training, rehearsal, and performance.

There is, however, one major difference which is important to note. When Chekhov refers to "the image" he generally does so in relation to a character. What he suggests is that the best way, indeed, the virtually *unavoidable* way, for an actor to begin work on a character is through imagining what the character looks like and translating that image into the body. In *ImageWork Training*, "image" refers rather to highly specific object/images, real and imaginary, and the ways they can be used to create specific resonances. How these two related concepts dovetail will be part of the succeeding sections.

The Psychological Gesture

All the great innovators in the field of acting training in twentieth-century Western theater—Stanislavsky and Strasberg, Brecht, Meyerhold, Meisner—are each automatically connected in our professional memories with one principal exercise for which they are best known: Emotional Memory, Biomechanics, the so-called "Alienation Effect," and the Repetition Exercise, respectively. Chekhov is no exception: the Chekhov Technique is primarily known for the Psychological Gesture or PG. The three strands of the training mentioned above—*improvisation/ creativity*, *body/imagination*, and *ImageWork*—all come together into a compact weave in the Psychological Gesture, since it contains it all: from the intuitive nature of its discovery, through its physicality and on into its profound psychophysical effect on the actor throughout the rehearsal process and in performance.

While it does share a centrality with the main exercises of the other techniques mentioned above, it seems to me that the Psychological Gesture, like the entire Chekhov Technique, has a unique advantage over the other training systems since it is based entirely on the *natural* psychophysical processes that occur when the actor crosses the threshold into the work space. Many of the other acting techniques require a fair measure of difficulty, if not downright suffering (or "torture," as Chekhov described it to his students in Hollywood). Method-trained actors, for example, who are used to a great deal of such "torture," are often baffled and downright suspicious when they are exposed to the Chekhov Technique for the first time because they find it so "easy"! As I understand it, this ease is a direct result of the fact that the main bases of the technique—the imaging function of our brain and the body/imagination symbiosis—are an integral, absolutely *natural* part of the creative process in the performing arts, and as such have to be *revealed* and then trained joyfully, rather than *acquired* with hard work and suffering. It is not surprising in this respect to find so much of Chekhov's writings imbued with a seductive, often naïve, but nonetheless wonderful, sense of beauty and ease.

NB

There is another reason for the ease and naturalness of Chekhov's training techniques which is worth noting: for the most part he developed his ideas for training actors in very much the same way that Freud developed his basic concepts of psychoanalysis—through self-analysis. A enormously talented actor with an inbred instinct for pedagogy, he analyzed his own creative processes, gave them names—Imaginary Body, Centers, Atmospheres, Image and so on— and then developed the training tools to turn these processes into a technique.

Training as rehearsal

From the point where a cycle of pure training comes to a temporary end (training should never actually *end*) there is a chasm to be crossed: the move from training to performance; the application of all the sophisticated techniques learned during a period of training to the creation of a theatrical persona and its communication to an audience in the real time of performance. This is often a difficult leap that many training disciplines—and actors after completing an initial training—find hard to make. The reason for this is that the sheer excitement of the creative improvisation that lies at the heart of most training disciplines is both exhilarating and seductive, and actors and acting trainers are often loathe to leave it behind.

However, the "underground current" connecting *ImageWork Training* and the Chekhov Technique, makes this move from the completion of the training cycle into work on character in the Chekhov Technique a seamless transition. Primed with the results of the training, with finely-tuned physical awareness, expanded physical expression, a solid grounding in the body–voice–imagination symbiosis and the practical use of imagery, in short, a thorough "pre-Chekhov" training, the actors can move effortlessly and with no less excitement into work on character using major elements of the Chekhov Technique. What is more, in the training format suggested below, the actors begin every rehearsal or training session with a full work-through of the WarmUp Sequences, and thus continue to develop their physical expression, their sense of Form and the Whole, and the body/imagination connections. Finally, since the actors are now working on specific characters, either for training purposes or for a production, these characters are sitting there in

No Motion in the back of their heads, or in their bodies, all the time, so that *everything* they do, including all the elements of the warm up, becomes part of the process of creating the character. This, among other things, is the meaning of the heading "Training as Rehearsal."

NB

Over the years I have had many discussions with my colleagues in the Chekhov work about the concept of "pre-Chekhov." Some purists insist that the Chekhov Technique is so all inclusive that there can be no such thing as "pre-Chekhov" training—it's all there in his writings. However, since the early 1990s when the renewed international interest in the Chekhov Technique began, and particularly since the establishment of the Michael Chekhov Association (MICHA, in 1999), the Technique itself and the methods used to train it have grown immensely. Through cross-fertilization, mutual influences, and organic growth, virtually every one of the master teachers has added his or her own ways of approaching the training of the Chekhov Technique, thus creating a large body of "pre-Chekhov" exercises, all of which are tied umbilically to the source of the work. It is perhaps a tribute to Michael Chekhov himself that his understanding of the art of the actor has spawned so many developments within the main precepts of his Technique. It is in this sense that *ImageWork* belongs to a rapidly growing body of exercises aimed at facilitating the learning and application of the Chekhov Technique—in a word: pre-Chekhov training.

A disclaimer before the fact

Since the turn of the new century, many new books have appeared about Michael Chekhov and his technique of acting training (see the Bibliography). Given this wealth of new material, it is important to note before we begin that what I describe is not a *complete* guide to the Chekhov Technique. What follows here is, rather, a very personal take on the way I train and use three of the most important elements of the Technique, which I have found to be the clearest natural continuation of *ImageWork Training* into character work, and as such have become a permanent part of my training and rehearsal techniques. For a more comprehensive elaboration of the Chekhov Technique, have a look at the Chekhov section in the Bibliography.

The training

This section is based on the assumption that the actors embarking on this journey into the Chekhov Technique have completed and incorporated the full cycle of *ImageWork Training*, and that they continue to fine-tune their training by beginning each workshop session, class, or rehearsal with a condensed, half-hour version of the WarmUp Sequence. Generally speaking, when I am working on a production, this includes:

Crossing the Threshold

NameBalls

Sticks (all the variations)

Staccato/Legato

The Walking Exercises (varied according to personal choice or need)

The Creative WarmUp (all the elements reduced to fifteen minutes)

Each of the techniques described below is given as a "class" with a clearly defined structure and format. The trajectory of these classes follows what I believe to be a graduated move into three basic elements of the Chekhov Technique that I use with my actors for the creation of characters: the *Imaginary Body*, *Centers*, and the *Psychological Gesture*.

A few procedural notes before we begin:

1. All these elements of the Chekhov Technique function on the basis of a funda-
    mental premise: *a character is nothing but words on a page*. In other words,
    assuming that the play is well-written and the characters are crafted in a
    psychologically sound manner, what is presented to the audience is not the
    character's psychology, but the *actor's incorporation of that fictional psychology
    into his own*. The character has no dreams, fantasies, or memories—or body
    for that matter; only the actor does, therefore what an actor needs to do is to
    go into the text, take out an element—as we shall see, an Imaginary Body, a
    Center, or a super-objective leading to a Psychological Gesture—then put the
    book away and look for correspondences to this textual evidence within
    himself, in other words, the sensation and/or feeling that that activity arouses
    in him, and the images that are excited up into his mind's eye. This is the
    essence of that central quality of transformation that is the core of acting: what
    the actor communicates to the audience is his reworking of the play's text for
    his character through the filter of his psyche, his dreams, his fantasies, his
    memories.
2. Each of the character-developing techniques elaborated here are possibilities

that are explored *individually* early on in the rehearsal process. They do not have to be used in any set order nor do they have any necessary mutual connection—except for the fact that they relate to the work on the same character. There is also no absolute necessity to use all of them all the time; the decision about which to apply is always a matter of expedience: the choice depends on the play, the directorial concept, and the actor(s) in question. What is more, a technique that works for an actor for the creation of one character may not work for her in another production for another character. There is only one golden rule to follow: if it works, use it; if it doesn't—throw it out!

3. The framework for these classes is a workshop, although rehearsal procedures will be referred to as a matter of course. What is more, these classes are an indication of subject matter, not a time frame. The actual time spent on each one depends, naturally, on the size of the group, the level of their training, the depth to which the teacher/director wants to go with his actors, and the tasks at hand in a given production.

The classes

Once the training moves into the Chekhov Technique the work is predicated on the idea that from the outset, *everything* the actors do in the training is connected, consciously or unconsciously, to the characters they are working on and to the play at hand. Therefore, the actors should be reminded to have diaries readily available at the edge of the work space (see the note about diaries in Chapter 3 under the heading "Fundamentals" on pages 22–23). They should be reminded that from the moment they enter the work space, they are free to go to them at any time (barring, of course, moments when other actors are doing individual work in the space), and write down anything they may have discovered and need to remember. Over a period of time, and with some encouragement from the teacher/director, the actors learn how to leave the work space to write something down without any break in their concentration. Later on, as we shall see, a technique is introduced to help make these transitions in and out of the work smooth, unobtrusive, and highly effective. Finally, when these raw insights are revisited later in the process, they often provide a wealth of temporarily forgotten or "submerged" material for further explorations of the character.

Class 1—The Imaginary Body

Premise

Whenever we read a book or a play our imagination supplies us with all the "visuals": detailed images of the characters that play out their story in our mind's eye. This, as far as Chekhov is concerned, is primal material—the intuitive, most profound and fruitful way of entering into the process of creating a character. This "imaginary body" of the character we are working on—even if it appears outlandishly different from our own—is the key to our creative transformation. No matter what we do while working on the character in rehearsals, the image of this "body" will remain embedded in our imagination as the virtual existence of the character we are about to portray, and everything else we do while working on the character will somehow partake of this primal or archetypal image.

Aim

To discover the image of the character, and refine it by acquiring as much information as possible about it, and then to "inhabit" that body in order to discover how you behave and feel inside that body, and to use this material as the basis for developing a character. As Chekhov points out at the very opening of his recorded master class, *On Theater and the Art of Acting*, transformation is the heart of the actor's process. Therefore, if we can imagine the character's physical appearance and get "inside" that body as we imagine it, we can begin to find our way toward a powerful transformation.

Procedure: Part one—Training

Reminder: A brief WarmUp Sequence should precede every rehearsal or class.

Step 1: To begin work on the Imaginary Body, the teacher/director should take the actors back to the Qualities and Centers exercise in Chapter 4 (Exercise 66), and sidecoach them through the exercise once again: abstract movement in response to a number of different qualities for their center, such as "thin," "round," "angular," "fragile." After a while, they should be sidecoached to begin paying attention not only to the physical aspect of their work, but also to the sensations that are aroused by each quality. The questions that should be posed here are, for example, "What do you *feel like* when your body is moving with the quality of 'angularity,' or the quality of 'softness'?"

NB

The body/imagination symbiosis is such a natural psychophysical phenomenon that it is an unavoidable part of any work an actor does in the work space. However, once we move out of the training and

into work on character, the body/imagination tandem generates something else which up until now we have kept mostly at bay: Chekhov's
"movement to emotion" sequence. Basically it goes like this: movement arouses images; images arouse sensations; sensations arouse
feelings; feelings lead to emotion. In this section of the training—work
on character—this sensation–feeling–emotion aspect of the body/
imagination connection must be brought into full consciousness, in
order to create what I refer to as an "emotional array"—as opposed to
a clearly-defined emotion.

Step 2:   Moving along the abstract-to-concrete trajectory from the training, we
now leave the generic, totally abstract qualities of the centers and move into more
concrete, physical details. The actors should now be given specific *physical* qualities such as "flabby," "wiry," "pale," and told to take them on gradually, beginning, say, from a hand, or head, or the legs, and gradually working the quality into
the entire body. Throughout the exercise, even in its initial stages, the actors
should ask themselves: "What does it feel like to move with a flabby (—wiry, pale,
etc.) body?" Once the actors have "acquired" the given physical quality, they are
now told to begin moving in the space, beginning from a simple walk, and then
performing simple everyday actions— sitting down, opening a window, combing
one's hair, and so on—as a way of checking the consistency of their new body in
different physical situations. In other words, they now begin moving and
performing actions from within a wholly imaginary body, which may be totally
different from their own; one that they have "put on" over their own.

Notes

1. While some visible physical transformations will take place, they are not absolutely necessary for this exercise to be effective. In order to move in a "tall"
   body, you do not have to get up on tiptoes; in order to move in a "small" body,
   you do not have to scrunch down or walk on your knees; in order to walk with a
   "flabby" body, it is not necessary to flop around the space like a jellyfish.
   Simply *imagine* your body as having these physical attributes and then, just as
   in the Qualities and Centers exercise (Exercise 66, p. 211) radiate this "flabbiness" wherever you move in the space. Create the body through the sheer
   power of your imagination and radiate it outward.
2. Be careful of clichés—both psychological and physical. Thin people are not all
   lithe, supple and quick moving, nor are they all angular and bony; fat people
   don't all lumber—some of them are often extraordinarily graceful. There is only
   one rule of thumb here—truthfulness. See the image of the character; take
   your time to incorporate it, and don't let intellectual preconceptions about these

physical types influence your work. Let the image in your body lead you and allow it to surprise you. With lessons in "remaining in the abstract" from *ImageWork* firmly embedded in the work, concentrate only on the physicality and let your body—not your mind—produce the sensations/feelings/emotions. This involves using what Chekhov refers to in his chapter on Imagination and Concentration in *On the Technique* as the "Sense of Truth" (1991, 6–7).

3. Using the Actor's Catechism, the actors should ask themselves as they are inhabiting each of these bodies, What does it feel like to be inside this body? How do I feel in it? What sensations does moving with this body arouse in me?

Step 3: In exercise 1 in *On the Technique of Acting*, Chekhov suggests looking at a piece of classical sculpture and trying, through observation and careful study, to "penetrate deeply into the architectural form and to experience it" (1991, 7). In this step of the work on the Imaginary Body, the actors should be told to undertake a similar exercise with sculptures, paintings, and photographs: look at the portrayed body, take on its physical characteristics—once again, without necessarily making any overt physical adjustments—and then try to find out what it feels like to live inside this body. The sidecoaching here is: "How do you walk?" "How do you run?" "How do you sit down in a chair?" And, in all of those experiments— "What does it feel like to do all those things with that kind of body? What sensations are aroused?"

Procedure: Part two—Character work

Step 1—Finding the body: Prior to this class, the actors should be asked to choose a character from a well-known play, read the entire play and write down their impressions of the character—any impressions at all—as they are reading. After working through the preparatory training for this exercise, the actors should be told to return to the play and read it again, this time paying special attention to the physicality of their chosen character as it appears to them in their imagination, and once again to write down their discoveries. This stage of the work on the Imaginary Body I often refer to as a kind of "séance": the actors are told not only conjure up the figure of their character in their imagination, but also to "guide" their imagination, using the intervention techniques learned in the early *ImageWork* exercises in Chapter 4 (Sound Pictures, Distant Analogies, and Random Talk, Exercises 56–60), and "ask" the character to do things for them, to move, run, take a chair and sit down, open a purse, lift up a window, and so on. Watching their character move and behave like that in their imagination provides the actors with a greatly expanded knowledge of their conception of the character, which they should note down for future reference.

NB

The use of the term "séance" comes from the nature of the activity this exercise involves: bringing your character up onto the screen of your imagination and then watching her and communicating with her in order to learn everything you can about her. Among the more bizarre experiments that Chekhov tried out in the private studio he opened in Moscow in the 1920s were mystical séances he held with his students, in an attempt to conjure up famous characters such as Hamlet, Medea, and so on in order to learn more about them. These experiments got Chekhov into serious trouble with the authorities for "excessive spiritualism," and caused his students to rebel against him, but they also failed miserably on a practical level. Assuming for a moment that séances actually work to begin with, Hamlet, Medea, Lear, or any other famous dramatic figure, are totally imaginary beings who never had any corporeal existence, and therefore could not "exist" in any material or spiritual form. Eventually, when he understood that these characters could only exist in the imagination, and thence through the imagination in the body of the actor, he modified this work and developed the concept of the Imaginary Body.

Step 2—Inhabiting the body.   The actors are now asked, individually, to stand in front of their colleagues, and describe their findings, and to take on—physically incorporate—each physical detail as they describe it. It is important to remind the actors that it's not necessarily about actual, physical transformation, but rather about radiating the attributes of the imaginary body into the space.

Notes

1. Emphasize to the actors that they should take their time! Every detail they mention should be incorporated—literally, put in the body—before going on to the next one. If, for example, an actor with long blond hair says that his character has short curly hair, then "having" short curly hair involves a different way of holding the head, and time should be taken to incorporate that detail and relate to the sensations it arouses. Like the technique of the Actor's Catechism, in which the important thing is not to find the answer but to ask the question, and thus initiate an inner search, here, too, the very thought of having hair of a different style and color than your own generates a physical "attitude" that may not be visible but is radiated out to the audience as an inner sensation.
2. The description of the character begins in the third person ("He has short curly hair"), or in a neutral form ("The hair is curly"). Often, as the exercise

progresses, actors unconsciously move into the first person and this is perfectly okay.

3. The teacher/director should pay careful attention to any physical adjustments actors may make as they are working. Sometimes an actor who is deeply connected to his image will make *unconscious* physical adjustments that derive directly from his response to the image, and it is up to the teacher/director to point this out. For example, the actor may be talking about his character's heavy hands and pudgy fingers and as he is doing so he might widen his stance a bit. The teacher/director should pick this up and ask, "You just widened your stance. Was that the character or you?" If the answer is, "It was the character"—as it is in most cases—then this is another bit of information about the character's physicality that the actor should be aware of and retain as part of the overall physicality he is working on. If the answer is, "That was me," then the adjustment will be ignored.

4. Once the description of the body is complete, and the transformation has taken place, ask the actor to move in the space—walking, running or "hurrying", sitting down, and so on—so that he can experiment with the consistency of the physical body he has just assumed, and with the sensations/feelings aroused in him by moving in that body.

5. In the training there is great emphasis on the fact that the moving body creates images. Therefore, as the actors move, walk, run, or sit in the Imaginary Body, they should also be aware of any images that may come up as they are working, and write down as soon as they can. Images that resonate powerfully for them in this exercise may remain with them and eventually function as keys in their performance.

NB

As I mentioned, this element of the Chekhov Technique, just like the others that follow, is used in the early stages of rehearsals, when the actors are looking for a way into their character, a toe-hold, something that will give them a basis for the beginning of their work on the character. I often use the metaphor of a tightly-raveled ball of wool, and each technique is then a method that helps us pull one thread out of the skein, to be used eventually, together with many others, in the final weave of the character. Eventually, the details of the Imaginary Body are "submerged," sent into the subconscious to continue influencing the actors' work on their characters from there. Note the following from *On the Technique*, "Gradually, the necessity of imagining the Invisible Body will disappear. This was only a preliminary, preparatory stage. A new experience in his own, real body will substitute for the imaginary one" (100).

The creative "séance"

Occasionally, this exercise takes on an extraordinary quality that is quite breath-taking to watch and sets a benchmark for the exercise as a whole. To a certain extent it skirts dangerously close to a kind of mystical event, but it does so by achieving its fundamental aim, no less than the epitome of the actor's art—a total transformation—which, at its best, is *always* a mystical event.

If the actor doing the exercise is totally centered and concentrated, and manages to assume the imaginary body fully, an amazing transformation takes place: she literally *become*s an other, *a completely different person*—before your eyes. This is as rare as some of the profoundly connected moments of creativity that I described in the training section (see the NB on pages 219–220), but when it does happen it is so extraordinary, so moving, exciting, and downright eerie, that the only possible reaction is a *gasp*! The very first time I saw this exercise in action was at a Chekhov conference in England in 1994, where my colleague, Lenard Petit, was leading a young woman from the Netherlands through the exercise. She had chosen to work on Miss Julie, and as he sidecoached her gently through the exercise, to my utter amazement she conjured up in her body, or morphed into—I have no other words for it—a wholly *different* person. It was a kind of magical transformation: her previous, daily self simply disappeared, and was replaced, without any dramatic physical adjustments of any kind, by a new persona—her totally incorporated, physical image of Miss Julie. When I managed to recover from my astonishment I wrote in huge letters across both pages of one of my ever-present notebooks: "IT'S A SÉANCE!!!" The closest equivalent I can think of to the nature of this event are the onscreen transformations actresses have undergone in films about multiple personality disorders, such as Joanne Woodward in *The Three Faces of Eve* (1957) or Sally Fields in *Sybil* (1976). In both cases the different personae simply emerge on screen, submerging one body and bringing out a wholly different, one on the same physical frame, as we watch. As in other such moments of pure creativity, the actor who undergoes such an extraordinary transformation generally cannot give an account of how it happened, or indeed *what* happened, except for that feeling of infallibility that I described earlier. What does remain, however, is a profound, intuitive grasp of the character that leaves a psychophysical resonance that is worth its weight in gold for the actor struggling to create a character.

Moments of pure creativity are rare, and these total transformations are no excep-tion. In most cases, using the Imaginary Body exercise leads to varying levels of physical transformation, which are, nevertheless, extremely useful as part of the rehearsal process. However, I always suggest to my actors that this kind of total transformation is the aim of the exercise—not dabbling in mysticism, from which I stay very far away—but developing the ability to wholly assume a *persona*: the character they are about to portray. It is also a very powerful, practical demonstration of the creative imagination as it manifests itself in the body and psyche of the actor in the performance space, and that is a lesson of prime importance at any level of training for the theater.

Step 3—Exploring the polarities: The grotesque: The Imaginary Body exercise sharpens the actor's concept of the character, and provides useful images, but most of all gives the actor a number of physical keys that help create a believable, three-dimensional character, and retain it throughout the run of the play. One of the ways to locate these resonant physical keys is by experimenting with a grotesque or caricature version of the Imaginary Body. After the actor has experimented moving in the imaginary body in various ways, she is then asked to stop and create a grotesque, or caricature version of the character, by emphasizing the most prominent physical aspects of the character as she sees it in her imagination. (NB: look at the photographs—Figures 26–27 that go with Mask–Body–Movement–Voice exercise in Chapter 4 [Exercise 50]: the grotesque of the Imaginary Body can—and should—go that far!) The actor is now asked to move around the space with *that* body, sit down, open a bag, be in a hurry, and so on.

After inhabiting that extreme version of her character, the actor should now be sidecoached, using a familiar procedure from *ImageWork* exercises, to gradually reduce the physical expression—draw in the exaggerations—until she is left with one or two physical attributes she feels she cannot do without; attributes without which she feels she will completely lose her character's physicality. In this way, the actor learns which of the attributes of her imagined character's body is the most important for her, which resonates most powerfully in her body, and these will then remain with her for the rest of the rehearsal period, and perhaps during performances as well, as physical keys to her character.

Notes

1. Actors new to the Technique—especially those coming from any kind of Stanislavsky or Method training—need to be encouraged by sidecoaching not to be afraid of creating an extreme physical caricature. Some actors tend to hold back from going into a grotesque, because it seems "silly" or "ridiculous" to them; a shooting for "results," objections that stem mainly from a fear of making fools of themselves. The teacher/director should help them overcome these fears by active sidecoaching.
2. The idea of using the grotesque in this exercise ties in to the Chekhov concept of "polarities." Generally, the polarities in the Chekhov Technique are associated with the twin terms of Expansion and Contraction. In this work I suggest to the actors that this too is a form of exploring polarities—the grotesque and

the minimal—which eventually leads to a more profound grasp of the character and to the discovery of all-important physical character traits, with the help of which the actor can assume his transformation.

3. It is perhaps needless to say at this point that all of the information gleaned from the grotesque should be written down in the actor's diary after the exercise.

Procedure: Part three—Body, voice, and text

The last element in the Imaginary Body cycle is the use of the voice. Once again we refer back to the voice exercises in the Training, particularly to the concept of the "necessary voice"—the one that emerges from a particular physical body and, as such, is deeply connected.

The actor is asked to go into the body—not the grotesque version—and use the Voice Precision exercise (see Exercises 51–55 in Chapter 4) to experiment with finding the "necessary voice" that emerges from that body. As is the case with the Imaginary Body itself, the voice does not have to change dramatically; it simply has to be connected to the new body that the actor now inhabits. Since, as we have seen, it is the moving body that produces the voice, the actor's concentration should be only on the body and on the basic mechanism of producing voice—breath passing over the vocal chords. If the actor has developed a sense of truth—an ability to concentrate on the image and radiate it out—then with a few adjustments, the voice should "fit," and be added to the growing body of knowledge she has about her character.

The final step in this section involves using text from the play that the actor is working on. And the procedure is the same: the actor goes into the Imaginary Body, finds the necessary voice, and then says a few lines from the play, examining all along the connection and the images that come to mind as she moves in the body.

Application

Depending very much on personal preference, the specifics of the characters, the trajectory of the play, or the director's concept, this can be a first step in the rehearsal process or a later step. And it is only one of the elements in the actor's toolbox, which can now be put back in the box—submerged into the actor's subconscious—as other tools are brought out and experimented with. Eventually, the information gleaned from the Imaginary Body will join the information developed from the other techniques to create the composite stage persona which is, of course, a great deal more than the sum of all the techniques used to create it.

Conclusion

To conclude this section, here is Chekhov, quoting Ethel Boileau, on the subject, in a paragraph entitled "To See Through Images":

> You will see images as in a vision mirrored in your imagination. You will give them form, substance, reality, but you will never quite know from whence they come. They are greater than yourself—and when you see them manifest a symbol, they will have a life of their own which is not your life—a mind which is not the reflection of your own. It is then you will ask yourself, "What is this that I have brought into being?" And the profounder their meaning and significance, the more you will question.
>
> (1991, 5)

Class 2—Centers and images

Introduction

In the Training section there is extensive reference to centers as a training tool for developing physical awareness, for facilitating radiation, as a repository for images, and as the locus of the connections between the body and the imagination. However, once we move out of the training and into the rehearsal process, centers are also a major tool for the development of a character, and usually go hand-in-hand with work on the Imaginary Body. As Chekhov writes, "The Imaginary Body can be elaborated very finely and with many details. To this refinement the actor must add the Imaginary Center (100)."

I have already noted that Chekhov followed Rudolph Steiner in referring to three main centers: Head, Chest, and Abdomen, which relate, respectively, to Thinking, Feeling, and Willing. Of these three, he refers to the Chest Center as the "Ideal Center," which, he claims "gives the whole body a harmonious appearance because, being in the middle of the chest, it draws the character nearer to the ideal body" (1991, 100). Chekhov goes on to suggest that the idea of the Center can also be viewed "from the point of view of characterization," as follows:

> As soon as the actor moves this Center to another place in his body, the ideal body changes and acquires a defined countenance ... [The] Center can be placed anywhere; in the shoulder; in one of the eyes (e.g. Tartuffe or Quasimodo); in the stomach (Falstaff, Sir Toby Belch); in the knees (Aguecheek) ... in front of the body (Prospero, Hamlet, Othello); behind the back (Sancho Panza). All variations imaginable are possible and correct if the actor finds them in accordance with his own and his director's interpretation of the part.
>
> (100–101)

For his own brilliant work on Strindberg's *Eric XIV*, Chekhov found the center in the wrist.

This idea of being able to "move" the center away from the Ideal Center, or from the three archetypal centers, gave birth to the concept of "Movable Centers" used by many of the Chekhov practitioners.

Premise

All of us have a center of energy, which, to a certain extent, defines our personality and our interaction with the world around us. If put to the test, most of us can identify our friends' or relatives' "centers of energy" which define them, more or less accurately, as Thinking, Feeling, or Willing people. When we pursue this concept in the theater, where we are dealing with characters, who are quintessences, so to speak, of human energies, it seems only natural that their centers should be extremely powerful distillations that govern much, if not all, of what they do in the play. Therefore, finding and using this center would seem to be a very effective way of discovering and maintaining the character's life-force throughout the play. What is unique in the Chekhov Technique is that it offers a way of translating this understanding into a psychophysical process, which, because it is intuitive, is easily incorporated into the actor's work on character.

Aim

To offer a technique for discovering and using the character's center of energy. Given that this is the "engine," the endless source of energy that drives the character from moment to moment through the intricacies of plot and relationships, once we find it and incorporate it, we have an important tool for the creation of a believable, three-dimensional character on stage.

Procedure

Prior to this class, the actors should be given some homework.

First of all they should go back to their imaginative communion with their characters, and use the "séance" to watch him or her in action, this time looking for the character's center or "hot spot," the place from where their character draws its energy.

Second, once they find the center, which, as Chekhov says, can be anywhere— including outside the body—they should also try and determine its quality: hard, soft, furry, cold, and so on. In other words, they are also looking for the *image* of the center. Based on their *ImageWork* training, they will instinctively look for an object/image that falls into one of the "families" of the Steiner categories: stick, ball, or veil (see Object/Image Dance I and II, Exercises 71 and 72 in Chapter 4).

With this homework in place we now move into the class.

NB

Since the technique that is going to be dealt with intensively in this class is Centers, the actors should be told during the WarmUp Sequences to pay particular attention to the center of energy as the source for all their movements.

Step 1—Training: The preliminary training for this element of the Chekhov Technique takes us back to the Object/Image exercise in Chapter 4 (Exercise 71). In keeping with the *ImageWork* abstract-to-concrete trajectory, the actors should be told to choose an image for this exercise, but *not* the one they found for their character's center. Since this is a training before the main event, they should wait with their character-image. (NB: in any case, as I mentioned earlier, *everything* the actors do in these sessions feeds into their work on the character, which is sitting in No Motion at the back of their heads, so that even an apparently unconnected image is connected.) They now go into the image/dance with their center in the *hara*, or working center. Remind the actors to pay particular attention to the elements of radiating and the overall psychophysical effect of their chosen image and its "location" in their body. Following what the actors have done in the previous class on the Imaginary Body, emphasis should also be placed on the movement-to-feeling sequence, i.e. what sensations are aroused while working with the image.

Step 2—Working the character image: Still remaining in the abstract, in this case delaying any direct connection to the character, the actors are now given time to work with the object/image they found for the character's center, in the physical location where they discovered it. This step of the training is worked in the same way as the Image/Dance exercise in Chapter 4 (Exercise 74): the actors work on their own and in pairs joined together and separated intermittently by the teacher/director.

NB

The procedure here is similar to the technique of remaining in the abstract outlined earlier (Note 1, page 251): they go into the text, extract something from it—a center with a particular quality—and then *forget the text and just work the image*. For the same reason, they should also avoid getting into voice or language. Remaining in the abstract like this helps them a) preempt the appearance of preconceptions that may limit their investigations into the character in future stages of rehearsal, and b) check the consistency and potency of the image and the location they have for their center. As always, the actors should be reminded to keep their notebooks near at hand and to write down any important information they may come up with in relation to their character.

Notes

1. This is a good place to bring in an axiomatic observation about the use of images. Simply put, *no one ever signs a contract with an image*. Therefore a) the actor may find, during the training, that the image or the center—which he found during the "séance"—doesn't really work for him, and b) an image that works very powerfully the first time, may fade with use. The solution in both cases is very simple: look for another image!

2. There are no magic solutions to the creation of a character; it is a process, and therefore trial and error are an integral part of it. Finding out on the floor that the image, or the center—or both—*don't* work as effectively as hoped is almost as important a piece of information about the development of the character as are the effective image and center.

3. Working in this way transforms the idea of "layering" mentioned in relation to the Training, into a rehearsal tool. The actor works with an image she has discovered for the character; through this image she gathers information—intuitively, imaginatively—about her connection to the character, and then, perhaps, changes the image and/or the center, and continues her research into the deep connections between her psyche and physical expression and the words on the written page that comprise the two-dimensional character. The work on the second image now overlays the first image, but whatever was discovered there is not wasted or discarded—like the layers of the Japanese *kata*, it becomes a "forgotten" part of the multiple layers of information that eventually make up the complete character.

Images and centers are powerful tools that have a number of applications, which are elaborated below:

Application 1—Character work

1. Developing the center with its location and qualities is an extremely important early step on the way to the creation of a character. Like the Imaginary Body, it is used early in the rehearsal process and then kept as a point of reference throughout the rehearsal period and into the performances.

2. The Image/Dance with character centers is a fecund tool that I frequently use

throughout a rehearsal period. It is, in effect, a movement-based substitute for the verbal "improvs" that are used in traditional rehearsal procedures. Worked as a purely abstract physical exercise, without the constructs of language or even voice, it opens the actors' energies into unexpected areas of investigation that ultimately strengthen their understanding of the character. With well-trained actors, who have incorporated the fundamentals of improvisation technique and the efficacy of remaining in the abstract, this is a highly creative procedure that often yields surprising results, and can be used intermittently during the rehearsal process.

Application 2—Problem solving

As I mentioned, one of the areas where *ImageWork* deviates from the Chekhov technique is in the basic concept of "the image" and its use as a rehearsal and performance technique. I have already noted that when Chekhov talks about "image" he refers to an image of the character, such as the one leading to the Imaginary Body. However, in my own work, the concept of images is more detailed and specific, relating to the use of "image/objects" not only as centers, but also as a technique for solving particular moments in a play. This is one of those elements of my work that I would have loved to discuss with Chekhov, and I believe that he would have gladly accepted the departure from his initial concept of centers.

Here are a few examples:

Example 1:   As a student at Manchester University Drama Department in the 1960s, I had the great good fortune of working with Stephen Joseph on a production of Marlowe's *Edward II*. One of the early scenes in the play, a meeting between King Edward's favorite, Gaveston, and his enemy, Young Mortimer, eluded us, and no amount of psychological soul-searching seemed to help—it simply fell flat on its face every time we tried it. Helping us out of the problem, Stephen provided all of us with an extraordinary example of the magic power of images. He asked us to go into a series of improvisations—in essence an *ImageWork* exercise—in which we were first "bouncing balls," then "concrete walls," then "twisted wires." After romping through the studio gleefully with these three images in our bodies, we now went back to the scene and Stephen gave us the key to all the fun: Gaveston comes into the scene like a bouncing ball, runs into Young Mortimer's concrete wall, and walks away like a twisted wire. Equipped with those totally physical, non-imaginational keys, the scene worked like a charm.

Example 2:   Early in my professional career as an actor, I played the Traveler in Pirandello's *The Man With the Flower in His Mouth*—a somewhat harassed family man who has spent the day in the big city and is returning home with presents for his family. Having missed the last train home, the Traveler sits down at the railway café, together with one other person seated at a nearby table. After a few words of introduction, the stranger joins the Traveler at his table and assails him with a torrent of words describing his experiences of the world, all of which, it transpires, are colored by the fact that he has a "flower" in his mouth—epithelioma, a terminal cancerous growth. Toward the end of the play, after having revealed to the Traveler his particular take on life and death, the man, played by my colleague, Gedalya Besser, walked slowly behind the bench I was sitting on, and said, very close to my ear: " . . . You see, I could easily *kill* someone like you who has missed his train." In rehearsals, I looked for some mechanism to convey the blind panic—and immobility—of a man caught between the desperate urge to flee to save his life and the need to wait for the dawn train that would take him home to his wife and daughters. Having had absolutely no experience of dealing with such a threat in my own life experience, I turned to an image arrayed in a psychophysical context: first, I clenched every muscle in my body into a painful cramp, and then ran an image in my imagination—swarms of birds careening wildly through the wintry Jerusalem skies at dusk. The result was that when Gedalya finally put his hand on my shoulder and said, laughingly, "But don't worry. I'm not going to kill you" I catapulted off the bench as though he had indeed fired a shot at me. The swooping birds were not in a center; it was as though my entire body had become the flight of the birds, radiating my desire to flee from within a tightly-held, immobile body. One of the more important discoveries I took away from this experience was that if I "remained in the abstract"—in this case, concentrated *only* on the physical tension and the image of the birds—Gedalya's hand on my shoulder had the same, totally surprising, effect *every time*. This was, perhaps, my first true experience of the great paradox of theater mentioned earlier: the first-time repetition.

Example 3:   In 1984 I directed Peter Weiss's *Marat/Sade* at Tel Aviv University. This extraordinary piece requires each actor to find the "base" character of an inmate of the insane asylum at Charenton, and overlay it with a persona from the Marquis de Sade's theatrical version of the death of Jean-Paul Marat in his bath at the hands of a mystically-inclined Charlotte Corday. The text clearly indicates that the inmate playing Corday suffers from a form of narcolepsy—an inability to stay awake—so that every time she has to play her part in the drama of Marat's death, she is forcibly woken up by the nuns and dragged into the performance. Like me in the Pirandello play, the young actress playing the part had no personal experience to draw on for this desperate need to remain immobile, and when I suggested that she look for an image as we had done in the training, she came up with an extraordinary one: a very sharp, triangular piece of glass with a drop of blood at one corner, which she "placed" in her intestines. From that moment on, she had a repeatedly effective key to her character's constant desire to sleep: through a powerful imaginative evocation of this sharp piece of glass embedded deep within her body, every move she made—getting up, walking, or lifting her hand to bring the knife down into Marat's back—caused the "glass" to "tear" her intestines, and just trying to avoid the excruciating pain that would ensue from the tiniest movement caused her to try and lie down and remain motionless—"asleep"—whenever possible.

Example 4: In 2002, I directed the great Jewish classic, *The Dybbuk*, at the Hungarian State Theater of Cluj in Romania. This is a play about thwarted love and spirit possession, which ends with a devastating exorcism during which the spirit of the dead lover, Hannan, that has sought refuge in the body of the beloved Leah, is forcibly torn out and banished to the nether world. At the height of the process, the exorcising rabbi, Reb Azriel, calls for the blowing of the *shofar*—the ram's horn blown on special occasions in Jewish ritual. He does so three times, each time using a different form of the trumpet-like blasts. This is a terrifying moment in the play, and one for which, clearly, the wonderful young actress playing the role, Imola Kezdi, had absolutely no personal experience to draw on. The solution, once again, was a use of images for two particular moments in the exorcism in order to generate the movement-sensation-feeling-emotion sequence in a very compact way. Neither of these images had anything to do with any other image she may have been using for her character; they were fashioned only to solve two specific moments in her performance. What is more, they had nothing to do with each other; each one was chosen in order to solve a particular acting problem: how to convey the frightening, soul-destroying desperation following each of the first two blasts of the *shofar*—*teki'ah* and *shevarim*—and stop the agonizing wrenching out of Hannan's spirit from within her body. The first image was a window that has just been hit by a stone in which cracks are snaking out very rapidly from the point of impact. Her image-task was to keep the window intact; not to allow it to disintegrate, and physically, forcefully, stop the cracks from spreading and turning the glass into dust. Like my use of the birds-image in Pirandello, she *became* the cracked window, frantically, powerfully trying to maintain its physical integrity. Once she succeeded and her Leah stood erect again to face Reb Azriel's next onslaught, she now had to "clear the screen" (as in the early imagination exercises in Chapter 4—Sound Pictures and Distant Analogies, Exercises 56 and 57), and prepare herself for the next blowing of the *shofar* which was soon to come. For this she used a totally different image, the key to which I had suggested to her: there is a saying in the Israeli Air Force that when a pilot runs out of fuel he "flies on the fumes" back to his base. Imola translated this idea of "flying on the fumes" into an image, probably by centering on some affective detail in the way I described in the early imagination exercises of the training. What that detail was is not important; what transpired onstage as a result was—and for the four years that the play was in repertoire, this image repeatedly created a stunning moment of theater—: barely able to stand up, she ran her text "backwards"—breathing the words *in* rather than out, trying desperately, so it appeared, to draw in air—fuel—from *somewhere* to continue the fight. Needless to say, having depleted her energies to this extent, and not even having "fumes" to draw on, she finally succumbed to the last blowing of the *shofar*. Hannan's spirit is torn out of her, as she collapses on the floor, soon to join him in the other world he inhabits.

Conclusion

When Chekhov talks somewhat disparagingly about other acting techniques that are based on the actor's "tiny experiential resources," and refers to the exhaustible nature of these resources, he directs us toward this concept of imaging because, unlike true-life experiences, the creative imagination of the actor is inexhaustible and an endlessly potent source of solutions for moments in the theater. Hopefully, these examples provide a clear idea about the use of imaging in rehearsal and performance. These images are not necessarily connected to centers, or to the Imaginary Body, and they are used individually to solve particular moments independently of any other technique or character image that the actor may be using. What characterizes all these examples, and the many others I have seen and used, is that they seem to evolve out of a *natural* imaging function of the actor in the performance space, which relies on an intuitive, non-analytical, but, nevertheless, highly precise and enormously effective procedure. Like all techniques in the arts, the fact that it is a natural phenomenon—like natural talent—is not enough. These techniques have to be deconstructed, incorporated through training, and *then* forgotten so that they turn into a part of the artist's creative process. This, in essence, is the core concept of *ImageWork Training*.

Class 3—The Psychological Gesture

Introduction

Undoubtedly, Chekhov's greatest contribution to the art of the theater, the Psychological Gesture—or PG—is perhaps the most important element of the Chekhov Technique, mainly because of its simplicity, infinite flexibility, and efficacy.

Chekhov's own definition of the PG is as follows: "the Psychological Gesture is composed of a Will-impulse painted by Qualities." Joanna Merlin, founder and president of MICHA who, as a very young actress, studied with Michael Chekhov in Hollywood during the last years of his life, defines the PG in these more practical terms: "It is the physicalization of the character's objective in archetypal form." Simply put, the PG is a strong, complete movement which is a translation into physical terms of the character's super-objective, defined as a simple, active verb—to crush, to embrace, to penetrate, and so on. Its applications are numerous, and they will be elaborated below, but basically it is a technique that provides the actor with an intuitive grasp of his character's life-force—the motivational will that directs all of his actions throughout the play. When all this is translated into a non-verbal physical gesture, it becomes, as we have seen in the training, a densely compacted form which directly affects the actor's psychophysical mechanism, bypassing the intellectual/analytical mechanisms of the brain and providing the actor with a simple, yet multilayered emotional and physical key to his character.

There are, I believe, a number of reasons for the longevity and popularity of the PG. First of all, as we shall see, the need to discover the character's super-objective and reduce it to a simple active verb in order to begin creating the PG, gives the actor a straightforward, highly effective tool with which to begin work on the character. Second, it is an extremely simple technique that requires mostly creative intuition. Third, it is a highly flexible technique with multiple applications: as a warm-up; as a vital key for the overall trajectory of the character and for every entrance; as a creative "charge" in the real time of the performance if concentration wanes; and, through the creation of an array of related PGs, it can also be used to key into individual scenes, moments, and transitions; and as a technique to create a score for the through-line of actions in the entire play. Finally, it has been my experience that of all the techniques that make up the Chekhov Technique as a whole, the PG is the only one that can effectively be used from the very first stages of the rehearsal process until the very last performance.

Premise

It is possible to reduce the overall life-force of a character in the play—it's super-objective—to a single active verb, and then, by translating the action implied by the verb into a powerful, archetypal gesture, to acquire a highly effective, easily accessible, intuitive psychophysical key to the character.

Procedure: Part one—The training

Before embarking on this class, there is homework to be done. Having chosen the character they want to play—and for teaching purposes it is helpful if the first choices are from well-known classics—the actors must read the play a number of times and try to discover their character's super-objective: what it is that the character wants more than anything else throughout the entire play. This is an entirely intuitive/imaginative process, not an intellectual one. They should try to define this basic will in a simple, active verb such as those mentioned above. They should be cautioned to stay away from any passive combination with the verb "to be" such as "to be loved" or "to be king," since a state of being is by definition non-active. How to arrive at the "bedrock" active verb, beyond which you cannot ask any more questions about the character's motives, will be elaborated below as part of the training.

Introduction—The archetypal gesture

While Joanna Merlin's definition of the PG is otherwise crystal clear, there is one word which gives us pause—"archetypal." What is an archetypal gesture? Why is it archetypal? In the section on *Psychological Gesture* from the Master Class DVD set, Joanna begins the lesson by noting the simple basis for the PG: Chekhov's contention that "Behind everything that we say or do there is a movement, there is a gesture." She then goes on to point out that standing there in front of a group of actors, her gesture as teacher is a "giving," and as she is saying this she makes a small opening gesture with her both hands, palms out toward the actors. Asked what they think their action toward her is, the actors all instinctively say, "receiving" or "drawing in" and make variations on the gesture of pulling in, gathering, or embracing. Both these gestures are "daily" body language gestures, physical adjuncts to amplify the spoken words. However, characters are not "daily" people; their entire existence is on a heightened, *dramatic* plane, governed by high concentrations of will, far beyond daily behavior. It is this powerful concentration of will that defines the difference between daily body language and archetypal gestures. What is more, as we shall see below, the archetypal nature of these gestures also derives from the fact that, in most cases, the super-objective—the governing desire—of a character in a play can be found within a fairly limited list of compact, highly evocative action/gestures. And this is where the training for the PG begins.

Step 1—The gesture: Definitions

In exercise 20 of *On the Technique of Acting*, Chekhov enumerates twenty different action/gestures: drawing, pulling, pressing, lifting, throwing, crumpling, coaxing, separating, tearing, penetrating, touching, brushing away, opening, closing, breaking, taking, giving, supporting, holding back, scratching. Chekhov talks about making these movements in a "moderate tempo," as broadly as possible, engaging the entire body, yet without any undue strain so that "you produce properly wide, broad but beautifully executed movements" (41). Over the years, the Chekhov master teachers have reduced these to a smaller number of archetypal gestures. Here are the ones I find most useful:

opening (expansion)

closing (contraction)

pulling

pushing

lifting

throwing/casting

embracing

smashing

wringing

penetrating

tearing

Opening and *closing*, otherwise known as Expansion and Contraction, are often taught separately in conjunction with other Chekhov concepts such as Radiating and Receiving, so they are perhaps the most important of the gestures in this list. While these two are fairly clear and can be done in any number of variations, the other gestures require a brief explanation.

Pushing, pulling, lifting: Here is Chekhov on the subject:

> The suggested movements must not become a kind of acting. You must avoid pretending, for instance, that you are pulling something with difficulty, and you are becoming tired . . . Your movements . . . must maintain a pure, archetypal form.
>
> (41)

So there should be no Iron Man efforts to pull a thirty-ton truck, or lift a steam-roller. Instead there is the archetypal *form* of each gesture, made with powerful, flowing, and sustained movements.

Throwing, or casting: The idea is not to throw a tennis ball or a softball, which is a very "realistic" gesture involving a fairly limited movement of the hand and the arm. Instead the idea is a gesture of throwing a heavy medicine ball or casting a fishing net, so that the entire body is involved and the gesture can be sustained and radiated at its peak.

Embracing and *smashing* are fairly clear, but *penetrating, wringing*, and *tearing* require an emphasis on the fullness of the body gesture involved. When doing these gestures in the exercise below, instead of looking for a total body move-ment, actors often "wring" a washcloth with a simple twisting action of the wrists, "penetrate" a chocolate pie with a forefinger, or "tear" a piece of tissue paper. In all of these the physical commitment is only partial, and they are basically too mime-like to qualify as archetypal in the sense that Chekhov is referring to. Care should be taken to ensure that all of these gestures involve total body movement.

Step 2—The gesture: the exercise

This initial training exercise involves developing an understanding of the maximal amplitude of these gestures. The actors are asked to center, and then told to perform these actions one after the other as the teacher/director calls them out. Each gesture should be experimented with in as many variations as possible, emphasizing the fact that they are a complete, powerful expression of each verb: to open, to close, to push, and so on.

After working each gesture physically in a number of variations, the actors are then told to choose one version of each gesture—preferably the one they feel is their best expression of each action—and perform it fully three times, and then once again as an inner, not visible but *sensible*, gesture, like they do in the third form of the Staccato/Legato exercise in Chapter 4 (Exercise 8).

There is a clear connection here to a number of *ImageWork Training* procedures that renders this part of the PG training very familiar: "impulse" as it appears in the "Move to Form" exercise in Chapter 4 (Exercise 44), the "Four Brothers" (the Feeling of Beauty, the Feeling of Ease, the Feeling of Form, and the Feeling of the Whole), and the inner movement phase of the Staccato/Legato exercise, or the "Move to Form—Repeat Without Moving" exercise in Chapter 4 (Exercise 45).

Notes

1. There is no one way of doing any of these actions, so the teacher/director should allow some time for the actors to experiment with different variations of each one before moving on to the next. The only criterion should be the full manifestation of each action.
2. Training habits from the Creative WarmUp, such as variety, should be brought in here—trying to create full expressions of each action with changes of direction, level, pace, amplitude, and quality.
3. Remind the actors also about the concept of sustaining and radiating that they use at the beginning of every workshop session in the Staccato/Legato exercise: every stretch in any direction continues into the space long after, and far beyond, the actual physical extension. By the same token, remind them too of the way in which they use their center in the Creative WarmUp: their total physical expression expands into the space with every move they make, far beyond the limits of their body. In this way, the actions continue moving into the space long after the actors reach the maximum expression of the action.

4. The idea of "not acting" is a way of ensuring that no emotional content gets into the initial work on the archetypal nature of each action. This element of content will be added later as an integral, but distinct, part of the process.

Step 3—The qualities

Following the list of gestures, Chekhov gives a list of qualities that can attend these gestures: "violently, quietly, surely, carefully, staccato, legato, tenderly, lovingly, coldly, angrily, cowardly, superficially, painfully, joyfully, thoughtfully, energetically" (41). With Chekhov's definition of the PG in mind—" a Will impulse painted by Qualities"—we now move into the third stage of PG training. Using the same set of archetypal gestures, the actors are led through them again as the teacher/director adds a variety of qualities for each action. For example they can be told to *embrace* carefully or violently, or hesitantly; *wring*—softly or forcefully, or thoughtfully; *throw*—wildly or joyfully, or staccato, and so on.

Emphasis should be placed throughout this exercise on what Joanna Merlin calls "the journey of the gesture." Fundamentally, this is a reference to Chekhov's "Feeling of the Whole," and it takes on particular importance at this point when actors begin working gestures with qualities. Each action with a quality has a beginning, a middle, and an end, so that from the moment the actor enters into the movement there is a four-part "journey" she should be aware of, once again drawing on *ImageWork Training* exercises: 1) the moment before—gathering the energies; 2) initiating the gesture ("stepping into the unknown"); 3) reaching the peak, and 4) following through (= sustaining and radiating). There is a parallel here to Meyerhold's three-part division of action in his Biomechanics training that is worth noting: *atkas* (a "refusal" or a move in a direction opposite to the direction of the intended action—as in "the moment before"); *passil* (the journey), and *tochka*, the peak point, the moment of sustaining and radiating.

Notes

1. Remember Chekhov's exhortation "not to act." (See *NB* below.)
2. After experimenting with any given version of a gesture it should also be exercised as an internal gesture.
3. The most important thing to look for—both in the visible, physical version and the inner version—is the fullness of the gesture; the "journey." A "smashing" done "tenderly" should still be a powerful, complete gesture.
4. Apart from the "emotional" qualities such as "angrily" or "violently" these gestures can also be informed by technical, or physical qualities from the training such as staccato, legato, or molding, flowing, flying, and radiating.

NB

Using different definitions for the quality of the gestures, such as "lovingly" or "angrily," seems to be at odds with Chekhov's insistence on "not acting," since it raises the issue of playing an emotion. However, this is only an apparent contradiction because we are not dealing here with a scene or a relationship between characters where there is a danger that actors might "push" their text in order to create the semblance of an emotion. In practice, when working this exercise, mention of qualities in relation to actions elicits an intuitive, totally physical response, which is mostly related to the tempo, direction, and amplitude of the gesture and no more. The teacher/director should pay attention to any tendency on the part of the actors to bring realistic elements into their gestures, which is usually indicated by a move into mime. However, the habits acquired in *ImageWork Training* of staying in the abstract, are all good safeguards against the emergence of superficial emotional charges in this exercise.

Procedure: Part two—The super-objective

Step 1—Discovering/defining the super-objective

Coming back now to the homework set for this exercise, we move closer to the PG itself as we try to work through our character's desires and motivations until we arrive at a single active verb that defines our character's overriding will-impulse.

NB

Earlier I defined one of the main benefits of the PG as the need to engage in an intuitive/imaginative process of reading and re-reading the play in order to discover what may seem as an extreme oversimplification—a single active verb that defines the character's overriding desire throughout the play. However, in fact, this is Michael Chekhov's physical version of Stanislavsky's concept of "through line" translated into what I believe to be a much more effective tool: a gesture, with all its psychophysical and imaginational resonances. Tellingly, perhaps, toward the end of his life, Stanislavsky himself moved far away from the early Emotional Memory exercises into a very Chekhov-like "Method of Physical Actions."

Let's take, for example, Oedipus. Our first, literary instinct is to suggest that what he wants is "to cure Thebes of the plague." But for the purposes of performance, this requires more detail, so we ask a question: *How* does he want to do this? The answer is: by revealing the root cause of the plague. While it is perhaps possible to remain with the verb "to reveal," there are many different ways of "revealing" and there is at least one more question to be asked—still without going into the area of quality: what is the nature of the action he employs in order to reveal? "Opening"? "Tearing away"? "Penetrating"? "Smashing"? Any one of these will do, and the choice will depend to a great extent on the directorial concept and the actor's understanding of the character within this framework. Whichever one we choose, it is fairly clear that we are at "bedrock" because there are no more questions we can ask about the mechanics of the action, only about the quality. And the answer to "How does he open (tear away, penetrate, smash)?" might be "relentlessly" or "determinedly," or even "lovingly," if that fits in with the overall direction of the production.

There is a very simple rule-of-thumb for gauging the effectiveness of a choice of super-objective: if, when we say the word, it arouses an image of the action in our imagination. When we say "to cure" we might briefly see in our imagination a nurse administering medicine to a patient, or a doctor examining an X-ray, but these are all realistic actions that are only *indirectly* active, and in any case "curing" involves an extended timeframe not a powerfully will-driven demand for immediate results. However, when we say the word "to reveal" or any of its avatars—opening, tearing, smashing—we will immediately see in our imagination any number of variations of that action, and more often than not we will demonstrate what we mean by "to reveal" by a body language gesture of the action, as Joanna does for "giving" in the DVD.

NB

1. Chekhov's suggestion for discovering the super-objective leading to the PG involves the Imaginary Body technique. In exercise 32 of *On the Technique*, he says the following:

   > Ask this character to act before your Imagination [moments in the play] and follow its acting in all its details. Simultaneously, try to see what the character is aiming at, *what* is his wish, his desire? . . . As soon as you begin to guess *what* the character is doing, try to find the most simple Psychological Gesture for it.

   (64)

2. It is important to point out to the actors that the *character* does not have a PG, nor is it likely that in his imagination the actor will see the character doing anything like the PG. What Chekhov is suggesting is something different: watch the character and try to

understand from what you see in your imagined recreation of the events in the play, what it is that the character wants, what is driving him or her, and then *extrapolate* from that behavior the PG that suits this desire.

Let's take another example: Lady Macbeth. Our initial reaction to the question "What does she want?" is, perhaps "power" or "wealth," or even "to rule." But these are not actions, just statements of fact that arouse no image of an action. At best we may conjure up a cliché image of a fierce-looking queen in medieval garb with a jewel-studded band around her head as in Orson Welles expressionist version of the play, or a svelte, leather-clad sorceress, as in Diana Rigg's filmed version. So we ask the question: If she wants wealth, power, or to rule—how does she go about getting them? Again, we are not talking about the quality, but the *modus operandi*. This leads us once more into the tricky area of interpretation—which is always there. For our purposes, let's say the answer is "By pushing Macbeth to take action." And immediately a number of images come to mind: the same fierce-looking queen, or svelte temptress, bent low and pushing with all her might a big-bodied soldier in chainmail carrying a huge sword. The action—the super-objective—now acquires a much clearer definition: *to push*, to which we can add whatever quality we feel is right for the play or for our interpretation of it.

There are other possibilities for Lady Macbeth which are worth looking into briefly. Let's take one of our first responses: "to rule." Initially there is no image, but when we ask *how* Lady Macbeth wants to rule the answer might be by "subduing everyone else." Once again, the litmus test of image-arousal brings only a fuzzy, generalized version of the action of "subduing," which is not very useful. So we dig deeper: how does one subdue anyone else? The answer: by smashing, taking down, holding down or pressing down, and with these we have touched bedrock—we know *what* she wants, what we need to find is "How does she do it?"—"With which quality?" If we take "wealth" as Lady Macbeth's guiding desire, then initially all we may see is a bright-eyed lady sitting in a stone-walled room in a castle, drooling over piles of gold and jewels, but there is no action. However, if we ask the question: "How does one go about amassing wealth?" immediately a picture comes to mind of this same woman "grabbing" or "pulling," or "embracing" in order to fulfill her desire to *amass* wealth.

In a production of *Macbeth* which I directed at the Tamasi Aron Theater in Romania in 2006, Gizella Kicsid, the talented young actress playing the role, initially defined Lady Macbeth's super-objective as "to be a queen"—not necessarily "to rule," just to be a queen with all the benefits that accrue to that lofty position. However, as I noted above, using the verb "to be" is by definition passive and therefore useless for our purposes. Working this in rehearsal, Gizella eventually translated the concept into "to grab": reaching with both hands high above her head and then "grabbing" or "pulling" something—the crown and all it symbolizes—forcefully down onto her head. Gizella also developed what might be called a subsidiary PG to give herself a key for Lady Macbeth's plight toward the end of the play, when all her finely laid plans go awry: a "holding on" as though what she had to deal with now was a rebellious "crown" that kept wanting to fly up off of her head into the air above her and that she was desperate to keep on. These gestures, of course, never actually appeared in the performance, but she used them as inner gestures to great effect throughout the play.

Notes

1. Having fine-tuned their physical awareness to a high degree in the training, and consequently acquired a high level of sensitivity to the psychophysical effect of even the minutest change in their physical expression, the details of each PG are extremely important. This is underlined by the very nature of the PG: it is, in the final analysis, a densely compacted *symbolic* gesture, so even the minutest part of it—down to the angle of the foot or the crook of a finger—is significant. A powerful pressing gesture coming from the verb "to rule" will have a totally different effect on the actor if he ends the gesture with his head down, looking in the direction of his pressing motion, or with his head up, looking out into the far distance. Here is Chekhov on the subject:

    > [T]he position of your head and shoulders, your arms, hands, elbows, the turn of your neck and back, the position of your legs and feet, the direction of your glance, the position of your fingers, all will call up in your creative spirit corresponding Qualities and Feelings. Go on exercising this way until you feel that even the slightest idea of a possible change makes you react to it inwardly.
    >
    > (1991, 79)

2. This process of asking questions about the analysis of the character and the definition of the action is an integral part of the use of the PG in rehearsal. More often than not actors unversed in the technique will start out with the realistic, psychological interpretation of their character's motives and have to be questioned until they reach a definition that arouses an image of an action and offers no room for any further questions.

Step 2—The Psychological Gesture

Having arrived at a viable super-objective, the next step is to translate the active verb into a PG. The steps toward it are the following:

1. The PG is nothing less than the character's entire life-force and *raison d'être*, condensed into a single movement phrase, therefore it can be nothing less than an enormously powerful gesture. This is true even if the gesture is colored by the quality of "gentleness." I have found that the most evocative way to elucidate this to actors is by telling them to put it into a context of "life or death": if the character does not get what he wants, he dies. So from the "moment before" until the last ounce of sustaining in the follow-through, the PG must be informed throughout by an extremely powerful will.

2. Depending on the form of the gesture, occasionally I will tell my actors to end the gesture before its completion—an "unfinished" gesture. The logic behind this is simple: if the gesture is the expression of the character's desire, say, to embrace, and the gesture itself is a complete embrace, then there is a kind of closure: upon completing the embrace, the actor feels as if he has achieved his objective. Since the PG is meant to charge the actor's will prior to carrying out the action, in some cases it is much more powerful if it remains just short of completion, leaving the actor with a powerful will to complete the action since the objective is so near yet so far away.

NB

The idea of the "incomplete gesture" has aroused some discussion among the Chekhov master teachers, since it is generally thought that, if the concept of sustaining and radiating has been truly incorporated, then the gesture of embracing will go on long after the actor has physically ended the gesture by wrapping his arms around himself, and therefore the PG should always be a complete gesture. This is undoubtedly true. However, in my own experience, I have found that the incomplete gesture is occasionally a very useful variation on the basic concept of the PG, depending on the actor, the character he or she is playing, and the chosen form of the gesture.

---

3. For training purposes, the PG should be performed three times in succession, and the actors should be sidecoached to regard each attempt as stronger than the one before. Just before actors go into the third time I usually remind them—"This is your last chance!"

4. After experimenting with the PG in this way, the actors should now add the final part of the "journey"—inner movement. The entire exercise now involves all four steps: three powerful physical gestures and a fourth, no less powerful, inner non-moving gesture.

Notes

1. If an actor doing a PG is on the verge of voice, the teacher/director should encourage him to produce the voice—no words—using the technique of the

Necessary Voice, the moving body producing the voice. In the same way that tennis players or discus throwers often can be heard grunting loudly at the peak of their efforts, so, at times, the power of the PG simply demands a voice, and there is no reason to hold it back. Indeed, when Joanna Merlin teaches the PG, she encourages the actors to add sound as part of the initial training. This certainly should be experimented with during the training.

2. Like anything else we do while working on a character, there may be a great difference between what we envision or write down at home and what we do in the work space. The PG is not immune to these kinds of disparities, and working on it can either strengthen the actors' conviction that the chosen gesture is the right one, or bring them to the realization that either the super-objective is not right, or the PG for that super-objective is not really as effective as they thought. The golden rule mentioned in relation to images applies equally here: *you never sign a contract with a Psychological Gesture*. If it doesn't work, or fades with use—look for another.

3. The use of inner movement is extremely important since the PG rarely if ever appears in the actual performance, yet it can be used throughout the perform-ance to sharpen an entrance, enhance a moment, or regain lost concentration by being performed as an inner gesture. An actor well trained in the PG will be able to use it at any time during the performance for any one of these purposes.

Step 3: The PG monologue

Once the basic technique of the PG has been practiced, we take it to the next step: a first practical application in a workshop context. (NB: in a rehearsal process you might skip this training exercise and apply it immediately to the text you are working on.) The actors are now told to learn a monologue and work on it in class in a procedure similar to the Moving Poetry exercise:

1. Do the gesture three times, each gesture more powerful than the one that preceded it, and complete the cycle with an inner gesture.
2. Do the monologue, using the PG at the beginning of every line or beat.
3. Do the monologue again, as realistically as possible, this time only with inner gestures of the PG.
4. Once again, to close the cycle leading back to the "unmoving actor moving an audience," do the monologue sitting down, with no visible physical move-ment—only the text and the powerfully radiated inner gestures of the PG.

Step 4—The subsidiary PG

Apart from the PG for the character, actors can go on to develop PGs for a beat, a specific moment in the play, or even a line. Chekhov's suggestion, as it appears in *On the Technique*, is to use the Imaginary Body technique of watching the character in your imaginative recreation of different scenes in the play, and to try and see what it is that the character wants in the given scene that you are studying. Once you discover the will, you then find and refine the gesture that expresses it. This can also be done by simply attaching an active verb to your understanding of a moment in the play, and finding the gesture for it according to all the directions detailed above.

In this way, an actor may develop an entire physical score for a play which is, in fact, the flip side of the concept of "sub-text". When we look for the subtext of a scene, we look for the will behind the lines—what it is the character *really* wanted to achieve by saying what he says. What Chekhov is suggesting is a minimally analytical and powerfully gestural approach to the same idea: either bypass the analytical effort altogether and find the PGs by "watching" your character in your imagination, or translate your analytical understanding of a line, a moment, or a beat immediately into a gesture, and, by doing so, you touch upon deep, intuitive resonances that develop into profound correspondences between the actor and the character.

For example, an actor may have a PG for *Richard III*—at least for the first part of the play, up to the coronation—which derives from the verb "to sweep away" or "to climb" (NB: after the coronation, Richard's super-objective—and PG—changes as he tries desperately to *hold on* to the crown he has won by so much blood.) But in Act I Scene 2—the famous "Lady Anne scene"—his will is entirely different: "to embrace" or "to penetrate." So a moment before entering the scene, the Chekhov-trained actor playing Gloucester will do the general PG of "sweeping away" which carries him as far as his order to the pallbearers to put down the coffin, and then, as he turns to Lady Anneand, at specific moments in the course of the scene, he will make use of a subsidiary PG—an internal gesture of "embracing" or "penetrating"—in order to work his evil charms on the unfortunate lady. Left alone at the end of the scene after Lady Anne's exit, the general PG returns—a sweeping away—before the final monologue: "I'll have her; but I shall not keep her long!"

NB

Occasionally in rehearsal I will use a variation derived from this technique—and similar to the Moving Poetry exercise in Chapter 4 (Exercise 75): after working with the actors on a score composed of transitional or subsidiary PGs, I will then ask them to play the scene only with gestures. The result is a silent, but highly evocative choreography of the scene, which, if allowed to continue as a physical improvisation (see Exercise 73, BodySong, in Chapter 4), can often bring to the surface important details for the actors about their characters and their relationships.

The PG and Plastiques

Since training goes on during the rehearsal process, whatever transpires during the warm ups is naturally affected by the actors' preoccupation with the play. From the moment they enter the work space the play and their character are there in No Motion as a silent point of reference. Consequently, they will frequently come up with new insights into their characters in different parts of the warm up sequence—which is yet another reason why their notebooks should always be within easy reach. This is particularly true of the last segment of the Creative WarmUp—the *Plastique* (see Exercise 46 in Chapter 4). There are two reasons for this. First of all, the actors working through the abstract movement that precedes the finding of a *Plastique* are looking for a form that resonates in them; one which they want to explore. Given the fact that work on their character goes on all the time, consciously or unconsciously, in the work space or in their daily lives, it is more than likely that what will resonate in them is some physical gesture that is either directly or tangentially connected to the play.

Occasionally, work on the *Plastiques* will produce a PG; more often than not it will produce "subsidiary" PGs, which in some of my productions were incorporated into the performance. For example, in a production of Lorca's *Blood Wedding*, at Tel Aviv University—a radical reworking of the text with two actors playing each role—one of the two actresses playing the Bride found a *Plastique* during the warm up which involved a clenched hand brought swiftly up to the head and a powerful sweeping movement from the forehead down and behind her body. It was only when she had finished working the *Plastique* and I asked her where this came from that Maya answered that it was probably from the moment in the play when the desperately indecisive Bride tears her orange-flower bridal wreath from her head and flings it to the floor. Expanded into an archetypal gesture, this was a "casting away" which characterizes much of the Bride's desires in the play: casting away the Groom who has been foisted on her; casting away her family to run off with Leonardo; and casting away the insoluble problem she is faced with—getting married to a man she doesn't love or running away with the man she does and dooming them both to exile and perhaps death. Since the production was movement-oriented, both Brides used this *Plastique* on stage at certain critical moments to give a dense expression of their innermost desire. Here is the "Zorba-syndrome" I spoke about in relation to the trajectories in the Introduction: "When a man is full, what can he do?—He dances!" The play, as I understand it, is a tragedy of indecision, and at certain critical moments, these multiple indecisions crowd in on the Bride to such an extent that words fail and the only thing she can do is express her desperation in the denser form of a gesture—a *Plastique* or its elder brother, a PG.

Note

Since the training is, in this way, a part of the rehearsal process, the director should watch every stage of the WarmUp sequence for material that might emerge knowingly or unknowingly in the actors' work. With actors who have trained with me the procedure is as follows:

1. In order to broaden their possibilities, every stage of the WarmUp Sequence must be done with a strong emphasis on staying in the abstract; in other words, without consciously thinking about the play or the character, just on the physical task at hand.
2. If the actor finds something important on his own, he will go and write it down; if I see something in his work that resonates in me in relation to the play or her character, I will go to him and suggest that he note it in his diary.
3. The procedure for writing anything down is as follows: first of all the actor repeats the *Plastique* a number of times, consciously paying attention to its exact form, trying to "embed" it in his body memory as he has trained himself to do in the various "repeat" exercises of the WarmUp Sequence; secondly, he writes it down as best he can, in words or sketches, adding whatever additional information he thinks is important about this gesture and its resonance; then, he returns to the space and does the *Plastique* again once or twice just to make sure it is indeed embedded, and then goes on looking for another *Plastique*.

In this way, throughout the rehearsal process, the actors have a chance, every day, to explore their character as if for the first time, paradoxically by *not* thinking about their character and only concentrating on the physical aspects of the warm up, trusting the permanent residence of their character in their No Motion to lead them to further discoveries.

While the connection between the *Plastiques* and the PG are clear, the same vigilance should be exercised by the director throughout the WarmUp sequence. Resonant moments can appear almost anywhere in the Warm Up Sequence, and if we start out from the concept that the warm ups are an integral part of the rehearsal process, then our task of picking out these important moments becomes much easier and more understandable.

The *ImageWork*/Chekhov Technique tandem

The Chekhov Technique comprises, of course, much more than these three major elements, and the entire canon falls into the categories outlined here: the *natural* connection between the body and the imagination as the key to that vital *sine qua non* of theater—transformation. Today there is a great deal of written, aural, and visual material that is available on the various elements of the Technique, not to mention the many possibilities offered by the Michael Chekhov Association for practical study of the technique with the master teachers and the growing number of new teachers that are now qualified to teach the Technique. Therefore, by way of summing up this section, I would like to give a brief description of the ways in which the combined techniques are used in rehearsal and performance.

Relating the two techniques

The integral relationship between the two techniques gives us the overall framework: intensive training in *ImageWork Training* as a preparation of the actors' instrument in order to take the fullest advantage of the benefits of the Chekhov Technique.

- In a school or workshop situation this means an extended period of *ImageWork* training (up to a year in acting schools), followed by training in the elements of the Chekhov Technique elaborated above—with the WarmUp Sequences as a permanent fixture in the work.
- When the training is in conjunction with a production this means an intensive workshop in *ImageWork* followed by a continuation of the WarmUp Sequences *as an integral part of the rehearsal procedure*, and the beginning of the rehearsal process with work on character using the Imaginary Body, Centers and Images, and the Psychological Gesture.

The toolbox

The first tool in the box is the continued use of the WarmUp Sequences before every rehearsal session. The various components of the sequences provide the actors with ongoing training to keep their creative instrument sharp and ready, and a veritable storehouse of exercises that will feed consciously or unconsciously into the rehearsal process in relation to the characters. What is more, as I noted in the section on the PG and *Plastiques*, the ongoing training feeds naturally into the rehearsal process, and is thus not a separate item in the day's schedule, but an integral part of the work on the play.

Second, in my own experience, the trajectory I have found to be most satisfying and fruitful begins with the Imaginary Body and Centers and Images, with all the variations detailed above, and then moves on to the more lasting technique—the PG—which will remain with the actors throughout the rehearsal process and the run of the performance. This progression, however, is only a recommendation and can be rearranged easily, depending on the specific needs of a given production.

However they are used, these techniques provide the actor with a range of keys that can be used throughout the rehearsal process and into performance.

Of the many other elements of the Chekhov Technique that are brought into rehearsals, here is a brief, annotated list. For more on all of these consult the Bibliography:

*   *Archetypes*   A follow-on technique related to the PG, which is a very effective early rehearsal procedure. The premise here is, first of all, that every character can be also be defined as an archetype: Beggar, King, Mother, Politician, Star, Witch, Diplomat, Dreamer, and so on. Secondly, since we all have, embedded within us from our childhood—and on into adulthood—preconceptions about these archetypes, they will inevitably influence our approach to any character we work on. Therefore, rather than leave this resource to our subconscious, we should try to define the archetype of the character, find its super-objective (for example, Beggar = to draw in, Star = to dazzle or radiate, Diplomat = to wring or penetrate, and so on), and work up its PG—which does not necessarily have to resemble the PG of the character. Eventually, like all these early rehearsal procedures, the knowledge about the archetype of our character, and the experience of its PG will be "submerged" or forgotten and join the other layers that we have created and forgotten on our way to our goal—the fully developed, complex, and utterly believable character.
*   *The qualities of movement—Molding, flowing, flying, radiating*   Used in many instances as simple physical solutions to complex psychological moments in a play. For example, Macbeth's reluctant entrance to Duncan's bedchamber can be a "molding"; Leah's headlong rush to the synagogue in *The Dybbuk* when she hears that her beloved Hannan has returned after a year's absence, can be a "radiating," and so on.
*   *The "Three Sisters"—Balancing, floating, falling*   Used in a similar way, for particular moments in the play. For example, in the brilliant scene at the end of *The Bacchae*, when Cadmus gently leads Agaue to a realization that what she is holding is not the head of a young lion, but that of her son, Pentheus, can be played using any one of these: "floating" can be used for her exhilaration upon returning to Thebes with the "lion's" head that she tore off with her bare hands; her denial of the terrifying fact that Cadmus is leading her so gently to can be worked as a "balancing"; while "falling" (or, in a more violent variation—"crashing down") is what happens to her as her eyesight clears and she finally understands the truth about the "lion's head." In some variations of this technique, such as the way Lenard Petit uses it, *parts* of the body can fall or float—the heart, the genitals, the head—to give the actor a physical/ imaginative image for a given moment.
*   *Atmospheres*   This is one of the more important elements of the Technique that is used extensively by many of the master teachers, and in general it is

very effective. However, as the early exercises in Chapter 4 in the mechanics of the imagination demonstrated (Sound Pictures, Distant Analogies—Exercises 56 and 57—and even the Statue exercises—Exercises 64 and 65), when we conjure up a picture in our mind's eye, we have a natural, *unavoidable* tendency to zoom in on an affective detail rather than seeing the entire panorama, and it is the detail that arouses the sensation derived from the chosen atmosphere. It has always seemed to me that "a cathedral" or "a cemetery" or "a railway station," are huge, unwieldy images that cannot be used effectively by the actors unless they are reduced to a single affective detail: a shaft of light for a cathedral; a smile on an evocatively engraved tombstone portrait for a cemetery; a banana peel in an overflowing trashcan for a train station. If you were to ask actors to come into the work space as if they were entering a cemetery, and then asked them what it was that appeared on the screen of their imagination, nine out of ten would answer that is was a tiny—*affective*—detail that created in them the sensation arising from the atmosphere of a cemetery. The tenth one will try to work on "the whole thing" and probably "telegraph" his false sensations of fear or haunting that would stand out a mile from the more authentic responses of the others.

Summing up

Often when trying to define the differences between the Strasberg Method and the Chekhov Technique, or to define the uniqueness of the Chekhov Technique through comparisons between the two, I suggest the following. The gesture of the Method is a *drawing down* of the fiction of the character from open-ended imaginative world of the play to the "tiny experiential resources" of the actor—and here I put my hands up above my head, widely spaced, and make the gesture of *pulling down* something from above my head, ending up with a severely reduced gesture of palms tightly clasped near my chest. The gesture of the Chekhov Technique, on the other hand, is a *reaching up* from my limited personal experience to the limitless expanses of my imagination—and here the tightly clasped palms move upward in a powerful gesture of *opening* which is sustained and radiated upward indefinitely.

A well-known anecdote about Chekhov and Stanislavsky provides an excellent demonstration of this difference. When, as a student at the Moscow Art Theater School, Chekhov was asked to do the Emotional Memory exercise, he told a heart-rending story about his father's death, reducing the entire class to tears. When it was over, Stanislavsky hugged his favorite pupil and congratulated him warmly in front of the class for the excellent exercise. One week later, the same Stanislavsky expelled young Michael Chekhov from the school for having "an overheated imagination" when he discovered that Chekhov's father was alive and well, and that the powerful recreation of his supposed death was a complete fabrication.

Chekhov's daring use of his imagination was his way of demonstrating, very early on in his career, what he believed in and taught until the end of his life: while our storehouse of truly powerful life experiences that we can draw on is limited, non-renewable and therefore prone to withering from overuse, the world of our imagination grows for as long as our minds are active. Everything we experience, in real life, in the fiction of a novel, a play, a film, a mini-series on TV, as well as in our dreams and fantasies—all these are instantly stored in our memories, consciously or unconsciously, and swell the storehouse of our imagination indefinitely. In the same way, it seems to me, the techniques of acting training that have developed ways to tap these riches and turn them into a practical creative technique, are open-ended and inexhaustible. The often chaotic and aleatory form of our imagination requires a framework, a logic, limitations and boundaries, in order to be effective, and it is within this paradox that both *ImageWork Training* and the Chekhov Technique exist in a fruitful reciprocal relationship.

Afterword

After years of languishing as a relatively unknown, somewhat disparaged, and largely misunderstood technique of acting training, kept alive only by a handful of devoted actors and directors, the Chekhov Technique has now come out of its anonymity and joined the ranks of the major acting techniques practiced in the West. Most indicative of this, perhaps, is the fact that of all the great masters reviewed in her book, Alison Hodge chose a photograph of Chekhov giving a class at Dartington for the cover of her wonderful book *Twentieth Century Acting Training*. With this new section of this book, joining preceding chapters on pure instrument training for actors in the tradition of great masters such as Meyerhold, Grotowski, and Barba, with its natural continuation into character work in the tradition of no less a master such as Michael Chekhov, I hope I have managed to make a significant contribution to this growing body of work which Chekhov set out for all of us in his concept of the Theater of the Future.

APPENDIX 1

Exercises by group, number, and page number

APPENDIX 2

The exercises in alphabetical order

Bibliography

These are the books that, over the years, have fed into my thoughts on acting training, some momentarily, some as frequently visited sources of inspiration. This is by no means an exhaustive bibliography, but it does reflect my preference for books on Training as a concept. Since, in any case there is a selection and a bias, I believe annotation might be superfluous. For this second edition, relating to the "Chekhov Connection," I have created a separate section devoted exclusively to books by, on, or about Michael Chekhov.

Barba, Eugenio, ed. *Towards a Poor Theatre*. New York, Simon & Schuster, 1968.
——. *The Floating Islands*. Holstebro: Thomasens Bogtrykkeri, 1979.
——. *The Dilated Body, Followed by the Gospel According to Oxyrhincus*. Rome: Zeami Libri, 1985.
——. *Beyond the Floating Islands*. New York: PAJ Publications, 1986.
Barba, Eugenio and Nicola Savarese. *A Dictionary of Theatre Anthropology, The Secret Art of the Performer*. London: Routledge, 1991.
——. *The Paper Canoe*. London: Routledge, 1995.
Bartal, Lea and Nira Ne'eman. *Movement, Awareness and Creativity*. London: Souvenir Press, 1975.
Braun, Edward, ed. *Meyerhold on the Theatre*, rev. edn. London: Methuen Drama, 1998.
Brook, Peter. *The Empty Space*. London: MacGibbon & Kee, 1968.
——. *The Shifting Point*. London: Methuen, 1988.
——. *The Open Door: Thoughts on Acting and Theatre*. London: Methuen, 1995.
Chaikin, Joseph. *The Presence of the Actor*. New York: Theater Communications Group, 1991.
Fo, Dario. *The Tricks of the Trade*. New York: Routledge, 1991.
Frost, Anthony and Ralph Yarrow. *Improvisation in Drama*. London: Macmillan, 1990.

Gordon, Mel and Alma Law. *Meyerhold, Eisenstein and Biomechanics*. New York: MacFarland, 1995.

Hodge, Alison, ed. *Twentieth-Century Actor Training*. London: Routledge, 2000.

Hornby, Richard. *The End of Acting: A Radical View*. New York: Applause Books, 1995.

Johnstone, Keith. *IMPRO: Improvisation and the Theatre*. New York: Theatre Arts Books, 1979. (A jewel of a book!)

LeCoq, Jacques. *The Moving Body: Teaching Creative Theatre*. New York: Routledge, 2000.

Mitter, Shomit. *Systems of Rehearsal*. London: Routledge, 1992.

Moffitt, Dale, ed. *Between Two Silences: Talking with Peter Brook*. London: Methuen, 2000.

Nachmanovitch, Stephen. *Free Play: Improvisation in Life and Art*. New York: Tarcher/Putnam, 1990. (An exquisite deconstruction of the creative moment!)

Oida, Yoshi and Lorna Marshall. *The Invisible Actor*. London: Methuen, 1997.

Rudlin, John and Norman H. Paul, trans. and eds. *Copeau: Texts on Theatre*. London: Routledge, 1990.

Saint-Denis, Michel. *Training for the Theatre*. New York: Theatre Arts Books, 1992.

Schechner, Richard and Lisa Wolford. *The Grotowski Sourcebook*. London: Routledge, 1997.

Spolin, Viola. *Improvisation for the Theater: A Handbook of Teaching and Directing Techniques*. Evanston, IL: Northwestern University Press, 1963.

Steiner, Rudolf. *Speech and Drama*. Spring Valley, NY: Anthroposophic Press, 1959.

Suzuki, Tadashi. *The Way of Acting: The Theatre Writings of Tadashi Suzuki*. New York: Theater Communications Group, 1985.

Watson, Ian. *Towards a Third Theatre: Eugenio Barba and the Odin Teatret*. New York: Routledge, 1993.

Zarrilli, Phillip B., ed. *Acting (Re)Considered: Theories and Practices*. London: Routledge, 1995.

An selectedly annotated Chekhov bibliography

Ashperger, Cynthia. *The Rhythm of Space and the Sound of Time: Michael Chekhov's Acting Technique in the 21st Century*. Amsterdam: Editions Rodopi B.V., 2008.

Black, Lendley C. *Mikhail Chekhov as Actor, Director, and Teacher*. Ann Arbor, MI: UMI Research Press, 1987.

Chamberlain, Franc, *Michael Chekhov*, London: Routledge, 2004. Appeared as a volume in Routledge's *Performance Practitioners* series.)

Chekhov, Michael. *To the Actor*. New York: Harper and Row, 1953.

——. *To the Actor, On the Technique of Acting*. A revised and expanded edition of the 1953 original, with an introduction by Simon Callow and a previously unpublished chapter on the Psychological Gesture (PG) by Andrei Malaev-Babel.

——. *On the Technique of Acting*. New York: Harper Perennial, 1991. Very similar to the 1953 original, with a good introduction by Mala Powers and a better organization of the material.

——. *Lessons for the Professional Actor*, New York: Performing Arts Journal Publications, 1985. A compilation of notes written down by Deirdre Hurst du Prey during a workshop series given by Chekhov in New York in 1941.

——. *The Path of the Actor*, Oxon: Routledge, 2005. An autobiography, written when Chekhov was 38, edited by Andrei Kirilov and Bella Merlin. It includes an abridged version of his later autobiographical work *Life and Encounters*.

Leonard, Charles, *Michael Chekhov's to the Director and Playwright*, New York: Limelight Editions, 1984.

Marowitz, Charles, *The Other Chekhov: A Biography of Michael Chekhov*, New York: Applause Theatre & Cinema Books, 2004.

Merlin, Joanna, *Auditioning: A Friendly Guide*, New York: Vintage Books, 2001. Joanna is one of the few surviving actors who studied with Chekhov in Hollywood in the 1950s. She was the moving force behind the establishment of MICHA, and is its present President. For many years one of the top casting directors in the US, this book sums up her many years of experience in the field with the special perspective of the Chekhov Technique.

Articles

The Drama Review, Volume 27, Number 3 (TPP) Fall 1983. The Chekhov Edition, with articles by Mel Gordon, Alma Law, Deirdre Hurst du Prey, and Atay Citron.
In Alison Hodge's excellent book *Twentieth Century Acting Training* (noted above), there is an article on Chekhov by Franc Chamberlain, *Michael Chekhov on the Technique of Acting: "was Don Quixote true to Life?"*

Material on Tapes, CDs, and DVDs

From Russia to Hollywood: The 100-Year Odyssey of Chekhov and Shdanoff. Pathfinder Home Ente's VIDEO DOCUMENTARY on Michael Chekhov and his long-time teaching associate, George Shdanoff. Starring Gregory Peck ~ Black & White, Color, 105 minutes. Available in VHS and DVD.

Master Classes in the Michael Chekhov Technique, produced by the Michael Chekov Association (MICHA) together with Routledge in 2007. Trying to be as objective as I can, this is one of the best training tapes in any technique that I have ever seen. It is concise without taking shortcuts, comprehensive without becoming tiresome, totally user-friendly and beautifully photographed and edited. The most important thing is that it also manages to convey the special spirit of creative joy that the Technique is based on. A must for anyone interested in a brilliantly clear visual introduction to the Chekhov Technique.

Michael Chekhov: On Theatre and the Art of Acting. The Five-Hour CD Master Class. A Guide to Discovery With Exercises, by Mala Powers. MCMXCII, MMIV Book Publishers Enterprises, 2004. Originally produced in 1992 on cassettes by Applause Books, this CD version comprises four 75-minute CDs of lectures Chekhov gave in Hollywood in 1955.

Finally—for those who would like to see Chekhov himself in action, there is his extraordinary performance as the psychoanalyst in Alfred Hitchcock's 1945 black and white thriller *Spellbound*, for which he was nominated for an Oscar as Best Supporting Actor. He appears there together with Gregory Peck and Ingrid Bergman, with nightmare sequences designed by Salvador Dali.

Index